T*SQ Transgender Studies Quarterly

Volume 5 ★ Number 4 ★ November 2018

Trans*historicities

Edited By Leah DeVun and Zeb Tortorici

ARTS & CULTURE

BOOK REVIEWS

General Editor's Introduction

SUSAN STRYKER

That *Perspectives on History*, the house organ of the American Historical Association, recently ran a lengthy feature on "transgender studies and transgender history as legible fields of academic study" says a great deal about how transness has become a significant object of both disciplinary and interdisciplinary inquiry at this historical moment (Agarwal 2018). In their introduction to this special issue of *TSQ* on "trans*historicities," guest editors Leah DeVun and Zeb Tortorici note the plethora of recent conferences, symposia, and journal issues on the contemporary interconnectedness of the topics of transness, time, and temporality, and ask, "What is it about the gesture of comparison to the past—be it ancestral, asynchronous, or properly contextualized—that provokes such urgency now?"

Perhaps urgency itself holds an answer to their question about the timeliness of trans*.

In his celebrated theses on the philosophy of history, Walter Benjamin asserts that "to articulate the past historically does not mean to recognize it 'the way it really was.'" In the present, rather, the past appears only as a fleeting image that can be grasped, or not, in the instant it appears in our vision, illuminated by the light of whatever calamities characterize the current moment. To write history, Benjamin said, means "to seize hold of a memory as it flashes up at a moment of danger." The danger he observed, writing in 1940 as the Nazis rolled over Europe, was all too clearly visible. He continued, "The tradition of the oppressed teaches us that the 'state of emergency' in which we live is not the exception but the rule. We must attain to a conception of history that is in keeping with this insight. Then we shall clearly realize that it is our task to bring about a real state of emergency, and this will improve our position in the struggle against Fascism" (1940).

Whether our own present "state of emergency" is best characterized as a "struggle against Fascism" or against some virulent new form of populist authoritarian reaction is up for discussion, but that we are in a "moment of danger," in which trans* lives are simultaneously more visible and more precarious, can scarcely be argued. Since 2016, when the United Kingdom awoke to news of Brexit's passage and the United States joined a growing list of countries where the government has lurched away from liberal democratic forms of governance, and as right-wing movements continue to make inroads across Europe, trans* lives are increasingly targeted as unwelcome presences in bodies politic animated by nativist, racist, and xenophobic fantasies.

Emma Heaney, in *The New Woman* (2017), her recent study of the "transfeminine allegory" that she finds to be a central if unmarked feature of transatlantic literary modernism, suggests that the figure of the feminine-identifying individual assigned male at birth, who occupies a lacuna between cis-feminist aspirations to overturn the debilitations of conventional femininity in order to enter the masculinist public sphere and cis-male homosexual efforts to assert masculinist privilege through the disavowal of effeminacy, has been enlisted to stage the conundrums of modern gender, identity, and public belonging ever since the advent of modernism in the late nineteenth century. Her literary analysis is compatible with biopolitical perspectives that cast the political oppression of trans* people as an expression of the "administrative violence" provoked by the difficulties gender-noncompliant bodies pose for the routine bureaucratic operations of civil society, through troubling the categories of personhood through which modern populations are settled on territories and their lives administered for collective political and economic ends, and by subverting the logics through which those categories are affixed to the flesh (Spade 2015). It is to be expected then, as Eurocentric modernity frays at the seams, perhaps on the verge of disintegration, that genres of beings who have long served as grist for modernist identity machines should be experiencing heightened levels of visibility, attention, scrutiny, and interrogation.

Trans* life at this moment in history, amid ecological and sociopolitical catastrophe, is rife with transformative potential. It demonstrates the fraught viability of enlivening movements across the hierarchized categories of being. It bears witness that deep change is truly possible—that the flesh can, at times, come to signify anew; that life canalized into familiar traces can overflow its banks and water other ways of being. Similarly, the radical alterity of the past itself offers testimony that deep change actually happens. Demonstrable difference over time is a promise that change will continue, that the present ordering of existence is not natural, inevitable, or eternal. But how, to follow Benjamin's injunction, can we attain "a conception of history," through the study of trans* oppression, that will allow us to grasp and enact the transformative potentials needed to make life otherwise than it is, for all of us who need another world?

The articles in this issue of *TSQ* provide no simple answers to that vital question. But in tackling the question of trans*historicity, they reframe the present in ways that let us see the past anew, and to perceive there, perhaps, in an electrifying flash, new pathways for life to follow.

Susan Stryker is associate professor of gender and women's studies and director of the Institute for LGBT Studies at the University of Arizona and general coeditor of *TSQ: Transgender Studies Quarterly*.

References

Agarwal, Kritika. 2018. "What Is Trans History? From Activist and Academic Roots, a Field Takes Shape." *Perspectives on History*, May. www.historians.org/publications-and-directories /perspectives-on-history/may-2018/what-is-trans-history-from-activist-and-academic -roots-a-field-takes-shape.

Benjamin, Walter. 1940. "On the Concept of History." www.marxists.org/reference/archive /benjamin/1940/history.htm.

Heaney, Emma. 2017. *The New Woman: Literary Modernism, Queer Theory, and the Transfeminine Allegory*. Evanston, IL: Northwestern University Press.

Spade, Dean. 2015. *Normal Life: Administrative Violence, Critical Trans Politics, and the Limits of Law*. Durham, NC: Duke University Press.

Trans, Time, and History

LEAH DEVUN and ZEB TORTORICI

Questions of time and chronology have risen to the forefront of scholarship in queer and trans studies in recent years.[1] Carolyn Dinshaw has advocated for anachronistic "touches" across time, Roderick Ferguson has envisioned queer "palimpsests with residues of earlier discourses and histories," and C. Riley Snorton has highlighted intersections of blackness and trans as a condition of temporal possibility—as "movement with no clear origin and no point of arrival" (Dinshaw 1999; Dinshaw et al. 2007: 180; Snorton 2017: 2). Beyond this, a wave of new conferences and publications has explored "trans temporalities," further demonstrating how methods of accounting for and thinking through time have become increasingly relevant to scholarship on trans subjects (e.g., Lau 2016; Fisher, Phillips, and Katri 2017).[2] In an influential essay, Kadji Amin has welcomed this "critical focus on the temporal underpinnings of transgender as a historical category [which] . . . may open the way toward a more transformative politics of justice" (2014: 219). It is to this crux of temporality and temporal crossing—always linked to overlapping modes of history, historiography, and historicity—that our issue of *TSQ* speaks. "Trans*historicities" joins surging interest in gender and sexuality as they relate to both patterns of time and the writing of history, advancing critical trans politics while simultaneously articulating and confounding our investments in reading, engaging, and cocreating historical pasts.

The notion of a historical past is intricately interwoven with considerations of chronology (time as succession), periodization (time as segmented into units), and the specific cultural experiences of movement and change that undergird how we view our position within time. Efforts to move ostensibly backward in time—to the historical underpinnings of trans—have long been attractive to scholars and activists. Pioneering works such as Kate Bornstein's 1994 *Gender Outlaw* and Leslie Feinberg's 1996 *Transgender Warriors* laid unabashed ancestral claim to gender-nonconforming lives in the past, and they did so to legitimate trans identities in the present. Bornstein, in ways that remain problematic yet

TSQ: Transgender Studies Quarterly ★ Volume 5, Number 4 ★ November 2018 **518**
DOI 10.1215/23289252-7090003   © 2018 Duke University Press

illustrative for us, invoked the history of indigenous cultures, writing, "My ancestors were performers. In life. The earliest shamanic rituals involved women and men exchanging genders. Old, old rituals. Top-notch performances. Life and death stuff. We're talking cross-cultural here. We're talking rising way way way above being a man or a woman. That's how my ancestors would fly. That's how my ancestors would talk with the goddesses and the gods. Old rituals" (143). Here, Bornstein draws (necessarily ahistorical) points of comparison between twentieth-century trans experience and that of a utopic, precolonial past, with which she expresses a deep affective bond. Bornstein's claim also naturalizes gender variance in the present by appealing to a shared transgender history, bracketing the "shamanic" as a romanticized, primordial system that exists outside civilizational time and place. As Evan B. Towle and Lynn Marie Morgan have noted, "The danger of portraying the transgender native in this way is that it can perpetuate stereotypes about non-Western societies, with their 'shamanic rituals' and panoply of gods" (2002: 478). It also risks consigning Native peoples to a past that is seemingly irreconcilable with the present or the conditions of modernity.

A number of scholars have rightly criticized Bornstein, Feinberg, and others for their decontextualization and appropriation of indigenous "ancestors," calling on such authors to "situate gender dynamics in specific historical and cultural contexts," as well as in specific relations of power (Towle and Morgan 2002: 471).[3] The editors of the recent *TSQ* issue "Decolonizing the Transgender Imaginary" have pointed out that the burgeoning field of trans studies has yet to adequately grapple, especially in historically nuanced ways, with whiteness, indigeneity, and settler colonialism, nor to "engage with *de*colonizing as an epistemological method and as a political movement" (Aizura et al. 2014: 309). As Kai Pyle argues in this issue, white queer "claims not only appropriate Two-Spirit history but also minimize the trauma of settler colonialism and heteropatriarchy that affects Two-Spirit people." Recent scholarship in trans studies has therefore warned against efforts to identify a universal transgender identity across time, even as they acknowledge that within the first iteration of the field, figures such as Feinberg and Bornstein "engaged in the kind of identity politics necessary to gain speaking positions within discourse, and consequently featured a good deal of autoethnographic and self-representational work" that did not prioritize historically grounded reflections on race or settler colonialism (Stryker and Aizura 2013: 3).

In some ways this trajectory of trans history resembles that of gay and lesbian history, which once saw social historians and cultural critics looking to the distant past to historicize same-sex desire and locate the origins of LGB identity. These early "ancestral" histories gave way to queer theories that—to use the phrase of Eve Kosofsky Sedgwick—drew on Michel Foucault's "Great Paradigm Shift" to suggest that homosexuality emerged as a discrete identity only toward the end of the nineteenth century (the debate between the two approaches became known, famously, as "essentialism" versus "constructionism"). Queer critiques emphasized the alterity of the past, respect for the contingency of historical phenomena, and the perils inherent in reading contemporary identities backward in time (Doan 2013). Indeed, such projects—inspired by Foucault's *History of Sexuality* (whose genealogical method remains a guiding force, as we see in this issue of *TSQ*)—have tended to foreclose the possibility of any continuous, transhistorical narrative of LGB experience that precedes the formation of modern concepts of sex and selfhood (Halperin 2002; Herring 2007). If we extend this logic, as some scholars have suggested, one cannot write a parallel history of "transgender" or "transsexual" before the advent of the very vocabulary that generated its subject; to do so would risk divesting past gender practice of what made it meaningful in its own time and place. It might also erase what scholar-activist Reina Gossett has called the "different and beautifully expansive" language of gender diversity in history (Boag 2005: 479–80; Beemyn 2013: 113; Walker 2015).

Unsatisfied by this stark choice between ancestral essentialism, on the one hand, and radical altericism, on the other, some scholars have preferred theories of queer or trans temporality—that is, visions of time as asynchronous and nonnormative, and thus enabling of community formation, often through "touches" or "binds" that connect marginalized peoples across time (Dinshaw 1999; Dinshaw et al. 2007; Freeman 2010).[4] Imagination often functions in such works as a means to rethink the past and our relationship to it: speculation about what might have happened, strategic anachronisms, and even defiance against the "tyranny of historicism" (Freccero 2006; Nardizzi, Guy-Bray, and Stockton 2009: 1) have all become hallmarks of queerly temporal projects. Maya Mikdashi and Carlos Motta, creators of the 2015 film *Deseos /* رغبات *(Desires)* and interviewed in this issue of *TSQ*, for instance, offer just such transhistorical speculation and the rejection of any imperative to be entirely faithful to the historical record. Their film stages an imaginary conversation between two women: Martina, who is "real" (based on archival documents), and Nour, who is "fictitious" (based on historical context rather than on any particular documented individual). In the words of Mikdashi and Motta:

> The criminal court of colonial New Granada prosecuted Martina in 1803 for being a "hermaphrodite" after being accused by her female lover of having a body that was "against nature." Martina was tried in a court of law and ultimately set free after medical doctors appointed by the court were unable to find evidence of her lover's accusation. This story is documented in the 1803 legal case found in the Archivo General de la Nación [General Archive of the Nation] in Bogotá, Colombia.

> Meanwhile in Beirut, Nour married her female lover's brother after her mother found them making love. Although Nour's story does not occur in a courtroom, nor is it found in a legal case, notions of Islamic and late Ottoman laws, cultures, and histories condition her narrative. (Motta 2015)

One the one hand, *Deseos* / رغبات speaks to the legibility of historical subjects who are marked in some way as "hermaphrodites," "sodomites," or "lesbians." At least provisionally, it accepts those categories and, in doing so, it offers answers that cannot be supplied by other means, and it spurs new forms of kinship with the past. On the other hand, the film's imaginative and temporal crossings rest on a refusal to assume that we can ever fully know historical subjects. And such a refusal ultimately "rests on differences—differences that confound, disrupt, and render ambiguous the meaning of any fixed binary opposition," be it between male and female, past and present, fantasy and historical record (Scott 1999: 177). Other scholars and artists have likewise explored aspects of "trans temporality" or "transgender time," offering further challenges to traditional chronology while highlighting the temporal dislocations necessary for self-narrativizing in autobiography, for refusals of settler colonial time, and for identifying echoes of transgender in history (Fisher, Phillips, and Katri 2017; Mills 2015).

History often lends legitimacy to a community's claim that it belongs in the here and now. Given the frequent citation of history by policy makers, there is no doubt that—at least in certain contexts—we imagine a political value in rendering communities visible within history (Currah 2017: 449–50). Take, for instance, the deeply historical statement on the occasion of the North Carolina "bathroom law" of 2016 by US Attorney General Loretta Lynch (2016): "This is not the first time that we have seen discriminatory responses to historic moments of progress for our nation. We saw it in the Jim Crow laws that followed the Emancipation Proclamation. We saw it in fierce and widespread resistance to *Brown v. Board of Education*. And we saw it in the proliferation of state bans on same-sex unions intended to stifle any hope that gay and lesbian Americans might one day be afforded the right to marry." In making such a statement, Lynch embedded the issue of trans access to bathrooms within a long genealogy of political struggles for rights—visualizing an overarching narrative of national progress—amid our inherited legacies of racism and homophobia.

Yet, as Reina Gossett, Eric A. Stanley, and Johanna Burton (2017) have noted, increasing trans visibility creates a double bind: while it promises legitimacy for certain individuals, it erases others, especially those who are economically precarious, who are of color, or whose means of self-representation are limited by systemic racism and sexism. Similar erasures result from what Johannes Fabian has termed the "denial of coevalness," that is, when academics write about racialized others in the present as if they lived in the past, or as if certain people's presents represent other people's futures (Fabian [1983] 2014: 35; Rifkin 2017). As Fabian shows, "such use of Time almost invariably is made for the purpose of distancing those who are observed from the Time of the observer," for they are negated a place in "our" here and now ([1983] 2014: 25). With this in mind, scholars have urged trans studies as a field to reject any interpretive stance that views racialized or "non-European gender-variant cultural practices as timeless 'traditions' bound to a particular location to which they are indigenous and authentic, and which are perpetually at risk of being polluted or diluted by the introduction of exogenous modern forms" (Stryker and Aizura 2013: 9).

How might we deal with these multiple and interconnected binds—of sameness and difference, presence and absence, "tradition" and "modernity" —while also acknowledging our own cravings for (queer and trans) histories? What is it about the gesture of comparison to the past—be it ancestral, asynchronous, or properly contextualized—that provokes such urgency now? How are scholars, artists, curators, and others negotiating these tensions through transhistorical work? We envision this issue as a moment of pause to reflect on new and diverse projects that explore these questions, and that offer a productive set of approaches to trans, time, and history that we call here "trans*historicities."

History and Its Others

Authors Susan Stryker and Aren Z. Aizura devote a section of their anthology *Transgender Studies Reader 2* to "Timely Matters: Temporality and Trans-Historicity." It is to this latter term, *trans-historicity*, that we turn our attention, and that serves as an inspiration for our framing of this issue. "Timely Matters" showcases the methodologically, conceptually, and geopolitically diverse work of five scholars—Mary Weismantel, Deborah A. Miranda, Karma Lochrie, Robert Hill, and Afsaneh Najmabadi—as they engage in cross-temporal analyses that resist ahistorical equivalencies. Through their essays, in the words of Stryker and Aizura, such scholars "envision different methods for excavating pasts that certainly contained gender-variant cultural practices, without necessarily imposing the name 'transgender' on those historical moments" (2013: 11). In doing so, they offer trans as a methodology for thinking about the potential of texts, bodies, artifacts, and narratives from different times and places to reshape our present. They are also attuned to questions of historical context and change over time (whether or not they explicitly use the term *historicity*).

While these scholars differ in their specific topics and approaches, what they share is an interest in making cross-temporal and interdisciplinary comparisons of "gender-variant cultural practices," yet without essentializing those practices or yoking them to progressive teleologies or to timeless traditions. This speaks to the possibility of writing trans history that precedes the relatively recent coinage of the terms *transsexual* and *transgender*—a project that scholars have already begun in earnest (e.g., Stryker 2008; Chiang 2012; Strassfeld 2013; Cleves 2014, 2018; Sears 2015; Karras and Linkinen 2016; Skidmore 2017; Campanile, Carlà-Uhink, and Facella 2017). Indeed, we do not abbreviate all histories of gender simply because past categories accord imprecisely with present ones; we write about women in the distant past even as we acknowledge that premodern subjects dovetail imperfectly with the modern term *woman* (which, of course, few gender studies scholars would characterize as a coherent and intelligible category even now). As Stryker and Aizura write, the field of trans studies wonders "why we think 'man' and 'woman' are any more transhistorical, or less contingent, than any other category of identity, and why we persist in the presentist fallacy of ontologizing a current framework and imposing it on the strangeness of the past" (2013: 6). Allowing the "strangeness of the past" to resonate across a chronologically expansive, historicized framework, as scholars have already suggested, can prompt us to view with new skepticism the seemingly unambiguous categories of "man" and "woman" (Block 2014). Such studies can also enrich our understanding of past gender variance, while preventing us from drawing facile conclusions about what is new or unique about our own era.[5]

At its most basic level, the goal of this issue of *TSQ* is to theorize *historicity* in relation to *trans*, taking Stryker and Aizura's formulation of "transhistoricity" as an invitation to think more carefully about their suturing. As we suggest below, both of these concepts are complex, paradoxical, and mutually illuminating: trans helps us think about time, historical analysis helps us think about trans, and historicity helps us interrogate the nature of evidence and its attendant notions of facticity and historical authenticity. We focus attention here on the prefix *trans* as a method for understanding crossings of time—as in the "trans-temporal" or "transhistorical"—and in ways that encompass the multiple and paradoxical meanings that have accrued to the term *historicity*. In doing so, we seek to put new scholarship—bridging trans studies, historicist inquiry, and queer temporality—into productive conversation to think specifically about history, its meanings, and its place in identity and community formation.

Our approach necessarily challenges the ways in which some queer theorists have set up the figure of "the historian" as a straw man, as if the discipline of history has a priori investments in empiricism and positivist claims of historical truth (for a summary, see Traub 2013; Doan 2013). In our view, such representations unfairly caricature historicist methods by ignoring how historians, at least since the nineteenth century, have engaged with and deeply theorized discursive constructions of (the discipline of) history, as well as their own conflicted relations with archival sources and other forms of historical evidence. While some historians no doubt still view their profession as a transparent retrieval of historical "reality"—keeping aloft the sentiments of nineteenth-century German historian Leopold von Ranke, who claimed that the goal of history was "to show how it essentially was (*wie es eigentlich gewesen*)" (Ranke 2011: 86)—historians have long grappled with problems of narration, representation, speculation, and imagination, as well as with multiple ways of accounting for time and its progression. But, even Ranke himself deeply questioned the meaning and so-called authenticity of historical sources (Berding 2005: 47).

At the same time, historians must acknowledge that in recent years much inventive rethinking and recasting of terms near and dear to them—*chronology, archives, the past*—have taken place outside the discipline of history (e.g., Cvetkovich 2003; Love 2007; Arondekar 2009; Freeman 2010). With this in mind, we suggest that responses to difficult questions about the methods and meanings of historical practice must be situated in debates across the disciplines and yet on the terrain of history. To advance this project, our present issue of *TSQ* unites perspectives from scholars located inside and outside the historical disciplines to look closely at how we might write histories of "trans before trans" and, beyond that, how the conjoining of *trans* and *historicity* might reconfigure our notions of chronology and periodization more broadly.

Genealogies of Historicity

By organizing this issue of *TSQ* around the concept of *trans*historicities*—with an asterisk and in the plural—we wish to push further on Stryker and Aizura's provocation and its implications for thinking about time and the past through the lens of trans. Why *historicity*? What does that term and concept offer us that *history* alone does not? Stryker and Aizura's use of *trans-historicity* (as opposed to *trans-history*) is suggestive, especially because they do not define the term explicitly in their volume. Its open-ended use points to just how much might be filled in, something that an even partial genealogy of the word suggests. *Historicity* is a term fraught with meaning, historically labile, and resistant to easy categorization. Its richness and unfixity resemble nothing so much as the heterogeneity and indeterminacy that we tend to associate with *queer* and *trans*. The linkage of *trans* and *historicity* in *trans*historicity*, moreover, suggests how these two analytics might be mobilized together usefully in ways that are relevant to the time-based relations we explore here.

While it is beyond the scope of this introduction to fully articulate all of the invocations and iterations of *historicity* in philosophy, history, literary criticism, and other fields, we want to draw attention to some of the central issues that orbit the term, and that bear directly on our present purposes, namely, problems of chronology, human agency, periodization, and imagination. Although never part of a unitary method, *historicity* can be traced back at least to the eighteenth century, when the concept became embedded in debates about the nature of time, as well as in considerations of the relationship between past, present, and future. *Historicity* has its etymological roots in the Latin *historicus*, which conveys a sense of both "history" and "the historical," and, at its most basic level, *historicity* is about making sense of things within their proper socio-temporal contexts. The *Oxford English Dictionary* defines the term today simply as "historical authenticity," and, indeed, *historicity* is often used interchangeably with *historicality* (that is, the historical actuality of persons, objects, and events as opposed to their grounding in myth, legend, or fiction). Yet we follow here scholarship that suggests that historicity's meanings are both more subtle and more capacious. Scholars have begun to identify *historicity* as a useful analytic—along the lines of *spatiality* or *materiality*—that communicates a dynamic, mutually conditioning relationship between subjects and objects (Hirsch and Stewart 2005). According to Eric Hirsch and Charles Stewart—editors of a special issue of *History and Anthropology* dedicated to "Ethnographies of Historicity"—*historicity* "draws attention to the connections between past, present and future without the assumption that events/time are a line between happenings 'adding up' to history. Whereas 'history' isolates the past, historicity focuses on the complex temporal nexus of past-present-future" (262). While we disagree that history (as a discipline, practice, method, or lived experience) necessarily "isolates the past," in what follows here we note that the operations identified by Hirsch and Stewart are hardly a new feature of *historicity*: for at least two centuries, the term has been essential to considerations of just this problem of individual and collective experiences of time.

Nearly from its inception, historicity has operated as a site of contention, serving to demonstrate opposing points of view. Some of its earliest proponents, for instance, sought to prove or disprove the bible as "fact" (and hence notions of divinely ordained time), while others challenged any notion of human experience as continuous, progressive, and ultimately culminating in a religious or secular enlightenment. Historicity developed most fully as a philosophical and historiographical concept through the divergent views proposed by two nineteenth-century schools of thought known as German Idealism and historism. Certain influential philosophers associated with German Idealism, such as Georg Wilhelm Friedrich Hegel (1770–1831) and Friedrich Wilhelm Joseph Schelling (1775–1854), staunchly committed themselves to teleological models, with the latter developing his ideas around the evolution of historical consciousness. Hegel proposed in *The Philosophy of History*, for instance, that the "History of the world is none other than the progress of the consciousness of Freedom," and that such consciousness was first recognized by the ancient Greeks and later realized by the Germanic nations, with human potentiality replacing divine providence as the engine of progress (1956: 19).

As the late twentieth-century philosopher Peter Koslowski explains, the "discovery of historicity was caused by the emphasis on world history and historical development in the philosophy of history expounded in German Idealism. When the German historians after Hegel further developed the historical method they felt the need to give more room to the singular, the unexpected, the unforeseeable, the contingent, and the free" (2005: 3). These later German historians, including Leopold von Ranke (1795–1886) and Johann Gustav Droysen (1808–84), helped found the nineteenth-century German philosophical and historiographical school that came to be known as historism. Proponents of historism criticized several aspects of historical teleology and, significantly, they did so primarily through the concept of historicity (particularly that of individual human experience), with the result that the term accumulated a wide range of meanings and implications as the twentieth century wore on. Awareness of historicity implied an intimate connection with the past, and it made possible the dialectic between human identity and historical narrativization—the latter conceived of as always partly imaginative. In Droysen's own words, man "is in history, and history is in him," and perhaps for this very reason "historical research draws an imaginary picture of the past" (quoted in Wittkau-Horgby 2005: 63, 65).

At its heart, historicity gave voice to impassioned critiques of the absolute—that is, it was invoked to make arguments *against* the existence of divine, natural, universal, or other fundamental laws, including reason itself —that supposedly governed human experience and provided temporal continuity through historical linearity. Embedded in the term was a distrust of any grand theory or absolute narrative of world history or development. Later generations of thinkers came to view with growing skepticism Hegel's notion of the existence of a single and absolute progression of time as ordained by God (critiquing, for example, Hegel's idea of world history that reaches toward human consciousness and the realization of human freedom). Indeed, even Ranke demonstrates a certain skepticism about such grand narratives. Yet, Ranke still placed history within a providential framework that he envisioned as both objective and scientific, if always a part of God's plan. He therefore shared in some version of the historical-theological view of history advocated by earlier thinkers such as Schelling and Hegel. Overall, however, proponents of historism were to become increasingly invested in historicizing the different branches of knowledge, finding diachronic laws of history (that is, how phenomena, especially language, evolved over time), acknowledging the importance of historical context, and basing their conclusions on specific historical sources and documents while, at the same time, interrogating the authenticity and reliability of those sources (Koslowski 2005: 5).

Perhaps, most importantly, the concept of historicity, as developed through certain strains of historism, came to subject everything to processes of historical change. Thus, even the divine was subject to the effects of temporality, a stance that made virtually all phenomena available for philosophical and political critique. From at least the nineteenth century, historicity was therefore wrapped up in explorations of the nature of time and its progression, and in deeply ontological questions of historical being. Moreover, historicity also stoked debates about history's relation to empirical truth: whereas some cited the concept of historicity to bolster the validity of history as a universal science, others, including Friedrich Nietzsche (1844–1900), pointed to the inherent dangers of ever envisioning history as an empirical field. For Nietzsche, history as "science" led to a fixation on the past and relativized all cultural phenomenon (Wittkau-Horgby 2005: 71–72).

A host of later continental philosophers—including Martin Heidegger (1889–1976), Jean-Paul Sartre (1905–80), Michel Foucault (1926–84), and Jacques Derrida (1930–2004), among others—were equally, if not more, invested in the concept of historicity. For Foucault, historicity's potential lay in its ability to account for processes of change, particularly the ways in which discrete cultures forged systems of power, through which identity could be produced or subverted (Malpas 2006: 60). As Foucault reminds us in *The Order of Things*, "a profound historicity penetrates into the heart of things, isolates and defines them in their own coherence, imposes upon them the forms of order implied by the continuity of time," but it too resists those very temporal taxonomies (2002b: xxv). Building on notions of historicity in existentialism, as well as of sequence and narrative among *Annales* school historians (including Fernand Braudel, Marc Bloch, and Lucien Fèbvre), Foucault, in the preface to volume 2 of *The History of Sexuality*, noted that his own turn to "the very historicity of forms of experience" led him to try to "bring to light the domain where the formation, development, and transformation of forms of experience can situate themselves: that is, a history of thought" (1984: 334). As Foucault explained, history was best understood in this context as discontinuous in sequence and constructed of multiple temporal series that "overlap and intersect, without one being able to reduce them to a linear schema" (2002a: 9). In Foucault's and his contemporaries' works, historicity could thus provide a means to interrogate linear or teleological notions of time, to foreground ruptures and discontinuities, and to evaluate the existence of transcendental ideas and experiences. As the literary theorist Krzysztof Ziarek has indicated, "historicity acts as a force of temporal dislocation. . . . [It] both lets the event emerge into presence and withholds (full) presence from it, keeping the event disjointed and incomplete" (2001: 14). From the nineteenth to the twenty-first century, historicity traveled a long way from its earliest associations with "historical authenticity."

Over the course of that period, debates also raged about the ontological and epistemological implications of historicity. For some, historicity became tightly bound to a (human) sense of historical awareness. Thinkers such as Droysen invoked historicity to assert that cognizance of the past (that is, how and why certain things exist in their proper historical context) was a characteristic that distinguished the human species. For Droysen, "the historical world is essentially the human world": it is only through man's own historicity that he "lives more than an animal, a human life" (quoted in Wittkau-Horgby 2005: 63). By this view, historicity and historical consciousness implied human exceptionalism—a point that later scholars, particularly those invested in posthumanism, would strongly contest. Historicity also raised the question of agency, which ostensibly required awareness of one's position in time. While Karl Marx had once suggested that historical progression was for the most part independent of individual human agency, for Heidegger, the past constituted the self and, hence, its future potential in time (Cohen et al. 1986; Bunnin and Yu 2004: 308). In Heidegger's formulation, *historicity* (*Geschichtlichkeit*) was categorically distinct from *history* (*Geschichte*). According to his view, *historicity* referred to the very "temporalization structure of temporality," through which *Dasein*—that is, the experience of being that is particular to humanity—stretched itself along past, present, and future (quoted in Guignon 1983: 137).

Directly related to this latter idea is yet another crucial aspect of historicity, that is, its ability to interrogate periodization, particularly efforts to distinguish past from present. As the historian Hayden White has argued, "critique means historicity," that is, while historicity is concerned with time-and-place specificity—the context that enables or hamstrings a thing and its expression—historicity, as he understands it, also means thinking about the present *as* history. Disassociation of past from present, he claims, is an ideological distortion that obscures how "by history we mean not simply 'the past' but the relation between the 'present' understood as a part of 'history' and the 'past'" (2007: 224). By fully investigating our own contingency, our own historicity, he says, we might lift the veil of necessity that clothes our present and, in light of this, envision new routes of escape. Such an analysis suggests not only that we think of history in more complicated terms than binaries of past/present and continuity/discontinuity, but also that we consider the radical potential of historicity (225).

Trans*Historicity's Radical Potential

Lest we think these opinions all the vestiges of a stale debate (tied to white, mostly dead European philosophers and historians), historicity continues to serve as an epistemological and ontological touchstone for scholars today, especially those working in critical race theory, posthumanism, colonial studies, and decolonial historiography. In *Silencing the Past: Power and the Production of History*, for instance, anthropologist Michel-Rolph Trouillot distinguishes what he calls "the two sides of historicity" (2015: 23). For him, "historicity 1" refers to the materiality of the sociohistorical process, pointing to those concrete traces—bodies and artifacts, buildings and monuments—of the past. On the other hand, "historicity 2" signifies future historical narratives, which are only partly based on those material traces (29). He asserts that only a focus on the processes and conditions of the production of historical narratives "can uncover the ways in which the two sides of historicity intertwine in a particular context. Only through that overlap can we discover the differential exercise of power that makes some narratives possible and silences others" (25). Historicity, in these two senses, functions to expose the fundamental power imbalances that go into the creation of any—though especially colonial and national—historical narratives.

Historian Marisa J. Fuentes also accounts for the differential exercise of power and its effects on the narration of history in her book *Dispossessed Lives: Enslaved Women, Violence, and the Archive*. She takes up the long discursive tradition of historicity to suggest a mode of *mutilated historicity*, which refers to "the violent condition in which enslaved women appear in the archive disfigured and violated. Mutilated historicity exemplifies how their bodies and flesh become 'inscribed' with the text/violence of slavery. As a result, the *quality* of their historicization remains degraded in our present attempts to recreate their everyday experiences" (2016: 16). The historical record of slavery in Barbados (as elsewhere), in Fuentes's view, consigns enslaved women to a mode of historicity that is precarious at best. Fuentes, as a result, turns to an imaginative encounter with her subjects—a story of what might have happened—through which she harnesses a sense of the possible and finds "an opening to represent the lives of the nameless and the forgotten, to reckon with loss, and 'to respect the limits of what cannot be known'" (141). Fuentes's approach forces us to consider what it means to narrate from a place of silence, as well as to feel deeply the entanglement of present with past—and its deep wells of terror and violence, which represent a continuing "danger to the researcher who sees her own ancestors in these accounts" (146). In Fuentes's work, historicity operates once more as a vehicle for questions of power, agency, speculation, and representation in relation to the narratives and life experiences of enslaved women in the Caribbean, and beyond.

Posthumanist scholars have also left their conceptual mark on historicity, in part by applying it to colonial and postcolonial subjects who have been denied historical consciousness by certain European travelogues, Western historiographies, and strains of anthropological discourse. Anthropologist Neil L. Whitehead, in *Histories and Historicities in Amazonia*, applies the concept of historicity to a range of Amazonian indigenous groups—the Guajá, Wapishana, Dekuana, and Patamuna—who have often been mistakenly perceived as having no conceptualization of "history" as we know it. Whitehead tells us that, for him, *historicities* refers to "the investigation of the cultural schema and subjective attitudes that make the past meaningful," whether or not those pasts operate along constructions of linear time (2003: xi). Whitehead's method operates partly by upending and inverting the originary Eurocentrism of the term *historicity*, and by challenging the temporal logic and absolute nature of settler colonialism (and settler colonial time). By grafting the concept of "historicities" onto Amazonian peoples and onto their nonlinear notions of history, Whitehead and his contributors show how, in comparison to the linear notions of time espoused by European colonizers and their mixed-race descendants in the nation-states that claim land throughout the Amazon River basin (namely, Bolivia, Brazil, Colombia, Ecuador, Guyana, Peru, Suriname, and Venezuela), many indigenous Amazonian peoples have radically different conceptions of both time and history.

If, as Hirsch and Stewart—along with other anthropologists and historians—argue, certain people's literatures, myths, dreams, songs, dramatic performances, perceptions of landscapes, and rituals of spirit possession can "usefully be classified as 'histories'" (even if neither teleological nor linear), then the very notion that any people could ever operate outside historicity is inherently flawed and colonialist (2005: 266). These scholars show that reconfiguring historicity to "index the fuller qualities of this social and personal *relationship* to the past and future makes it a complex social and performative condition, rather than an objectively determinable aspect of historical descriptions" (262). Trans*historicities, for us, conveys this sense of historicity as an embodied reality, an imaginative process, and a performative condition that resonates across time and place. Far from historicity implying any simple notion of "historical authenticity," as its dictionary definition would have it, it finds its own radical potential in this clash of meanings.

In this spirit, the contributions we include in this issue of *TSQ* approach trans, time, and history in novel, diverse, and productive ways that likewise harness historicity's radical potential. They also prompt us to consider what might fit within the purview of "trans before trans." Our first set of essays does this, in part, by analyzing the multiplicity and mutability of gender within transhistorical iterations of spiritual devotion and transformation. How do studies of particular historical subjects—such as a "passing" medieval saint queerly depicted in ico-nography (as discussed by Robert Mills in "Visibly Trans? Picturing Saint Eugenia in Medieval Art") or members of the Russian religious sect known as the *skoptsy*, who underwent mastectomies and castration to curb desire (as described by Jennifer Wilson in "Dostoevsky's Timely Castration")—enrich our approach to whether or not certain practices should be considered or named "trans"? How does a "trans" lens shed new light on such social and discursive phenomena? For Mills, this means visualizing the many possibilities of Saint Eugenia's life "through a transgender prism," which brings out the saint's embodied and iconographic "genderqueer potential" but in ways that simultaneously generate partial erasures of that very trans potential. For Wilson, it means asking how the "apocalyptic beliefs of a chaste religious group [*skoptsy*] who rejected identification according to gendered sexual organs challenge contemporary assumptions about the rela-tionship between sexual alterity and teleology." The two essays leave us with no simple view of the relation between past and present: Mills suggests that "the flash of recognition that some modern viewers may experience when confronted with such images draws attention to the possibility that representing and contemplating nonbinary notions of gender is not simply a privilege of the present"; yet Wilson sees little affinity between trans identities in the present and those of the *skoptsy* in the past, that is, no "queer antecedents or a community that one might want to, in the vein of Carolyn Dinshaw, 'touch across time.'"

All of our contributors explicitly move beyond the question of "Is a par-ticular historical figure or community trans, and how do we know?" to the further questions of "What does such a history do? How does it trouble our certainty about the past, present, or future?" Kai Pyle, for instance, in "Naming and Claiming: Recovering Ojibwe and Plains Cree Two-Spirit Language," explores how to access (and thereby partly recover) the range of meanings behind native "Two-Spirit" Ojibwe and Plains Cree figures through written and oral records. Pyle focuses on "trans*temporal kinship" as a means to claim transgender ancestors in the past and descendants in the future, exploring how such relations might make transgender Two-Spirit individuals legible within their own communities, as well as announce the continuity of their presence across time. Trans, in this sense, becomes a site of struggle with terms and translations, as well as a way to consider that language's service to identitarian and post- and decolonial projects. Asato Ikeda also considers terms and translations in her account of the process of curating the exhibition *A Third Gender: Beautiful Youths in Japanese Prints* at the Royal Ontario Museum in 2016. Ikeda reflects on the difficulties of representing Edo-period *wakashu* without imposing on them modern terms or categories, yet while also doing justice to requests from members of Toronto's LGBTQ+ communities to use language reflecting contemporary concerns about gender, identity, and pronouns in the exhibition. Ikeda asks, "To what extent should we consider contemporary communities' requests for particular language or other interpretive gestures, especially when we consider these communities' temporal and geocultural distance from Edo-era Japan?" Both Pyle and Ikeda describe efforts to preserve the specific language and context of historical subjects while also acknowledging the identitarian impulses of present communities, showing how trans*historicities enable us to play with the tension "between recognizing similarities and situating differences, rather than simply picking a side," as Pyle puts it.

As several of our contributors suggest, when we train our eyes toward the past, we find that "trans" might operate not just as a marker of gender but also as a collapser or extender of time. We see this, for instance, in Kadji Amin's "Glands, Eugenics, and Rejuvenation in *Man into Woman*: A Biopolitical Genealogy of Transsexuality," which analyzes the autobiography of Lili Elbe, subject of the recent movie *The Danish Girl*. As Amin writes, Elbe's story is as much about rejuvenation as it is about changing the bodily markers of sex: the surgical transplantation of a young woman's ovaries into Elbe's body ostensibly renders Elbe not only female but also newly youthful. Yet rejuvenation was part of a eugenicist strategy to enhance the fittest forms of life. As Amin shows, Elbe's story shows how transgender history corresponds with the racial "improvement" of European stock; rather than recovering a rosy story of the "first transsexual," Amin instead shows how the history of medical transition was deeply implicated in eugenics, as well as in attempts to manipulate time's progression. Returning to Wilson's piece, the *skoptsy* too tried to intervene in time through surgical interventions. Their physical alterations were thought to accelerate time and cause premature aging; thus, in their case too, corporeal shifts were once more linked to temporal ones.

Fernanda Carvajal's article, "Image Politics and Disturbing Temporalities: On 'Sex Change' Operations in the Early Chilean Dictatorship," explores the political stakes behind the sensationalist press coverage of Marcia Alejandra, the first trans woman to legally change her sex and gender following the 1973 military coup d'état that installed dictator Augusto Pinochet in Chile. Juxtaposing a set of visual images of the (chaotic) "yesterday" and (orderly) "today" of the Chilean coup alongside press images of the "before" and "after" of Alejandra's sex change, Carvajal shows how the dictatorship discursively molded the idea of the sex change operation as a temporal and political device that ultimately served the purposes of the state, bringing trans in line with the heteronormative family of "today." At the same time, these images disturbed any sense of temporal linearity, for the political repressions of the past invariably continued to haunt the present. In Julian Gill-Peterson's "Trans of Color Critique before Transsexuality," trans also functions as an interstitial space between what we can and cannot know about history and about the body. Employing medical records and "hermaphroditic" patient files from the 1910s to the 1950s held at Johns Hopkins Hospital, Gill-Peterson articulates how the medical archive simultaneously enables and distorts the "very historicity of black trans and trans of color life through the recording of differing types of absence, silence, or opacity." Gill-Peterson looks at how certain medical practitioners—like Hugh Hampton Young, who led the Brady Urological Institute at the hospital—rendered the bodies of so-called hermaphrodites "modern" through invasive surgical interventions. Black and brown bodies were, time and time again, deemed less worthy of receiving "modern" forms of medical care and intervention as a result of the framework of "racial plasticity" that Young and others espoused to determine which bodies they viewed as sufficiently alterable. In essence, Gill-Peterson asks how the overexposure of medicine as an available archive of transgender history has produced an incalculable deflation of trans of color life's intelligibility, especially black trans life. Both Carvajal and Gill-Peterson thus show how available archives, whether taken from the Chilean sensationalist press or the North American medical clinic, limit the intelligibility and linearity of political "progress," of sex change, and of transgender histories.

The final section of this issue of *TSQ* includes both a curated interview (with Maya Mikdashi and Carlos Motta) and a roundtable (with M. W. Bychowski, Howard Chiang, Jack Halberstam, Jacob Lau, Kathleen P. Long, Marcia Ochoa, and C. Riley Snorton), compiled by the editors in an effort to highlight the theoretical and political potential of trans*historicity. Motta and Mikdashi's film and interview, as we have already suggested, engages history simultaneously as both archival and imaginative. Infusing historical narration with the radical potential of the imagination enables new possibilities for the conditions of queer and trans experiences across time and place. As Mikdashi writes, one of the goals behind *Deseos /* رغبات was to "imagine the cacophony of imperial and colonial temporality, a temporality that our current lives—living in a settler colony that is also the world's imperial hegemon—are also unfolding within." Finally, the contributors to the "'Trans*historicities': A Roundtable Discussion" gesture at the many ways in which queer notions of time and temporality enable trans histories that crisscross different periods from the medieval to the present. As Jacob Lau writes, "queer temporality can and does operate within the normative scripts of historicism yet lends itself to nonnormative historicities by pushing against the social scripts enacted on queer and nonnormative subjects already feeling out of sorts with the paths they are told to follow." This roundtable offers a glimpse at current interdisciplinary thinking around time, trans, and history with both established and emerging scholars in trans theory and history.

As we suggest, this group of writings collectively documents phenomena and demonstrates methods that we name here "trans*historicities," providing language to describe embodiment across time, and forging a creative space in which evidentiary and imaginative gestures might meet. Many of these analyses depend on explicit comparisons between trans in the past and trans in the present, and a number of them foreground the emotional needs of living trans people now. They also ask: To what extent must such comparisons assume that we can recognize trans-like phenomena, whether *now* or *before*, and that *now* and *before* constitute discrete and incommensurate temporal regimes?[6] While a number of our contributors avoid contemporary terms to describe past subjectivities, they nevertheless stake a claim in *trans* as a sign for corporeal practices that have existed outside or across interrelated binaries. Through their work, they also show how trans might be theorized through (a)historical comparison without making definitive or appropriative claims about what counts as a trans past (or present), but also without dismissing the investments that shape our relations to historical subjects, and their effects on both identity and community.

We thus offer this issue as an opportunity to focus on, and think more analytically about, trans*historicity as an interpretive prism—one that scholars and artists are already using to weigh historical specificity against desires for a "usable past" and a more chronologically expansive history of trans. We make no effort in this issue to locate the "origins" of trans, nor to trace its development across a continuous temporal framework. We also avoid resolving the differences that exist between various disciplines and their distinct approaches to history, some of which entail incommensurate views of causality, change, evidence, and other issues. We do not seek to codify any single methodology or gloss over debates about how or why to proceed with history (indeed, we welcome ambivalence, contradiction, and acrimony). We intend our brief engagement with historicity's past iterations above, however, to demonstrate how the term might hold in productive dialogue multiple visions of epistemology and temporality, as well as competing theoretical, methodological, and historiographical modes. Further, we question how much distance really lies between historicist and imaginative approaches to the past. As Howard Chiang points out in this issue, as in all kinds of histories, "researching, writing, and theorizing trans history *demands* robust speculation and imagination. . . . This also might just mirror the creative ways with which subjugated historical actors have had to speculate or imagine ways of survival across time and place."

As many before us have pointed out, the "now" is fleeting, ephemeral, and lost to the past. Yet "now" might also be an "expanded now"; "now" might extend seamlessly into the past or future; "not now" might erupt into "now"—and all might become entangled in visions of a more radically transformative future (to paraphrase Dinshaw 1999; Muñoz 2009; Butler 2018). It is in this paradoxical, polyvalent spirit that we embrace "trans*historicities." As a synthetic paradigm, trans*historicities cinches together different ways of thinking about time, the historical record, and relations of power—including careful contextualizations, queer touches, temporal drags, and blatant distortions—each as a possibility among possibilities. Together, these fractious modes expand our knowledge of what history is and how we go about finding, crafting, and responding to it. We offer *trans** here with an asterisk to signal the overlapping, sometimes contradictory, modes of embodiment and representation that the term has come to signify. The plural *historicities*, moreover, rejects the imposition of any single narrative of events that would demand coherence or continuity, and—even as we acknowledge the complex emotions that often accompany our work—it refocuses us on the pleasures (of identifying or disidentifying; of avowing or disavowing; of imagining, filling in, or leaving blank) that arise when we—through language, image, and sound—are caught up in history. Trans*historicities, we hope, holds a space for these pleasures.

Leah DeVun is an associate professor of history at Rutgers University. She is the author of *Prophecy, Alchemy, and the End of Time* (2009), winner of the 2013 John Nicholas Brown Prize, as well as articles in *GLQ, WSQ, Osiris, ASAP/Journal, postmedieval*, and *Radical History Review*, among others.

Zeb Tortorici is an associate professor in the Department of Spanish and Portuguese Languages and Literatures at New York University. He is the author of *Sins against Nature: Sex and Archives in Colonial New Spain* (2018), editor of *Sexuality and the Unnatural in Colonial Latin America* (2016), and coeditor of *Centering Animals in Latin American History* (2013).

Notes

1. We would like to thank Susan Stryker, Paisley Currah, Abraham Weil, Leif Weatherby, Marvin J. Taylor, Carolyn Dinshaw, and all those who contributed to or gave feedback on this issue. We write this essay from our perspectives as cisgender, white queer historians (one the partner of a trans person) writing about trans, hermaphroditism, sodomy, and the "sins against nature" in a medieval (European), early modern (Iberian Atlantic), and colonial (Latin American) contexts.

2. See, for instance, papers presented at conferences such as "Trans Temporalities" at University of Toronto in April 2016; "Technicity, Temporality, and Embodiment," at University of Queensland and Southern Cross University in November 2016; and "Priors and Priorities: Conceiving Time and Other Bodies" at Harvard University in April 2018.

3. As a number of scholars have noted, this dichotomy has become reversed, with the "liberal West" now playing the foil to a presumably primitive, unenlightened global South and its stunted temporality (e.g., Puar 2007; Haritaworn, Tauqir, and Erdem 2008; among others).

4.   Despite any assumptions that the "turn" to temporality in queer studies represents the inauguration of a new field, de/postcolonial, critical race, and feminist scholarship has long theorized asynchronicity and the temporal dimensions of power; see, for instance, Bhabha 1997; Chakrabarty 2000; Quijano 2000; Lugones 2007 and 2008. For some queer theorists, "queer time" occupies a position opposite "straight time," grounded in normative linear and teleological progress, as well as in diachronic history.

5.   On broad chronological frameworks, see also the recent focus on "deep" or "big" history, "reception studies," and other modes of transhistorical comparison within the discipline of history, e.g., Shryock and Smail 2012; Hunt 2013; Holmes 2012; among others.

6.   As David Valentine has shown us, even in the twenty-first century, we find sufficiently competing terms and variable categories to demonstrate that, even now, we cannot ever know or define what trans is (2007).

References

Aizura, Aren, et al. 2014. "Introduction." *TSQ* 1, no. 3: 308–19.

Amin, Kadji. 2014. "Temporality." *TSQ* 1, nos. 1–2: 219–22.

Arondekar, Anjali. 2009. *For the Record: On Sexuality and the Colonial Archive in India*. Durham, NC: Duke University Press.

Beemyn, Genny. 2013. "A Presence in the Past: A Transgender Historiography." *Journal of Women's History* 25, no. 4: 113–21.

Berding, Helmut. 2005. "Leopold von Ranke." In *The Discovery of Historicity in German Idealism and Historism*, edited by Peter Koslowski, 41–58. Berlin: Springer.

Bhabha, Homi K. 1997. "Race, Time, and the Revision of Modernity." In *Postcolonial Criticism*, edited by Bart Moore-Gilbert, Gareth Stanton, and Willy Maley, 166–90. London: Longman.

Block, Sharon. 2014. "Making Meaningful Bodies: Physical Appearance in Colonial Writings." *Early American Studies* 12, no. 3: 524–47.

Boag, Peter. 2005. "Go West Young Man, Go East Young Woman: Searching for the *Trans* in Western Gender History." *Western Historical Quarterly* 36, no. 4: 477–97.

Bornstein, Kate. 1994. *Gender Outlaw: On Men, Women, and the Rest of Us*. New York: Routledge.

Bunnin, Nicholas, and Jiyuan Yu. 2004. *The Blackwell Dictionary of Western Philosophy*. Oxford: Blackwell.

Butler, Judith. 2018. "Susceptibility and Solidarity." Lecture, New York University, February 12.

Campanile Domitilla, Filippo Carlà-Uhink, and Margherita Facella, eds. 2017. *TransAntiquity: Cross-Dressing and Transgender Dynamics in the Ancient World*. New York: Routledge.

Chakrabarty, Dipesh. 2000. *Provincializing Europe: Postcolonial Thought and Historical Difference*. Princeton, NJ: Princeton University Press.

Chiang, Howard, ed. 2012. *Transgender China*. New York: Palgrave Macmillan.

Cleves, Rachel Hope, ed. 2014. "Beyond the Binaries in Early America." Special issue, *Early American Studies* 12, no. 3.

———. 2018. "Six Ways of Looking at a Trans Man? The Life of Frank Shimer (1826–1901)." *Journal of the History of Sexuality* 27, no. 1: 32–62.

Cohen, G. A., et al. 1986. "Historical Inevitability and Human Agency in Marxism [and Discussion]." In "Predictability in Science and Society." Special issue, *Proceedings of the Royal Society of London. Series A, Mathematical and Physical Sciences* 407, no. 1832: 65–87.

Currah, Paisley. 2017. "Transgender Rights without a Theory of Gender?" *Tulsa Law Review* 52, no. 3: 441–51.

Cvetkovich, Ann. 2003. *An Archive of Feelings: Trauma, Sexuality, and Lesbian Public Cultures.* Durham, NC: Duke University Press.

Dinshaw, Carolyn. 1999. *Getting Medieval: Sexualities and Communities, Pre- and Postmodern.* Durham, NC: Duke University Press.

Dinshaw, Carolyn, et al. 2007. "Theorizing Queer Temporalities: A Roundtable Discussion." *GLQ* 13, nos. 2–3: 177–95.

Doan, Laura. 2013. *Disturbing Practices: History, Sexuality, and Women's Experience of Modern War.* Chicago: University of Chicago Press.

Fabian, Johannes. (1983) 2014. *Time and the Other: How Anthropology Makes Its Object.* New York: Columbia University Press.

Feinberg, Leslie. 1996. *Transgender Warriors: Making History from Joan of Arc to Dennis Rodman.* Boston: Beacon.

Fisher, Simon D. Elin, Rasheedah Phillips, and Ido H. Katri, eds. 2017. "Trans Temporalities." Special issue, *Somatechnics* 7, no. 1.

Foucault, Michel. 1984. "Preface to *The History of Sexuality*, Vol. 2." In *The Foucault Reader*, edited by Paul Rabinow, 333–39. New York: Pantheon.

———. 2002a. *Archaeology of Knowledge.* Translated by A. M. Sheridan Smith. London: Routledge.

———. 2002b. *The Order of Things: An Archaeology of Human Sciences.* New York: Routledge.

Freccero, Carla. 2006. *Queer/Early/Modern.* Durham, NC: Duke University Press.

Freeman, Elizabeth. 2010. *Time Binds: Queer Temporalities, Queer Histories.* Durham, NC: Duke University Press.

Fuentes, Marisa J. 2016. *Dispossessed Lives: Enslaved Women, Violence, and the Archive.* Philadelphia: University of Pennsylvania Press.

Gossett, Reina, Eric A. Stanley, and Johanna Burton, eds. 2017. *Trap Door: Trans Cultural Production and the Politics of Visibility.* Cambridge, MA: MIT Press.

Guignon, Charles B. 1983. *Heidegger and the Problem of Knowledge.* Indianapolis, IN: Hackett.

Halperin, David M. 2002. *How to Do the History of Homosexuality.* Chicago: University of Chicago Press.

Haritaworn, Jin, Tamsila Tauqir, and Esra Erdem. 2008. "Gay Imperialism: Gender and Sexuality Discourse in the 'War on Terror.'" In *Out of Place: Interrogating Silences in Queerness/Raciality*, edited by Adi Kuntsman and Esperanza Miyake, 71–95. New York: Raw Nerve.

Hegel, Georg Wilhelm Friedrich. 1956. *The Philosophy of History.* Mineola, NY: Dover.

Herring, Scott. 2007. *Queering the Underworld: Slumming, Literature, and the Undoing of Gay and Lesbian History.* Chicago: University of Chicago Press.

Hirsch, Eric, and Charles Stewart. 2005. "Introduction: Ethnographies of Historicity." *History and Anthropology* 16, no. 3: 261–74.

Holmes, Brooke. 2012. *Gender: Antiquity and Its Legacy.* Oxford: Oxford University Press.

Hunt, Lynn. 2013. "Globalization and Time." In *Breaking Up Time: Negotiating the Borders between Present, Past, and Future*, edited by Chris Lorenz and Berber Bevernage, 199–215. Gottingen: Vandenhoeck and Ruprecht.

Karras, Ruth Mazo, and Thomas Linkinen. 2016. "John/Eleanor Rykener Revisited." In *Founding Feminisms in Medieval Studies: Essays in Honor of E. Jane Burns*, edited by Laine E. Doggett and Daniel E. O'Sullivan, 111–22. Woodbridge, UK: Boydell and Brewer.

Koslowski, Peter. 2005. *The Discovery of Historicity in German Idealism and Historism*. Berlin: Springer.

Lau, Jacob Roberts. 2016. "Between the Times: Trans-Temporality and Historical Representation." PhD diss., University of California, Los Angeles.

Love, Heather. 2007. *Feeling Backward: Loss and the Politics of Queer History*. Cambridge, MA: Harvard University Press.

Lugones, María. 2007. "Heterosexualism and the Colonial/Modern Gender System." *Hypatia* 22, no. 1: 186–209.

———. 2008. "The Coloniality of Gender." *Worlds and Knowledges Otherwise* 2 (Spring): 1–17.

Lynch, Loretta E. 2015. "Attorney General Loretta E. Lynch Delivers Remarks at Press Conference Announcing Complaint Against the State of North Carolina to Stop Discrimination Against Transgender Individuals." Remarks as prepared for delivery. US Department of Justice. www.justice.gov/opa/speech/attorney-general-loretta-e-lynch-delivers-remarks-press-conference-announcing-complaint.

Malpas, Simon. 2006. "Historicism." In *The Routledge Companion to Critical Theory*, edited by Simon Malpas and Paul Wake, 55–65. New York: Routledge.

Mills, Robert. 2015. *Seeing Sodomy in the Middle Ages*. Chicago: University of Chicago Press.

Motta, Carlos, dir. 2015. *Deseos /* غبات. Written by Maya Mikdashi and Carlos Motta. carlosmotta.com/project/2015-deseos-%D8%B1%D8%BA%D8%A8%D8%A7%D8%AA/.

Muñoz, José Esteban. 2009. *Cruising Utopia: The Then and There of Queer Futurity*. New York: New York University Press.

Nardizzi, Vin, Stephen Guy-Bray, and Will Stockton. 2009. "Queer Renaissance Historiography: Backward Gaze." In *Queer Renaissance Historiography: Backward Gaze*, edited by Vin Nardizzi, Stephen Guy-Bray, and Will Stockton, 1–12. Farnham, UK: Ashgate.

Puar, Jasbir. 2007. *Terrorist Assemblages: Homonationalism in Queer Times*. Durham, NC: Duke University Press.

Quijano, Anibal. 2000. "Colonialidad del poder, eurocentrismo y America latina" ("Coloniality of Power, Eurocentrism and Latin America"). In *Colonialidad del Saber: Eurocentrismo y Ciencias Sociales* (*Coloniality of Knowledge: Eurocentrism and Social Sciences*), edited by Edgardo Lander, 201–46. Buenos Aires: CLACSO-UNESCO.

Ranke, Leopold von. 2011. *The Theory and Practice of History*. Edited by Georg G. Iggers. New York: Routledge.

Rifkin, Mark. 2017. *Beyond Settler Time: Temporal Sovereignty and Indigenous Self-Determination*. Durham, NC: Duke University Press.

Scott, Joan Wallach. 1999. *Gender and the Politics of History*. New York: Columbia University Press.

Sears, Clare. 2015. *Arresting Dress: Cross-Dressing, Law, and Fascination in Nineteenth-Century San Francisco*. Durham, NC: Duke University Press.

Shryock, Andrew, and Daniel Lord Smail, eds. 2012. *Deep History: The Architecture of Past and Present*. Berkeley: University of California Press.

Skidmore, Emily. 2017. *True Sex: The Lives of Trans Men at the Turn of the Twentieth Century*. New York: New York University Press.

Snorton, C. Riley. 2017. *Black on Both Sides: A Racial History of Trans Identity*. Minneapolis: University of Minnesota Press.

Strassfeld, Max K. 2013. "Classically Queer: Eunuchs and Androgynes in Rabbinic Literature." PhD diss., Stanford University.

Stryker, Susan. 2008. *Transgender History*. Berkeley, CA: Seal.

Stryker, Susan, and Aren Aizura. 2013. "Introduction: Transgender Studies 2.0." In *Transgender Studies Reader 2*, edited by Susan Stryker and Aren Aizura, 1–12. New York: Routledge.

Towle, Evan B., and Lynn Marie Morgan. 2002. "Romancing the Transgender Native: Rethinking the Use of the 'Third Gender' Concept." *GLQ* 8, no. 4: 469–97.

Traub, Valerie. 2013. "The New Unhistoricism in Queer Studies." *PMLA* 128, no. 1: 21–39.

Trouillot, Michel-Rolph. 2015. *Silencing the Past: Power and the Production of History*. Boston: Beacon.

Valentine, David. 2007. *Imagining Transgender: An Ethnography of a Category*. Durham, NC: Duke University Press.

Walker, John. 2015. "Connecting Stonewall to Baltimore: A Conversation with Some Filmmakers Exploring Trans History." *Splinter*, June 4. splinternews.com/connecting-stonewall-to-baltimore-a-conversation-with-1793848182.

White, Hayden. 2007. "Afterword: Manifesto Time." In *Manifestos for History*, edited by Sue Morgan, Keith Jenkins, and Alun Munslow, 220–31. London: Routledge.

Whitehead, Neil L. 2003. Introduction to *Histories and Historicities in Amazonia*, edited by Neil L. Whitehead, vii–xx. Lincoln: University of Nebraska Press.

Wittkau-Horgby, Annette. 2005. "Droysen and Nietzsche: Two Different Answers to the Discovery of Historicity." In *The Discovery of Historicity in German Idealism and Historism*, edited by Peter Koslowski, 59–76. Berlin: Springer.

Ziarek, Krzysztof. 2001. *The Historicity of Experience: Modernity, the Avant-Garde, and the Event*. Evanston, IL: Northwestern University Press.

Visibly Trans?

Picturing Saint Eugenia in Medieval Art

ROBERT MILLS

Abstract What happens when medieval depictions of gender-crossing saints get refracted through a transgender prism? Focusing on objects and artifacts associated with St. Eugenia of Rome, this article considers the extent to which medieval artists confronted the genderqueer potential of Eugenia's legend. Often the saint was overtly feminized, patently obscuring her road to sanctity as a gender crosser. But sometimes the crossing itself was rendered at least partially visible—notably in scenes representing the moment when, after a period living as a male monk, Eugenia is placed on trial and forced to reveal her "true" identity as a woman. Some depictions of Eugenia may therefore resonate with more recent expressions of queer and trans identity. This prompts critical reflection on the concepts of *passing* and *trans visibility* in histories of transgender.
Keywords cross-dressing, Eugenia, medieval, saints, visibility

Hagiography has long been recognized as providing a sanctioned space for representations of bodily and gender transformation in premodern Europe. Written stories about holy women who assume a masculine disguise, or cultivate bodily attributes such as tonsures or beards that conventionally mark out holy men, have provided grist to the mill in debates about gender and sexuality in the Middle Ages (for overviews, see Anson 1974; Hotchkiss 1996: 13–47). Yet relatively little attention has been devoted to the presence of these figures in visual and material culture. This article considers a selection of artifacts associated with one such individual, Eugenia of Rome, who, to follow a Christian calling and maintain a life of chastity, spent several years dressing and living as a man.

In what follows, I propose casting a queer eye over representations of Eugenia in medieval art, viewing depictions of the saint's life through a transgender prism. This offers a means of reaching beyond the questions of attribution, quality, and artistic style that have tended to direct research on these objects to date. Such a perspective not only helps bring into focus the genderqueer potential of Eugenia's road to sanctity but also speaks to the partial erasure or obfuscation

TSQ: Transgender Studies Quarterly ∗ Volume 5, Number 4 ∗ November 2018 **540**
DOI 10.1215/23289252-7090017 © 2018 Duke University Press

of that same potential. Just as it is vital to trace the development of trans eradicating impulses in modernity, so it behooves scholars engaged in historical work to acknowledge the epistemological violence that has been done to nonbinary bodies and genders across time and within academic scholarship (Cromwell 1999; Weismantel 2013). Additionally, however, in our efforts to advance trans affirmative modes of historical inquiry, we need to remain attuned to the spaces for thought and action that the objects under consideration may conceivably have generated. Both at the time of their creation and in the centuries before *transgender* emerged as a category of identity and gendered selfhood, images of gender-crossing saints would not necessarily have held the same significance as they do for today's queer and trans communities. Yet, emphasizing only the violence of representation risks impoverishing our sense of the past as a field of possibility, plurality, and difference.

At the outset, it is worth acknowledging the distinct and varied meanings that gender crossing held for late medieval Europeans. Some scholars (see, e.g., Bullough 1982; Bynum 1987: 291) have suggested that women dressed as men mainly for practical reasons, a pattern that conforms to theological advice in the period. In her *Scivias*, a text styled as a series of visions voiced by God himself, the abbess and visionary Hildegard of Bingen (d. 1179) condemns cross-dressing, by men or women, "so that their roles may remain distinct"—unless the man's life or woman's chastity is in danger, in which case the practice is permitted out of necessity and "fear of death" (1990: 278; see Mills 2015: 90–98). Others have argued that, at least for some women, notably Joan of Arc, donning male attire was a "powerful symbol of self" (Crane 2002: 73), one at least partly indicative of "spiritual advancement" (Hotchkiss 1996: 68). Some legal records, meanwhile, paint a different picture. Women arrested for wearing male clothing in London at the end of the Middle Ages tended to be accused of concubinage or prostitution, thus associating cross-dressing with sexual licentiousness in the company of men; references to women attempting to pass as men for extended periods were extremely rare (Bennett and McSheffrey 2014). Unusual too were cases in which women were condemned at courts of law for posing as men to sustain erotic relations with other women (see, e.g., Puff 2000). Taken together, such cases nonetheless support the view that "medieval benevolence toward female crossdressers was clearer in fiction than action" (Bennett and McSheffrey 2014: 6).

The objects gathered together in this article provide no straightforward clues as to their reception or interpretation by premodern audiences. Today's female cross-dressers, trans, and nonbinary people may well recognize aspects of their experiences and identities in some of the examples discussed. But a question mark remains over whether, before terms such as *transgender* came into their own in the 1990s, people would have found, in visual depictions of a legendary saint and martyr, critical resources for sustaining their own gender-crossing or gender-nonconforming lives. We can of course speculate about the likelihood of a given interpretation (and imagination is a powerful tool in queer and transgender history; see Karras and Linkinen 2016). But while it is beyond the scope of this article to reflect in detail on every single interpretive possibility or set of contexts, Eugenia's example can usefully inform current debates about the existence of transgender in periods before our own.

Contributors to this special issue were asked to consider what emerges "if we look for trans∗ before *trans*∗." What is at stake in imagining and recovering trans experiences and identities before the advent of modern concepts and terminology? Here I pose a series of related questions. Under what circumstances, historically, has gender's multiplicity and transformability been rendered visible? When does the idea of crossing, implied by the prefix *trans*, come into view as a facet of gender? And how is *queer*, itself implicated in notions of moving across, represented visually? While some textual accounts of Eugenia's life and martyrdom have been discussed at length, notably the versions in Latin and Old English, artworks associated with Eugenia have been much less studied. As such, the story is known today primarily through texts; one of the aims of the present study is to redress the balance in favor of visual as well as textual treatments. By expanding the archive of trans experiences and identities in the direction of objects that convey or respond to gender diversity through nonverbal forms, we enrich our understanding of "trans∗historicities" as a frame.

A focus on visuality also allows me to draw out the connections between trans historicity and trans visibility. Visibility is a key issue in contemporary experiences of transgender. Never have trans people been under such a glaring spotlight as they are today. Representations of individuals who transition from male to female or from female to male have exploded in the public sphere. It is a phenomenon that *Time* magazine recently dubbed "The Transgender Tipping Point" (Steinmetz 2014). But the individuals who are the subjects of this seemingly relentless exposure tend, for the most part, to be viewed as "passable." Passing is a common but controversial trope in modern accounts of trans experience. The key factor at play in the ability to pass is whether the person represented is readily identifiable as transgender. Is their gender queerness visible in some way, or do they manage to get through life as a cis-looking trans person? The imagery disseminated in the wake of this so-called tipping point is seemingly marked by a preference for effective or convincing modes of passing, for conformity to perceived gender norms and binaries (photographs illustrating the *Time* article are a case in point). One problem with this bias is that it diminishes the visibility and viability of people who actively identify as nonbinary, or who experience themselves and are perceived by others as genderqueer or gender fluid.

Trans visibility is bound up with temporality. When a trans person comes into view *as* transgender, he or she has ostensibly failed to pass, a failure that threatens to expose what Jack Halberstam calls "a rupture between the distinct temporal registers of past, present, and future. . . . Visibility, under these circumstances, may be equated with jeopardy, danger, and exposure, and it often becomes necessary for the transgender character to disappear in order to remain viable" (2005: 77–78). Halberstam's analysis is directed at representations of transgender experience in film, but the comments are equally applicable to images of St. Eugenia. The saint's exposure as female, after a period spent living as a male, causes a ripple in historical time. Recognition of the saint's womanly past spells the restoration, as least outwardly, of femininity and subsequently comes to define Eugenia's future as a (female) virgin martyr. But another past—Eugenia's time as a man—also exerts a shaping influence on the saint's vocation as a virile virgin. Meanwhile, in the narrative present that coincides with the act of exposure and revelation, Eugenia's gender is rendered mobile, even undecidable. One possible outcome here is trans legibility: Eugenia's gender queerness becomes visible, albeit momentarily, when the saint's different pasts collide. But that same queerness can also be made to disappear, whether through acts of suppression, erasure, or looking away. My argument is that medieval image makers prevaricated, adopting different perspectives and representational strategies depending on the context.

On one level, Eugenia's legend can be interpreted as incorporating an episode of successful male passing. According to medieval hagiographers, Eugenia was the daughter of a Roman patrician, Philip, who took his family from Rome to Alexandria in Egypt, where he had been appointed prefect, during the reign of Emperor Commodus (180–92 CE). A gifted student, Eugenia discovers Christian teachings during her time in Alexandria and subsequently determines to spurn marriage and devote herself to a life of chastity. Aged sixteen, she gets permission from her unwitting parents to go on a rural retreat with her eunuch slaves Protus and Hyacinthus, who share their mistress's passion for learning. Encountering a procession of Christians, Eugenia decides to enter the nearby monastery dressed as a man. Wearing male garb and introducing herself as Protus and Hyacinthus's brother "Eugenius," Eugenia is welcomed by the community's miracle-working abbot, bishop Helenus, who sees through the young woman's disguise but agrees to admit the trio anyway. Personally overseeing their baptism, Helenus keeps Eugenia's female embodiment secret from the monastery's other inhabitants.

Three years later, following the death of their mentor, Eugenius becomes abbot of the house; leading by example, he is praised for his exceptional humility, discipline, and healing powers. A wealthy widow, Melantia, comes to Eugenius to be cured of a fever and subsequently develops an intense passion for the abbot.

Attempting to woo the object of her affections with thoughts of worldly pleasures and marriage, Melantia is harshly rebuked by Eugenius. Frustrated by the rejection, the widow subsequently accuses him of attempting to rape her, and a case is brought before the prefect Philip in Alexandria, who no longer recognizes his daughter now she has assumed a male persona. During the public trial, Eugenia explains that just as loving God is a "manly" (*uiriliter*) pursuit, so have they "performed the perfect man" (*uirum gessi perfectum*) by donning male attire and maintaining chastity for Christ (quoted in Whatley 2012: 107; cf. Stimm 1955: 78).[1] Then, as a last resort, the protagonist rips off their clothing as proof of innocence. Recognizing the accused's womanly identity as his daughter, Philip converts to Christianity, along with his wife Claudia and Eugenia's brothers; Philip is subsequently elected bishop of Alexandria before being assassinated by the prefect who arrives to replace him. Eventually, after returning to Rome, the saint, her eunuch companions, and other family members are arrested as Christians and martyred. Eugenia herself is beheaded on Christmas Day, after undergoing various torments and a stint in prison, and subsequently appears to her mother in a heavenly vision at the saint's tomb.[2]

People who, like Eugenia, are perceived as conforming to traits associated with the gender they identify as rather than the gender (or sex) assigned at birth, may get by—at least for some of the time—without their transgender status becoming visible. Blending or passing well enough to be taken as cisgender, such individuals are discernibly queer or trans only within certain well-defined parameters. Eugenia's own birth gender is revealed to audiences within the story at a specific juncture, during the saint's trial. Forced to reveal her bodily sex, in an act that violates what might be called Eugenia's access to "passing privilege," the saint had previously been taken for a man by everyone except her eunuch companions and the bishop who originally admitted her to the monastery. As if to prove the point, even another woman falls for Eugenia-as-abbot. While Melantia's passion arguably raises the specter of sexual relations between women, the saint is depicted as embodying the traits (including visual characteristics) associated with maleness so successfully that homosexual passion comes into focus only fleetingly (see Clark 2009: 192–93; Mills 2015: 207–8). For the duration of her extended sojourn in the monastery, Eugenia is effectively presented as a passing male. In these terms, the saint is neither visibly trans nor genderqueer.

The dissemination of Eugenia's legend in medieval art raised the stakes considerably. Whereas textual renditions of the legend highlighted the saint's perceived status as a gender crosser, image makers tended to maintain an overriding emphasis on Eugenia's femininity, thereby rendering invisible or seriously underplaying her temporary acquisition of male identity and prerogative. Conversely, a small number of depictions of Eugenia in art present alternative perspectives. Very occasionally, the images in question seem visibly to convey dimensions in the saint's story that cannot easily be assimilated to a language of passing, troubling gender in ways that appear to resonate with some modern-day experiences and expressions of trans visibility and gender queerness. From one perspective, the examples surveyed call into question the assumption that holy gender crossers can straightforwardly be reclaimed as "transcestors," to use a recent coinage. From another, they help us appreciate how, in premodernity as today, gender queerness was intermittently discernible in the field of vision.

As Saisha Grayson has demonstrated, in an article exploring what she terms the "problem of transvestite saints for medieval art," artists who tackled Eugenia's story in the Middle Ages tended to represent only the narrative's conclusion—the moment when, following the restoration of her female identity, Eugenia died a martyr. For instance, in a fifteenth-century illuminated copy of a French translation of the *Golden Legend* analyzed by Grayson (2009: 150–52), Eugenia is depicted dressed in characteristically female garb while her eunuch companions wear neutral-looking monastic habits.[3] Several other representations of the saint similarly emphasize Eugenia's feminine appearance following the trial. Varzy, a small town in Burgundy on the pilgrimage route to Santiago de Compostela, had a collegiate church dedicated to Eugenia, and it had reputedly been in possession of the saint's relics since the tenth century (Anfray 1951; Boisseau 1905: 11–14, 64–66; Jobert 1867; Lussier and Palet 1934). Although the Collégiale Sainte-Eugénie was largely destroyed during the French Revolution, and remnants of the site are now mainly in private hands, the local museum and another church in Varzy dedicated to St. Peter still possess several Eugenia-related objects. These include a late fifteenth- or early sixteenth-century statue (fig. 1), which represents the saint wearing the crown of martyrdom, carrying a book (presumably a sign of Eugenia's dedication from an early age to learning), and dressed in the garments of a late medieval noblewoman (Cario et al. 1990: 47). The statue is identified by an inscription on its base and by repetition of the phrase "Santa Eugenia" along the edge of the saint's tunic.[4]

There is also a stained-glass window roundel, roughly contemporary with the statue, which depicts the saint nimbed, clasping a book, and carrying a palm of martyrdom (fig. 2). Significantly the glass, although it highlights Eugenia's ultimate trajectory as a female virgin martyr, retains a textual trace of the saint's former identity as a male monk by seemingly using a masculine form of the name, *S. Eugène*, as opposed to the feminine *Sainte Eugénie*.[5] Conversely, at the back of the statue (fig. 1), Eugenia is depicted with a head of wavy, golden hair stretching almost to her waist, as if to emphasize the restoration of femininity following the saint's years of being shaved and tonsured. Lengthy or extravagant locks are also a feature of several other Eugenia images, as we shall see. Cumulatively, these

Figure 1. St. Eugenia. Polychromed statue, ca. 1500. Choir of Saint-Pierre, Varzy (Nièvre). Photos: Robert Mills

representations give the impression that image makers were inclined to subject Eugenia to a process of compensatory refeminization in response to the virile virgin topos that intermittently shapes the legend. With the possible exception of the gendering of the name on the glass panel, after all, viewers would be hard pressed to find visible traces of the saint's manly past in the images just cited.[6]

The moment in the story with perhaps the greatest potential for subverting gender binaries is the trial, when Eugenia, dressed as a male monk, reveals their previous identity as a woman. Once again, however, some artists appear deliberately to have steered away from showing Eugenia explicitly as a gender troubling figure. Thus, a fifteenth-century illumination discussed by Grayson (2009: 165–66) shows Eugenia clearly dressed as a female nun, replete with veil, rather than as a tonsured male abbot.[7] The saint's habit, hitched up to reveal a white petticoat, signals visually that this is the moment of the big reveal, thus eliding the text's emphasis on breasts. An illustration in a French translation of Vincent of Beauvais's *Speculum historiale* (fig. 3) from around 1335 seems less tame by comparison: it features a nimbed, long-haired woman opening a dark blue tunic

Figure 2. St. Eugenia. Glass roundel, late fifteenth century. Musée
Auguste Grasset, Varzy. Photo: Musée Auguste Grasset

Figure 3. Eugenia on trial. Miniature in Jean de Vignay, *Miroir historial*, translation of Vincent
of Beauvais, *Speculum historiale*, ca. 1335. Paris, Bibliothèque nationale de France, MS Arsenal 5080
réserve, fol. 154r (detail). Photo: Bibliothèque nationale de France

with a red lining to her father's gaze, revealing her pubic region even as she draws a hand across her breasts. As in the Vézelay sculpture discussed below, Philip raises his right hand, but Eugenia is now shown in the process of stripping from head to toe. A woman in a headdress to the right, presumably the saint's mother Claudia, holds out a new red tunic, a garment doubtless deemed appropriate to the resumption of womanly status (it has a pattern of golden stars and circles, which distinguishes it from the "monastic" garb being removed by Eugenia); two other women, one with her hands in a gesture of prayer, observe from the sidelines. This is the last of four images illustrating the Eugenia legend in the manuscript. The others show Eugenia being instructed in philosophy by her father, the saint's baptism in the company of Protus and Hyacinthus, and Melantia visiting Philip to accuse the woman she thinks is a man of violating her sexually.[8] While in the miniature representing baptism, the presiding bishop, Helenus, throws water over three individuals shown naked from the waist up, Eugenia's long hair contrasts markedly with the tonsures of her companions, which again suggests that her masculine performance has been filtered through an emphatically feminizing lens. Grayson is surely correct in her assessment that such depictions steer away from rendering visible what she calls the "disruptive guise" (2009: 169) of a woman in male garb.

The earliest and best-known depiction of Eugenia's trial in medieval art is a twelfth-century carved capital in the abbey church of Vézelay in Burgundy (Ambrose 2004; Ambrose 2006: 39–44; Crane 2002: 94–95; Grayson 2009: 155–61; Loos-Noji 1990; Mills 2015: 200–208). In the high Middle Ages Vézelay became significant as one of the starting points for pilgrims traveling through France to the shrine of Santiago de Compostela in northern Spain. This carving (fig. 4) is one of only a handful of surviving images that visibly convey what might be termed, with the benefit of hindsight, the narrative's genderqueer potential. Again, the focus is on the act of revelation, but the twelfth-century sculptor has adopted a different strategy from the later medieval manuscripts just cited. A short-haired, tonsured Eugenia is portrayed in the center of the capital, looking toward the prefect while opening their tunic; to the left stands the widow Melantia, who points to the accused with one hand as she holds her own, long hair with the other. The sculpture balances strongly gendered figures to the left and right, with a more ambiguously gendered persona in the center. Here is an image that potentially resonates with modern debates about trans visibility. The scene does not connote gender passing so much as gender crossing. Frozen in time to a moment just before the chest is revealed fully, Eugenia's boyishness lingers even as "he" is on the verge of becoming "she." Yet the anticipation of that revelation, at least in the mind's eye, provokes a vision of the saint's gender that seemingly transcends the binary frame in which it is simultaneously embedded.

Figure 4. Eugenia on trial. Carved capital, ca. 1120–40. North aisle of nave, La Madeleine, Vézelay. Photo: Robert Mills

One of the most striking depictions of Eugenia's trial from the Middle Ages is a fourteenth-century altar frontal, believed to have been commissioned for Santa Eugènia de Saga (Ger), a small church located in the Cerdanya region of Catalonia (Blanc 1998: 56–58; Cook 1959; Crane 2002: 94–95; Easton 2009: 343–45; Melero-Moneo 2005: 93–99). Now in a museum in Paris, the frontal tells the story of Eugenia's life and martyrdom across eight panels. In the first two scenes Eugenia escapes with her eunuch companions, before receiving baptism at the hands of the Christian bishop. The bishop, presiding over the monastery in which they seek refuge, keeps Eugenia's bodily sex hidden from the other monks. Interestingly, the scene of baptism depicts Eugenia facing the viewer frontally: her head is surrounded by a nimbus to indicate that she is already saintly, but she also holds her hands in front of her chest, thus obscuring precisely the physical attribute—breasts—that comes into view in the story's climax. Next, we see Eugenia transformed into Eugenius the abbot, visiting the sick widow with one of his fellow monks (fig. 5, left); still nimbed, to enable viewers to track the protagonist from one panel to the next, Eugenius has the same clean-shaven,

Figure 5. Eugenia visits Melantia (left); Eugenia on trial (right). Detail from St. Eugenia altar frontal, ca. 1330–35. From church of Santa Eugènia de Saga (Ger). Tempera on pinewood and base of lacquered silver. Musée des Arts Decoratifs, Paris. Photo: Robert Mills

tonsured appearance as other religious figures in the painting. Then the trial in Alexandria is depicted (fig. 5, right), in a scene that adopts a strikingly similar arrangement to the Vézelay capital and could plausibly be influenced by it (the frontal was probably created in a town with links to the Camino de Santiago).[9] This time Melantia kneels before Eugenia's father, the pagan judge, and a fourth figure, wearing a monk's habit, has been introduced. But in the Catalan painting, as at Vézelay, the father is bearded and raises his right hand; again, events are fixed temporally to the moment just before Eugenia reveals their body, producing a queerly disjunctive vision of female masculinity.

Scenes then follow that relate Eugenia's subsequent martyrdom in Rome. One image shows the Roman ruler pronouncing judgment, while in another Eugenia begins her ordeal as a martyr. The torments commence with the saint being thrown into the River Tiber to be devoured by fishes and miraculously saved. Next, she is pushed by an executioner into the furnace of the imperial baths, from which she reportedly emerged unharmed; this scene is combined with another episode also described in the written legend, in which Eugenia is visited by Christ in prison. Finally, the saint is shown being decapitated, her soul carried up to heaven. In these last four scenes Eugenia's appearance has been restored to that of a typical noble woman, wearing a trailing garment and long hair. The frontal contrasts masculine or bigendered imagery in the upper register with feminine imagery in the lower register. As in the Vézelay carving, the painting maintains a strong dichotomy between male and female, even as it also highlights a moment when that binary is disrupted. In the trial scene itself, of course, the ambiguities of the saint's gender identity are kept in play—and it is this kind of depiction, I am arguing, that potentially resonates with some modern articulations of gender queerness. Refusing to show a final, embodied act of displaying female breasts, Eugenia is effectively suspended in a state of continuing maleness, which conveys the spiritual transformation the saint has undergone by maintaining sexual purity. Eugenia's experience does not simply involve a temporary change of clothing; it also entails a sort of inner transformation. The altar frontal concludes, like some of the manuscript illuminations and sculptures discussed above, by highlighting Eugenia's trajectory from virile woman (or differently bodied man) to female virgin martyr. But it places greater emphasis than some of the other illustrative sequences on Eugenia's performance as a man.

Painted perhaps a few decades after this extraordinary painting is a cycle of frescoes devoted to Eugenia in Nevers cathedral, the existence of which affirms Burgundy's status as the most prominent locus for Eugenia-related imagery in medieval Europe.[10] Unfortunately, the paintings are badly preserved, so it is not clear whether they originally included a representation of the saint's trial in Alexandria; what remains appears only to relate to the martyr's torments in Rome. But the selection of episodes reportedly still visible in the nineteenth century (Guérin 1882: 467), namely, Eugenia's arrest, attempted drowning in the Tiber, attempted burning in the furnace of the imperial baths, and imprisonment during which she is sustained by a visit from Christ, corresponds remarkably closely to the arrangement of the lower register of the Catalan altar frontal. This suggests that narrative cycles depicting Eugenia's life and passion were not necessarily as rare as has sometimes been claimed by recent commentators (Grayson 2009: 155), and that her story may have been disseminated visually via international as well as regional networks, notably those associated with pilgrim roads to Santiago.

Lending support to this hypothesis is a late Gothic altarpiece (figs. 6 and 7) in the church of Santa Eugenia in Astudillo (Palencia) in northwestern Spain (Cantero 2000; Yarza Luaces 1987: 46–47; Wethey 1936: 98–99), which has received scant attention in literature on Eugenia's cult to date. Astudillo is located just a few miles from the Camino de Santiago, around three days' walk west from the city of Burgos. The altarpiece, which has been linked stylistically with the workshop of the celebrated Burgos sculptor Gil de Siloé (ca. 1400–1505), incorporates several polychromed wood carvings representing episodes from the saint's life. In the large, central scene Eugenia appears with book in hand, flanked by her eunuch companions Protus and Hyacinthus (fig. 6). There is a strong resemblance between this image of the saint and the statue at Varzy depicting Eugenia with extravagantly long golden locks (fig. 1). Immediately to the left of this scene, however, is another showing Eugenia exposing their breasts during the trial (fig. 7). Dressed in a black

Figure 6. Eugenia flanked by Protus and Hyacinthus. Detail from Santa Eugenia altarpiece. Late fifteenth or early sixteenth century, with later additions. Iglesia de Santa Eugenia, Astudillo (Palencia). Polychromed and gilded wood. Photo: Robert Mills, by permission of the bishopric of Palencia

habit, and wearing a tonsure that intriguingly suggests that the assumption of masculine appearance also prompted a change of hair color, Eugenia proudly displays their chest—replete with prominent nipples—to the gaze of Philip and his entourage. In other scenes on the altarpiece representing the saint's life, Eugenia assumes a distinctly feminine appearance, even in the carvings identified as showing the saint taking the vows of a monk and visiting the enamored widow Melantia; the final scene appears to show Eugenia enthroned and receiving a crown from Protus and Hyacinthus, who each place a hand on the golden tresses spread across her shoulders.[11] Arguably, these images place an overriding emphasis on the saint's "womanly" identity; but, as with some of the other renditions of the trial, beholders are also afforded a glimpse of different gendered possibilities.

The Astudillo trial scene cannot really be described as imaging a transman-in-the-making. Nor will terms such as *butch* fully account for the meanings such imagery conveys: narrative, visual, and cultural contexts evidently work against such

Figure 7. Eugenia on trial. Detail from Santa Eugenia altarpiece. Late fifteenth or early sixteenth century, with later additions. Iglesia de Santa Eugenia, Astudillo (Palencia). Polychromed and gilded wood. Photo: Robert Mills, by permission of the bishopric of Palencia

sanguine—and patently anachronistic—interpretations. Indeed, the denouement of the trial generates a reverse scenario: Eugenia's female masculinity is effectively *un*made. But the flash of recognition that some modern viewers may experience when confronted with such images draws attention to the possibility that representing and contemplating nonbinary notions of gender is not simply a privilege of the present. Willfully anachronistic deployments of terminology clearly have a role to play in tracing a genealogy for queer and trans subjectivities as they are currently conceived; but a fleeting sense of connectedness with images and objects created half a millennium ago also draws attention to the possibility that, long before terms such as *transgender* and *transsexual* entered the English language, gender was already being envisioned as a plural and potentially mutable phenomenon. This is important because it affirms the existence of alternatives to the homogenous gender norms and patriarchy customarily associated with the

Figure 8. Eugenia on trial. Detail from Master of Dinteville Allegory (Bartholomeus Pons?), *Triptych of St. Eugenia*, 1535. Oil on wood. Choir of Saint-Pierre, Varzy (Nièvre). Photo: Musée Auguste Grasset

period we call the Middle Ages. Even as the alternatives are ultimately imaginary (the "real" St. Eugenia is as elusive as the historical Jesus), such representations open our eyes to the prospect that, even during an epoch renowned for its conservative gender politics, different inflections and nuances of gender were sometimes rendered visible.

Another, better-known depiction of Eugenia's trial features in a triptych commissioned in 1535 by the bishop of Auxerre for the saint's church in Varzy (Boisseau 1905: 81–85; Cario et al. 1990: 100–103). As with the Astudillo altarpiece created a few decades earlier, the left-hand panel (fig. 8) representing the trial again shows Eugenia moving between genders (or possibly "transitioning"), except that the saint now openly displays a breast. At some point in the 1800s the bare breast was covered over with black pencil or paint, seemingly acknowledging the erotic potential of the image.[12] Alternatively, what disturbed the nineteenth-century censor may have been the disjunctive combination of a masculine tonsured head with visibly female morphology; again, the image arguably conveys the possibility of nonbinary genders and bodies. As in the Catalan altar frontal, the saint's femininity is restored in the central panel showing her martyrdom. And, in an additional move that confirms Eugenia's status as a reassuringly female virgin martyr, the right-hand panel shows the saint with a full head of hair, ringed with a crown of martyrdom, appearing to her mother Claudia at the site of her burial. The painter of the triptych has been identified as the Master of the Dinteville Allegory due to the work's similarities to another panel now in New York representing the powerful Dinteville brothers (Elsig 2005; Thuillier 1961); François II de Dinteville was the bishop who commissioned the work. A likely contender for the role of the "master" in question is a Dutch artist called Bartholomeus Pons, who is recorded as working in Burgundy around this time (Bruyn 1984). Setting aside the question of the painter's identity, however, it is worth acknowledging the resonances with earlier depictions of Eugenia's trial. Here is further evidence that in theory, and sometimes in practice, gender crossing was not simply a textual possibility but also representable in art.

Recently, some scholars have set out to explore how the human experiences and potential that we currently label *trans* resonate with representations of gender variance and diversity in premodernity (see, e.g., Gutt 2018; Karras and Linkinen 2016; Mills 2015; Raskolnikov 2010; Weisl 2009). If, in the words of Judith Butler, it is necessary today to develop a "new legitimating lexicon for the gender complexity that we have been living with for a long time" (2004: 51), then the images of Eugenia collated here arguably contribute to a deeper awareness of a medieval chapter in that long-running history. Although, as we have seen, artists often deliberately reined in the possibilities of Eugenia's story, refraining from visualizing the saint's trial in Alexandria or recoding the episode to reduce its impact, every so often their responses took a seemingly more open course.

Finally, it is worth acknowledging the political dimensions to this project. Collating and analyzing such imagery crucially demonstrates how, even as efforts are made to normalize gender crossing or to render it invisible, gender queerness endures as a possibility. While gender-crossing saints such as Eugenia were represented as experiencing the benefits of passing privilege, their example reminds us that passing is a situational activity, one that often remains fraught with danger. While being visibly trans is (understandably) not a desirable alternative for those striving to avoid such risks in the real world, discovering instances of trans visibility in the Middle Ages can nevertheless be a powerful corrective to the idea that gender normativity and gender binaries are in any way "natural" or anchored in "tradition." And if, as I have been arguing, images of gender queerness can indeed sometimes be discovered in medieval art, they convey a field of possibility that is as rich and provocatively complex as any of the experiences that today might be grouped under the umbrella of transgender.

*   *   *

In conclusion, I turn to a final example of Eugenia-related imagery that allows me to approach the issue of trans visibility from a different angle. Secreted away in a small treasury attached to the parish church of Saint-Pierre in Varzy, where several artifacts from the former Collégiale Sainte-Eugénie have ended up, is a remarkable thirteenth-century reliquary associated with the martyr (Bouillet 1901; *Les trésors des églises* 1965: 427). The box, shaped in the form of a small, shrine-like edifice or edicule, is surrounded on each side by the name—and in three cases portrait—of a female virgin martyr (fig 9). The inscriptions identify the individuals in question as Agnes, Agatha, Cecilia, and Eugenia. The words *Sancta Eugenia* currently appear below a statuette of an uncrowned figure carrying a book (fig. 9, lower left), but a colored lithograph (fig. 10) made by the nineteenth-century sculptor and scholar Jules Dumoutet, who in 1859 embarked on a project to produce a detailed and lavishly illustrated study of the collegiate church in Varzy, suggests that at one time this name appeared in a different position, at the base of a small window surrounded by a gilt frame (fig. 9, upper left). Later photographs also confirm that Dumoutet's illustration accurately conveys the shrine's original appearance.[13] Thus, at some point between the creation of these reproductions and recent times, the base of the reliquary has been turned to a new position. In what I take to be the correct, earlier configuration, however, the window was designed to draw the viewer's eye toward the relics contained within, allegedly pieces of skull, which the inscriptions on the base identified as belonging to Eugenia and other saints.[14]

The representational strategies adopted by the makers of this object are seemingly twofold. On one level, the reliquary is resolutely figurative, indicating what kind of person Eugenia really is. Emphasizing Eugenia's connections with a series of feminine-looking portraits, the object visibly suppresses the saint's stint as a male abbot in favor of her status as a female virgin martyr. Yet staying with the figurative, it is worth acknowledging connections between Eugenia's story and those of the other saints: Agnes, for instance, miraculously grew her hair to disguise her body and protect her chastity, while Agatha's breasts were removed and miraculously restored in an episode that potentially resonates with Eugenia's own movement between genders; for her part, Cecilia is said to have exerted control over her husband Valerian by persuading him not to consummate their marriage, as well as assuming a preaching and teaching role by instructing Valerian and his brother in the intricacies of Christian theology (Jacobus de Voragine 2012: 101–4, 154–57, 704–9). Each saint thus registers the potential for virginity to bleed into

Figure 9. Reliquary of Saint Eugenia. First half of thirteenth century. Silver, gilded and silvered copper, glass, over wooden core. Treasury of Saint-Pierre, Varzy (Nièvre). Photos: Robert Mills

Figure 10. Reliquary of Saint Eugenia. Lithograph in Jules Dumoutet,
*Monographie des monuments de la collégiale de Varzy (Nièvre) consacrée
à Sainte-Eugénie. 1ème et 2ème livraisons* (Paris: Lemercier, 1859).
Photo: Musée Auguste Grasset

virility in some way. Even what looks like an insistently "feminizing" interpretive
prism turns out, on closer inspection, to be less securely gendered.[15]

Moreover, the reliquary's refusal (at least in its original configuration) to
image Eugenia directly registers the potential for bodies to change and to be changed
over time. Notably, the monstrance displaying the saintly relics is surrounded by
signs of the four evangelists: Matthew, Mark, Luke, and John. While these symbols
were possibly added after the thirteenth century, their presence signals that when
audiences view the reliquary they are not simply being confronted with the material
remnants of a woman called "Eugenia." They are also seeing, through a glass darkly
as it were, the God-man with whom the martyr has become spiritually united.

If, as St. Jerome (ca. 340–420) once famously declared, woman "wishes to
serve Christ more than the world, then she will cease to be a woman and will be

called man, because we all wish to attain the perfect man" (*Commentariorum in Epistolam ad Ephesios*, quoted in Mills 2015: 206). Of course, Jerome's perfect man is Christ, represented figuratively on the reliquary in the form of a tiny figure of Christ crucified (fig. 9, upper left), held aloft by an angel that is thought to have been added in the fifteenth century (*Les trésors des églises* 1965: 427). But these figurative devices operate in tandem with a meditative framework. Eugenia's body is beheld via its relics; but, tantalizingly, an anchoring image of that very body is simultaneously withheld from view. There, in the gap between the body's evocation and its image, lies the possibility of contemplating gender transformation more abstractly. This is a mode of contemplation that is cognitively generative, in other words. Displaced from the field of earthly vision into the domain of the imaginary, viewers are being invited to behold Eugenia's transcendent state. Picturing Eugenia in abstract, then, other bodies, other genders might be thought.[16]

Robert Mills is professor of medieval studies at University College London, where he teaches history of art. Recent publications include *Seeing Sodomy in the Middle Ages* (2015) and *Derek Jarman's Medieval Modern* (2018).

Notes

1.   I refer to Eugenia as "they" when discussing the trial, in a nod to the episode's gender-queer potential.

2.   The Latin legend's sources, expertly analyzed by E. Gordon Whatley (2012), include the *Acts* of another gender-crossing saint, Thecla; the episode of Joseph and Potiphar's wife in Genesis 39; and a pre-Christian tale recorded by the mythographer Hyginus about the first Athenian female physician, Agnodice, who cross-dresses to enable her to practice medicine. My summary draws on those in Whatley 2012 (109–11), Bonner 1920, and Boisseau 1905 (86–127), as well as the versions included in Jacobus de Voragine's *Golden Legend* (2012: 551–53) and a thirteenth-century Old French version in a manuscript —Bibliothèque nationale de France, français 818—that contains texts with Burgundian forms (Stimm 1952: 7–9; 1955: 67–87).

3.   Morgan Mâcon, *Golden Legend* (Flanders, 1445–65), translated by Jean de Vignay, New York, Pierpont Morgan Library, MS M.672, fol. 74v.

4.   Inexplicably, the saint's right sleeve is also inscribed with the words "Santa Genovefa," possibly denoting an error on the part of the sculptor or the repurposing of a sculpture initially intended to represent Paris's patron saint.

5.   Nonetheless, in the Old French text edited by Helmut Stimm (1955), the masculine form is given as "Eugenios" and the feminine form as "Eugeni," so the "Eugene" spelling in the glass roundel is possibly a variation on the latter.

6.   On the "virile woman" theme in medieval Christianity more generally, see Newman 1995. Whatley (2012: 108–9) points out that the early Latin legend also concludes by reinscribing Eugenia's femininity, notably aligning her typologically with the beautiful

"virgo" Eve, which implicitly identifies her as bride to the second Adam Christ. Also, the Old French text edited by Stimm (1955) refers almost exclusively to the saint using the feminine form of the name "Eugeni," even during the period when she is dressed as a monk. It is only during the saint's entry to the monastery and in some of her interactions with Melantia that the masculine form "Eugenios" is deployed.

7. Jean de Vignay, *Miroir historial*, translation of Vincent of Beauvais, *Speculum historiale* (France, 1463), Paris, Bibliothèque nationale de France, français 50, fol. 393v.

8. Paris, Bibliothèque nationale de France, MS Arsenal 5080 réserve, fols. 152r (instruction), 152v (baptism), 153v (accusation).

9. Marisa Melero-Moneo (2005: 94–95) detects the presence of "linear Gothic" aesthetic principles, a style associated with Anglo-French influences, and suggests that the workshop in which the frontal was painted was likely located in Puigcerdà, a town in Cerdanya at the head of one of the Catalan tributaries of the Camino de Santiago. Catalonia is also peppered with numerous other buildings and places named after the saint, many originally Romanesque foundations, which reveal a fervent devotion to Eugenia in the region. These include Santa Eugènia de Berga (Osona), Sainte-Eugénie de Saillagouse (Cerdagne), and Sainte-Eugénie de Souanyas (Pyrénés-Orientales).

10. For a brief notice, which cautiously identifies and dates the surviving paintings in the north arm of the cathedral transept, see *D'ocre et d'azur* (1992: 297). Though current research favors a late fourteenth-century date, previous commentators have described the murals as emanating from the thirteenth century (Locquin 1913: 28) or earlier (Crosnier 1858: 151; Guérin 1882: 467). Locquin mentions making use of an account or drawing by a nineteenth-century museum curator in Nevers, Louis Du Broc de Ségange, which I have not been able to locate.

11. Or is the object being raised above Eugenia's head a comb? This would lend further weight to the possibility that the sculptors deliberately accentuated the perceived restoration of femininity following the trial. Harold E. Wethey (1936: 98) tentatively identifies the scene as showing the saint in prison, but it seems more likely, given the presence of the throne, that she is being depicted in a heavenly state following martyrdom. Thanks to José Luis Calvo Calleja, Delegado Diocesano de Patrimonio Cultural y Artístico de Palencia, for granting permission to allow me to photograph the altarpiece in situ.

12. A reproduction of the panel in its unrestored state, showing the bowdlerization, appears as plate 2 in Hervey and Martin-Holland 1911. Émile Boisseau (1905: 84) documents the use of pencil to conceal the saint's exposed chest.

13. One photograph is reproduced on a postcard dated 1892, which shows the reliquary flanked by two arm reliquaries from the treasury of Saint-Pierre in Varzy. Others were taken by Luc Joubert in conjunction with an exhibition at the Musée des Arts décoratifs, Paris (see *Les trésors des églises* 1965). Another late twelfth- or early thirteenth-century arm reliquary emanating from the church of Sainte-Eugénie in Varzy, known as the "Bras d'Or de Sainte Eugénie" (Cario et al. 1990: 143; *Les trésors des églises* 1965: 426) was destroyed in 2000 by thieves trying to recover its precious metal. A third reliquary, in the form of a bust, was recorded in the eighteenth century (Jobert 1867: 152, citing a 1792 inventory taken at the time of the church's suppression) but has also subsequently been lost (Crosnier 1858: 152; Guérin 1882: 468). I am very grateful to Jean-Michel Roudier of the Musée Auguste Grasset for facilitating my visit to the treasury in 2016, which enabled me to inspect and photograph the extant reliquary and other objects associated with Eugenia's cult.

14.   One seventeenth-century report suggests the reliquary also contains fragments from the skulls of all four martyrs (Jobert 1867: 144, transcribing from a manuscript by the seventeenth-century monk and scholar Georges Viole). In view of the reliquary's provenance, however, it seems likely that Eugenia's relics had particular significance for the inhabitants of Varzy and that the original arrangement, as documented in Dumoutet 1859, was designed to draw special attention to Eugenia's bones.

15.   Other connections also presumably determined the choice of martyrs, notably the fact that Agnes, Cecilia, and Eugenia all met their deaths in Rome. Auxerre cathedral's collection of relics included bones reputedly belonging to all four saints, as well as a host of other female virgin martyrs (Lebeuf [1743] 1855, 4:241–42). The bishops of Auxerre had strong connections with Varzy, building a palace there and sponsoring the Collégiale Sainte-Eugénie; in 925 bishop Gaudry was gifted Eugenia's relics by the pope during a trip to Rome and donated the lion's share to the church in Varzy (Boisseau 1905: 13; Guérin 1882: 468; Lebeuf [1743] 1855, 1:232).

16.   For an interrogation of how abstraction, in modern sculpture, provokes reflection on gender's multiple capacities, see Getsy 2015. For medieval theories of imagination and the process, termed "abstraction," through which the intellect extracts an intelligible kernel from a sensible shell, see Karnes 2011.

References

Ambrose, Kirk. 2004. "Two Cases of Female Cross-Undressing in Medieval Art and Literature." *Source: Notes in the History of Art* 23, no. 3: 7–14.

———. 2006. *The Nave Sculpture of Vézelay: The Art of Monastic Viewing*. Toronto: Pontifical Institute of Mediaeval Studies.

Anfray, M. 1951. *Architecture religieuse du Nivernais au moyen âge: Les églises romanes* (*Religious Architecture from the Nivernais in the Middle Ages: Romanesque Churches*). Paris: Picard.

Anson, John S. 1974. "The Female Transvestite in Early Monasticism: The Origin and Development of a Motif." *Viator* 5: 1–32.

Bennett, Judith M., and Shannon McSheffrey. 2014. "Early, Erotic, and Alien: Women Dressed as Men in Late Medieval London." *History Workshop Journal* 77, no. 1: 1–25.

Blanc, Monique. 1998. *Retables: La collection du musée des arts décoratifs* (*Retables: The Museum of Decorative Arts Collection*). Paris: Union centrale des arts décoratifs—Réunion des musées nationaux.

Boisseau, Émile. 1905. *Varzy (Nièvre): Son histoire, ses monuments, ses célébrités* (*Varzy [Nièvre]: Its History, Its Monuments, Its Personalities*). Paris: Societé anonyme de l'imprimerie Kugelmann.

Bonner, Campbell. 1920. "The Trial of Saint Eugenia." *American Journal of Philology* 41, no. 3: 253–64.

Bouillet, A. 1901. "L'art religieux à l'exposition rétrospective du Petit-Palais en 1900" ("Religious Art at the Petit-Palais's Retrospective Exhibition in 1900"). *Bulletin monumental* 65: 138–66.

Bruyn, J. 1984. "Over de betekenis van het werk van Jan van Sorel omstreeks 1530 voor oudere en jongere tijdgenoten (4). De Pseudo–Félix Chrétien: Een Haarlemse schilder (Bartholomeus Pons?) bij de bisschop van Auxerre" ("On the Significance of the Work of Jan van Sorel around 1530 for Older and Younger Contemporaries [4]. The Pseudo–Félix Chrétien: A Haarlem Painter [Bartholomeus Pons?] with the Bishop of Auxerre"). *Oud Holland* 98, no. 20: 98–110.

Bullough, Vern L. 1982. "Transvestism in the Middle Ages." In *Sexual Practices in the Medieval Church*, edited by Vern L. Bullough and James A. Brundage, 43–54. Buffalo, NY: Prometheus.

Butler, Judith. 2004. *Undoing Gender*. New York: Routledge.

Bynum, Caroline Walker. 1987. *Holy Feast and Holy Fast: The Religious Significance of Food to Religious Women*. Berkeley: University of California Press.

Cantero, Rodrigo Nebreda. 2000. "Retablo mayor de la iglesia de Santa Eugenia, Astudillo (Palencia): Agonía de una magna obra" ("Principal Retable of the Church of Santa Eugenia, Astudillo [Palencia]: Agony of a Great Work"). *Restauración y rehabilitación: Revista internacional del patrimonio histórico* (*Restoration and Rehabilitation: International Journal of Historical Heritage*), no. 47: 16–17.

Cario, Fabrice, et al. 1990. *Trésors caches des églises de la Nièvre* (*Hidden Treasures from the Churches of Nièvre*). Exhibition catalog. Nevers: Camosine.

Clark, David. 2009. *Between Medieval Men: Male Friendship and Desire in Early Medieval English Literature*. Oxford: Oxford University Press.

Cook, Walter W. S. 1959. "A Catalan Altar Frontal in Paris." In *Studies in the History of Art Dedicated to William E. Suida on his Eightieth Birthday*, edited by Samuel H. Kress Foundation, 17–20. London: Phaidon.

Crane, Susan. 2002. *The Performance of Self: Ritual, Clothing, and Identity during the Hundred Years War*. Philadelphia: University of Pennsylvania Press.

Cromwell, Jason. 1999. "Passing Women and Female-Bodied Men: (Re)claiming FTM History." In *Reclaiming Genders: Transsexual Grammars at the Fin de Siècle*, edited by Kate More and Stephen Whittle, 34–61. London: Cassell.

Crosnier, Augustin-Joseph. 1858. *Hagiologie nivernaise, ou Vies des saints et autres pieux personnages qui ont édifié le diocèse de Nevers par leurs vertus* (*Nivernais Hagiology; or, Lives of Saints and Other Pious Figures Who Built the Diocese of Nevers by Their Virtues*). Nevers: I.-M. Fay.

D'ocre et d'azur: Peintures murales en Bourgogne (*Wall Paintings in Burgundy*). 1992. Exhibition catalog. Dijon: Musée archéologique de Dijon.

Dumoutet, Jules. 1859. *Monographie des monuments de la collégiale de Varzy (Nièvre) consacrée à Sainte-Eugénie: 1ème et 2ème livraisons* (*Monograph on the Monuments of the Collegiate Church of Varzy [Nièvre] Dedicated to Saint Eugenia: First and Second Installments*). Paris: Lemercier (lithographs); Firmin-Didot (text).

Easton, Martha. 2009. "'Why Can't a Woman Be More Like a Man?': Transforming and Transcending Gender in the Lives of Female Saints." In *The Four Modes of Seeing: Approaches to Medieval Imagery in Honor of Madeline Harrison Caviness*, edited by Evelyn Staudinger Lane, Elizabeth Carson Pastan, and Ellen M. Shortell, 333–47. Farnham: Ashgate.

Elsig, Frédéric. 2005. "Les limites de la notion d'école': Remarques sur la peinture à Troyes au XVIe siècle" ("Limits of the Notion of 'School': Remarks on Painting in Troyes in the Sixteenth Century"). In *Études transversal: Mélanges en l'honneur de Pierre Vaisse* (*Transversal Studies: Miscellany in Honor of Pierre Vaisse*), edited by Leila El-Wakil, Stéphanie Pallini, and Lada Umstätter-Manndeova, 41–46. Lyon: Presses universitaires de Lyon.

Getsy, David J. 2015. *Abstract Bodies: Sixties Sculpture in the Expanded Field of Gender*. New Haven, CT: Yale University Press.

Grayson, Saisha. 2009. "Disruptive Disguises: The Problem of Transvestite Saints for Medieval Art, Identity, and Identification." *Medieval Feminist Forum* 45, no. 2: 138–74.

Guérin, Paul. 1882. *Les petits Bollandistes: Vies des saints de l'Ancien et du Nouveau Testament (The Little Bollandists: Lives of Saints from the Old and New Testaments)*. 15 vols. 7th ed. Paris: Bloud et Barval.

Gutt, Blake. 2018. "Transgender Genealogy in *Tristan de Nanteuil*." *Exemplaria* 30, no. 2: 129–46.

Halberstam, J. 2005. *In a Queer Time and Place: Transgender Bodies, Subcultural Lives*. New York: New York University Press.

Hervey, Mary F. S., and Robert Martin-Holland. 1911. "A Forgotten French Painter: Félix Chrétien." *Burlington Magazine* 19, no. 97: 48–49, 52–55.

Hildegard of Bingen. 1990. *Scivias*. Translated by Columba Hart and Jane Bishop. New York: Paulist Press.

Hotchkiss, Valerie R. 1996. *Clothes Make the Man: Female Cross Dressing in Medieval Europe*. New York: Garland.

Jacobus de Voragine. 2012. *The Golden Legend: Readings on the Saints*. Translated by William Granger Ryan. Introduction by Eamon Duffy. Princeton, NJ: Princeton University Press.

Jobert, M. l'abbé. 1867. "Extrait des manuscrits de dom Viole, religieux bénédictin de Saint-Germain d'Auxerre [. . .] de l'église collégiale de Sainte-Eugénie de Varzy" ("Extract from the Manuscripts of Dom Viole, Benedictine Monk of Saint-Germain d'Auxerre [. . .] on the Collegiate Church of Sainte-Eugénie de Varzy"). *Bulletin de la Société nivernaise* (2nd ser.) 2: 129–56.

Karnes, Michelle. 2011. *Imagination, Meditation, and Cognition in the Middle Ages*. Chicago: University of Chicago Press.

Karras, Ruth Mazo, and Tom Linkinen. 2016. "John/Eleanor Rykener Revisited." In *Founding Feminisms in Medieval Studies: Essays in Honor of E. Jane Burns*, edited by Laine E. Doggett and Daniel E. O'Sullivan, 111–22. Woodbridge, UK: Boydell and Brewer.

Lebeuf, Jean. (1743) 1855. *Mémoires concernant l'histoire civile et ecclésiastique d'Auxerre et de son ancien diocèse (Memoirs Concerning the Civil and Ecclesiastical History of Auxerre and Its Former Diocese)*. 4 vols. Revised and expanded by Ambroise Challe and Maximilien Quantin. Auxerre: Perriquet et Rouillé.

Les trésors des églises de France (Treasures from Churches in France). 1965. Exhibition catalog, Musée des Arts décoratifs. 2nd ed. Paris: Caisse nationale des monuments historiques.

Locquin, Jean. 1913. *Nevers et Moulins*. Paris: H. Laurens.

Loos-Noji, Pamela, 1990. "Temptation and Redemption: A Monastic Life in Stone." In *Equally in God's Image: Women in the Middle Ages*, edited by Julia Bolton Holloway, Joan Bechtold, and Constance S. Wright, 220–32. New York: Peter Lang.

Lussier, Réné, and Jacques Palet. 1934. "La collégiale Sainte-Eugénie de Varzy" ("The Collegiate Church of Sainte-Eugénie de Varzy"). *Bulletin de la Société Nivernaise des Lettres Sciences et Arts* 27: 547–66.

Melero-Moneo, Marisa. 2005. *La pintura sobre tabla del gótico lineal: Frontales, laterales de altar y retablos en el reino de Mallorca y los contados catalanes (Linear Gothic Panel Painting: Frontals, Altar Laterals, and Retables in the Kingdom of Mallorca and the Catalan Counties)*. Memoria Artium 3. Barcelona: Museu Nacional d'Art de Catalunya.

Mills, Robert. 2015. *Seeing Sodomy in the Middle Ages*. Chicago: University of Chicago Press.

Newman, Barbara. 1995. *From Virile Woman to WomanChrist: Studies in Medieval Religion and Literature*. Philadelphia: University of Pennsylvania Press.

Puff, Helmut. 2000. "Female Sodomy: The Trial of Katherina Hetzeldorfer (1477)." *Journal of Medieval and Early Modern Studies* 30, no. 1: 41–61.

Raskolnikov, Masha. 2010. "Transgendering Pride." *postmedieval: a journal of medieval cultural studies* 1, nos. 1–2: 157–64.

Steinmetz, Katy. 2014. "The Transgender Tipping Point." *Time*, May 29. time.com/135480/transgender-tipping-point/.

Stimm, Helmut. 1952. *Studien zur Entwicklungsgeschichte des Frankoprovenzalischen* (*Studies on the Developmental History of Franco-Provençal*). Akademie der Wissenschaften und der Literatur. Wiesbaden: Franz Steiner.

———, ed. 1955. *Altfranksprovenzalische Übersetzungen hagiographischer lateinischer Texte aus der Handschrift der Pariser Nationalbibliothek fr. 818* (*Old French-Provençal Translations of Hagiographic Latin Texts from the Manuscript of Paris, Bibliothèque nationale fr. 818*). Akademie der Wissenschaften und der Literatur. Mainz: Akademie der Wissenschaften und der Literatur; Wiesbaden: Franz Steiner.

Thuillier, Jacques. 1961. "Études sur le cercle des Dinteville: L'énigme de Félix Chrestien" ("Studies on the Dinteville Circle: The Enigma of Félix Chrestien"). *Art de France* 1: 57–75.

Weisl, Angela Jane. 2009. "How to Be a Man, though Female: Changing Sex in Medieval Romance." *Medieval Feminist Forum* 45, no. 1: 110–37.

Weismantel, Mary. 2013. "Towards a Transgender Archaeology: A Queer Rampage through Pre-history." In *The Transgender Studies Reader 2*, edited by Susan Stryker and Aren Z. Aizura, 319–34. New York: Routledge.

Wethey, Harold E. 1936. *Gil de Siloe and His School: A Study of Late Gothic Sculpture in Burgos*. Cambridge, MA: Harvard University Press.

Whatley, E. Gordon. 2012. "More than a Female Joseph: The Sources of the Late-Fifth-Century *Passio Sanctae Eugeniae*." In *Saints and Scholars: New Perspectives on Anglo-Saxon Literature and Culture in Honour of Hugh Magennis*, edited by Stuart McWilliams, 87–111. Cambridge: D. S. Brewer.

Yarza Luaces, Joaquín. 1987. "Definición y ambigüedad del tardogótico palentino: Escultura" ("Definition and Ambiguity in the Late Gothic Province of Palencia: Sculpture"). In *Arte, Arqueológica y Edad Antigua* (*Art, Archaeology and Antiquity*), vol. 1 of *Actas del I Congreso de Historia de Palencia* (*Proceedings of the First Palencia History Congress*), 23–59. Valladolid: Diputación Provincial de Palencia.

Dostoevsky's Timely Castration

JENNIFER WILSON

Abstract This article is a profile of "the skoptsy," a Christian sect that emerged in tsarist Russia whose followers, in an effort to divest themselves from the organs of sin, practiced castration as a form of religious piety. The skoptsy believed that before the fall of Adam and Eve, men and women did not have sexual organs; that its—they did not conceive of the original man and woman as being differentiated by their genitalia. The skoptsy were also millenarians, and as such they imagined the world would be transformed following an apocalyptic reckoning. In exploring how the temporal register of the skoptsy was depicted in the novels of Dostoevsky, the author proposes that the apocalyptic religious and political movements that were developing across imperial Russia can deepen contemporary discussions about queer temporality, in that they offer a counterpoint to arguments that the future is the realm of the normative reproducing subject.
Keywords Russia, Fyodor Dostoevsky, castration, temporality, nihilism

In the late eighteenth century, records emerged of a peasant by the name of Andrei Ivanov Blokhin who convinced a dozen people in the region of Orel (an area two hundred miles south of Moscow) to castrate themselves as a sign of their commitment to God.[1] Blokhin called his followers "*skoptsy*," Russian for "the castrated ones." The skoptsy lived by a literal interpretation of a verse from the Gospel of Matthew that reads, "There are some eunuchs, which were so born from their mother's womb: and there are some eunuchs, which were made eunuchs of men: and there be eunuchs, which have made themselves eunuchs for the kingdom of heaven's sake."[2] They considered themselves the latter, believing that once the world was populated by 144,000 skoptsy (this number was inspired by verse 14:1 in the Book of Revelations),[3] their sect would be admitted to heaven. A belief that sexual intercourse was sinful animated much of the skoptsy dogma, but abstinence alone was insufficient in their estimation of religious piety. The skoptsy believed that sexual organs themselves were inherently sinful; it was their conviction that Adam and Eve were given testicles and breasts by God as punishment for eating from the tree of knowledge, and that in their original sinless state of being, the first man and first woman were without distinction on the basis

TSQ: Transgender Studies Quarterly ∗ Volume 5, Number 4 ∗ November 2018   **565**
DOI 10.1215/23289252-7090031   © 2018 Duke University Press

of sexual genitalia (Heretz 2008: 92). The skoptsy persisted under the tutelage of Kondratii Selivanov (1732–1832), a vagrant from the Orel region who had previously been a member of a Christian sect of self-flagellants but left after finding the group's method of battling against the flesh to be insufficiently thorough. Only castration, which Selivanov referred to as "*ognennoe kreshchenie*" (fiery baptism) could render a person wholly purified (Engelstein 2003: 40).

The skoptsy were initially criminalized as schismatics; that is, their beliefs were deemed sectarian and in tension with Russian Orthodoxy, the official state religion. However, the skoptsy posed other threats to the fabric of traditional Russian society. For one, they were peasants (the same class that made up the serf population), and their ability to amass a following without the power of the state or the mark of aristocracy rendered them suspicious (just a few decades before the emergence of Blokhin, a Don Cossack named Yemelyan Pugachev led a mass uprising of 3 million people, mostly peasants, against the government of Catherine the Great). More still, their ability to perform castration with surgical precision (brought about by their familiarity with animal husbandry) and their seeming wealth of knowledge about medicine made them a threat to new efforts by the Russian state to professionalize the medical vocation and to centralize expertise within the walls of the recently formed institutions like the Saint Petersburg Military Medical Academy and the Medical Department within the Ministry of Internal Affairs (Engelstein 2003: 61).

There is nothing to suggest that the skoptsy, in the act of removing their genitalia, relinquished the gender identities assigned to them at birth. From their diaries and other testimony, nothing implies that the men of the skoptsy felt they were shedding male identity by removing their penises, nor did women impute such significance to the labiaectomies or mastectomies they underwent for religious purposes. Their memoirs and other testimonies do not reveal any sense of feeling "trapped in the wrong body"—rather they felt trapped for having a body—for being not divine but of the flesh. Writing about the skoptsy, the historian Laura Engelstein notes, "The Skoptsy clung to conventional gender roles and apparel . . . they were as patriarchal and misogynistic as the rest of the common folk" (2015: 123).

This essay, which briefly explores Fyodor Dostoevsky's portrayal of the skoptsy in two of his major novels (*The Idiot* and *The Brothers Karamazov*), is not an attempt to "re-populate the ancient past with modern trans men and women" (Weismantel 2013: 321), though I stand in solidarity with scholars like Valerie Rohy who argue that the pushback against ahistoricism runs the risk of "sound[ing] like the theories that have historically labeled homosexuality regressive and premature, belated and derivative" (2006: 67). While in their announcement for this special issue of *TSQ*, editors Zeb Tortorici and Leah DeVun observed that "scholars and activists have looked to the distant past for antecedents that might legitimate and inform present trans* identities," I do not see in the skoptsy such queer antecedents or a community that one might want to, in the vein of Carolyn Dinshaw, "touch across time" (1999: 21). Instead, I ask, how might looking at the apocalyptic beliefs of a chaste religious group who rejected identification according to gendered sexual organs challenge contemporary assumptions about the relationship between sexual alterity and teleology? Rather than employing ahistoricism to "unsettle what today's queer discourse takes for granted about sexuality" (Rohy 2006: 77), I am much more interested how it might unsettle what today's queer discourse takes for granted about time. In writing about the skoptsy (and their representation in nineteenth-century Russian literature, namely, the work of Dostoevsky), I use transhistoricity as a means to delicately puncture contemporary discourses around queer temporality with the small matter of nineteenth-century Russian millenarianism.

As nonreproducing, the skoptsy found themselves inserted into Dostoevsky's larger critique of the chaste asceticism of the burgeoning nihilist movement, whose followers purported to abstain from sex as a way of displaying a monastic devotion to revolution (which for the politically conservative Dostoevsky was another form of apocalypse). By the time he wrote his major novels, Dostoevsky had undergone a significant political conversion. Earlier in life, he had flirted with utopian socialism and was arrested for his involvement in a left-leaning group called the Petrashevsky Circle. He was then sentenced to four years in a Siberian labor camp and emerged from prison believing that Russian Orthodoxy, not social reforms, would solve the major ethical crises of his time (Frank 1983; Ruttenberg 2010).

An important touchstone for the nihilist movement was the 1863 novel *What Is to Be Done?* by Nikolai Chernyshevsky, a text that was meant to be for its readers a manual on how to lead a revolutionary life. Chernyshevsky presents the character Rakhmetov, an ascetic who sleeps on a bed of nails and abstains from wine and sumptuous foods, as the paragon of revolutionary commitment. Dostoevsky was long engaged in a polemic against Chernyshevsky's worldview and the nihilist crusade, and his critique, both of the nihilists and the skoptsy, often took the shape of painting chaste subjects as pathologically destructive. In both *The Idiot* and *The Brothers Karamazov*, which are two of Dostoevsky's four "murder novels," characters in some way associated with the skoptsy are implicated in the crimes. In both cases, these figures are guided by unscrupulous principles, often associated with excessive desire for material wealth, which Dostoevsky contrasted with the generosity of those fully enmeshed in family affairs.[4] Further still, the skoptsy are often connected to ideas of prophecy, premature aging, accumulation of wealth (all ways of engaging the future), whereas Dostoevsky elsewhere depicts characters focused on questions of family as preoccupied with the present moment.

The title of Dostoevsky's novel *The Idiot* (1869) refers to the main protagonist, Prince Myshkin, a Christ-like figure marked by a kind of exaggerated naïveté who arrives in Saint Petersburg to find the capital city full of avarice and vice. He crosses paths with a representative of Russia's new merchant class, a man by the name of Rogozhin. When Rogozhin takes Myshkin to his home, the latter is horrified to hear that all of the rooms are rented out by members of the skoptsy sect. About the house Rogozhin tells Myshkin, "В нем всё скопцы жили, Хлудяковы, да и теперь у нас нанимают" (Castrates, the Khludyakov family, have always lived here. Even today they still rent from us) (Dostoevsky 1972–90: 8:172). Rogozhin, we soon learn, is desperate to win the hand of Nastasya Filippovna, who is cast as the novel's fallen woman. Nastasya, castigating Rogozhin at one point for his mercantile lifestyle and mores, makes a prediction that invokes the specter of the skoptsy, again placing the sect in the prospective sphere of prophecy:

> You would start to amass [*kopit'*] money and, like your father, you would stay in this house with your castrates [*skoptsy*]. I guess that towards the end you would convert to their faith; and since you'd be so in love with your money, I guess, you'd amass [*skopil*] not 2 million, but 10 million. (translation from Comer 1996: 92)

> (А так . . . стал бы деньги копить и сел бы, как отец, в этом доме с своими скопцами; пожалуй бы, и сам в их веру под конец перешел, и уж так бы "ты свои деньги полюбил, что и не два миллиона, а, пожалуй бы, и десять скопил.) (Dostoevsky 1972–90: 8:178)

William Comer, writing about this exchange, notes with the above translation that Dostoevsky uses two different meanings of the Russian verb *skopit'* to make a judgment not only about Rogozhin but also about the skoptsy themselves. He points out that the verbs *to castrate* and *to amass* (typically money) are linguistically connected; the Russian word *skopit'* in its imperfective form refers to the former, and in its perfective form to the latter. Comer writes, "This play on the meanings of skopit' is the linguistic expression of a seemingly widespread cultural myth of the mid-nineteenth century. It was thought that the skoptsy, having lost their sexual organs, redirected their sexual drive into a passion for amassing wealth" (1996: 92).[5] What begins to emerge is that rather than depicting the skoptsy as without children and thus without a future, Dostoevsky presents the apocalyptic sect as teeming with futurity, merely channeled elsewhere, into wealth accumulation, into the world of prophecy (through the words of Nastasya Filippovna), a clear reference to the prophetic tradition of millenarianism.

Skoptsy also play a significant role in Dostoevsky's *The Brothers Karamazov* (1880), in which they are similarly associated with the novel's villain, Smerdyakov. The novel explores the murder of Fyodor Karamazov, father of the titular brothers. While Fyodor's eldest son Dmitry is blamed for the crime, his

Figure 1. Smerdyakov reveals his white stocking to Ivan. Fritz Eichenberg, illustration from a 1949 edition of Fyodor Dostoevsky's *The Brothers Karamazov* (New York: Heritage Press). Art © Estate of Fritz Eichenberg/Licensed by VAGA, New York, reproduced courtesy of the Department of Rare Books and Special Collections, Princeton University Library

illegitimate son, Smerdyakov, confesses to Dmitry's younger brother Ivan that he in fact killed Fyodor. In the process of confessing, Smerdyakov reveals to Ivan that he is wearing a white stocking, which causes Ivan to recoil in shock (fig. 1). White stockings were thought to be worn by the skoptsy.

Thus, like Rogozhin, Smerdyakov is closely associated with the skoptsy, though in this case, it is implied that he is actually a member of a sect (and does not, like Rogozhin, merely live among them). At one point in the novel, Smerdyakov goes on a trip to Moscow, and when he returns, his physical appearance changes significantly; according to the narrator: "Он вдруг как-то необычайно постарел, совсем даже несоразмерно с возрастом сморщился, пожелтел, стал походить на скопца" (He had suddenly somehow become curiously old, wrinkled to a degree not proportional to his age. His skin appeared jaundiced. He started to look like a castrate) (Dostoevsky 1972–90: 14:114). In focusing on the tendency of the skoptsy to appear prematurely aged, Dostoevsky places the sect and their practices on the temporal plane of the future; they are out of sync with time because they are too fast, hurrying toward an apocalyptic horizon. If the skoptsy can be said to occupy Jack Halberstam's definition of queer time, a time based on "the potentiality of a life unscripted by the conventions of a family, inheritance, and child rearing" (2005: 2) (and certainly they and the nihilists do not abide by the first or last), then they provide an example of queer time that is not belated, delayed, or without a future but one that rushes to the future, unencumbered by the quotidian demands of the present. It is precisely this overwhelming futurity that makes them antisocial to Dostoevsky.

Indeed, in his novel *The Possessed* (1872), Dostoevsky suggests that the antidote to the nihilist impulse is to be enmeshed in the present, which Dostoevsky specifically codes as the temporal sphere of the domestic, of the family. In the novel, a group of nihilist conspirators appear at the door of a character named Shatov, a former member of their group who has since abandoned his socialist ideals, a conversion cemented by the return home of his pregnant wife. The conspirators believe the presence of Shatov's wife, Marya, provides them with an advantage, as it will so consume Shatov with the present moment that he will be unable to see his future (an assassination) coming; the narrator remarks that the presence of a wife "отнял от него обычную прозорливость" (deprives [Shatov] of his habitual foresight) (Dostoevsky 1972–90: 7:536). By associating what is traditionally thought of as heteronormative time, defined by linear teleology toward the future, with an apocalyptic sect like the skoptsy, Dostoevsky reverses our understanding of how nonnormative sexual practices have been coded temporally. In essence, the case of the skoptsy contributes to recent scholarship by Elizabeth Freeman that seeks to disrupt the thinking espoused by Lee Edelman in *No Future: Queer Theory and the Death Drive* that the future is a space wholly occupied by the child and that reproduction is somehow synchronized with the forward teleology of US industrialization. In *Time Binds: Queer Temporalities, Queer Histories*, Freeman writes instead, "Emotional, domestic, and biological tempos are, though culturally constructed, somewhat less amenable to the speeding up and micromanagement that increasingly characterized U.S. industrialization" (2010: 7). In arguing this point, Freeman cites the work of Eli Zaretsky, historian and author of *Capitalism, the Family, and Personal Life*, in which Zaretsky asserts that, "the family, attuned to the natural rhythms of eating, sleeping, and child care, can never be wholly synchronized with the mechanized tempo of industrial capitalism (1986: 33).

The skoptsy never reached their goal of 144,000, though they came remarkably close. By the time of the Russian Revolution of 1917, they counted 100,000 members among their constituency (Lane 1978: 95). However, after the revolution, their numbers declined dramatically, dropping to two thousand as of 1929 (95). In the latter half of the twentieth century, small isolated groups could be found who had perpetuated their group by raising orphans of the Second World War (95). As a force for creative thinking about the nature of the body as a site of self-making in a repressive society like tsarist Russia, they exist only now in the archives and in the novels of Dostoevsky where they were mostly used as a proxy for the novelist's larger fears of a political apocalypse in the form of nihilist revolution. In writing about the skoptsy in the context of transhistoricity, I mean to question whether the apocalyptic beliefs of the sect, inscribed on their very bodies, can push against the conventional wisdom that the future is the realm of the normative. Perhaps the skoptsy project (and the nihilists for that matter) can add to the queer archive imagined by Freeman wherein queerness is a "form of future-making, of re-creating the social, though perversely enough, not in the name of the future" (Freeman et al. 2007: 188).

Jennifer Wilson is an assistant professor in the Department of Slavic and Eastern European Languages and Cultures at the Ohio State University.

Acknowledgment

I would like to first express my gratitude to Zeb Tortorici and Leah DeVun for their tireless work and curatorial brilliance. Their feedback on my essay and the conversations we had about how it fit into their overall vision for this issue were tremendously helpful as I revised my thoughts on Dostoevsky's potential contribution to the idea of transhistoricity. I would also like to thank the anonymous reviewers for their thorough and generous reports; having interlocutors whose breadth of knowledge was so vast (from the arcane religious practices of tsarist Russia to contemporary discourses of queer temporality) was truly inspiring. I would also like to thank the participants of the Queer Russia Symposium at Davidson College for their feedback, especially Roman Utkin, who brought us all to North Carolina. Lastly, thank you to the heroic Massimo Balloni who helped me track down the beautiful Fritz Eichenberg lithograph that is reproduced in these pages. The translations from Dostoevsky's novels that appear in this essay are, unless otherwise noted, my own.

Notes

1.   On the arrest and capture of Blokhin, see Engelstein 2003 (26). Laura Engelstein's book on the skoptsy is considered the authoritative historical account of the group, its beliefs, and how the tsarist government responded to their bodily practices. There does exist a second book on the skoptsy (Etkind 1998, available in Russian), but Engelstein and others have questioned much of its methodology and findings. For Engelstein's review of Etkind, see Engelstein 1999.

2.   The verse is Matthew 19:12. This is quoted from Engelstein (2003: 11), where she offers more on skoptsy exegesis.

3.   The verse reads, "Then I looked, and behold, on Mount Zion stood the Lamb, and with him 144,000 who had his name and his Father's name written on their foreheads." For more on the significance of this number in the context of skoptsy apocalyptic mythology, see Heretz 2008 (92).

4.   Due to space constraints, this piece can only focus on representations of the skoptsy in Dostoevsky and cannot wholly or even adequately account for the complexities with which Dostoevsky approached questions of gender and sexuality. For more in-depth studies on this topic, see (to name just a few) Fusso 2008, Knapp 2004, Doak 2015, and Straus 1994.

5.   Laura Engelstein has pointed out that this myth was wildly overstated and relied on much of the same stereotyping as anti-Semitism in the nineteenth century (and in fact, Dostoevsky was unapologetically anti-Semitic). Engelstein writes, "Portraying the skoptsy as ferociously money-loving became a cliché of anti-sectarian writing. . . . Like the Jews, some did, in fact deal in precious metals and lend money at interest. For this reason, as well as their entrepreneurial success, both groups were said to profit at the common people's expense" (2003: 69).

References

Comer, William. 1996. "Rogozhin and the 'Castrates': Russian Religious Traditions in Dostoevsky's The Idiot." *Slavic and East European Journal* 40, no. 1: 85–99.

Dinshaw, Carolyn. 1999. *Getting Medieval: Sexualities and Communities, Pre- and Postmodern.* Durham, NC: Duke University Press.

Doak, Connor. 2015. "Masculine Generation in Dostoevsky's Demons." In *Russian Writers and the Fin de Siècle: The Twilight of Realism*, edited by Katherine Bowers and Ani Kokobobo, 107–25. Cambridge: Cambridge University Press.

Dostoevsky, Fyodor Mikhailovich. 1972–90. *Polnoe sobranie sochinenii v 30 tomakh (Collected Works in Thirty Volumes).* Leningrad: Nauka.

Engelstein, Laura. 1999. "Review of Aleksandr Etkind, *Khlyst: Sekty, literatura i revoliutsiia.*" *Slavic Review* 58, no. 2: 482–83.

———. 2003. *Castration and the Heavenly Kingdom: A Russian Folktale.* Ithaca, NY: Cornell University Press.

———. 2015. "Prisoner of the Zeitgeist." In *Adventures in Russian History Research: Reminiscences of American Scholars from the Cold War to the Present*, edited by Samuel H. Baron and Cathy A. Frierson, 115–26. New York: Routledge.

Etkind, Aleksandr. 1998. *Khlyst. Sekty, literatura i revoliutsiia (Khlyst: Sects, the Literature, and Revolution).* Moscow: New Literary Observer.

Frank, Joseph. 1983. *Dostoevsky: The Years of Ordeal, 1850–1859.* Princeton, NJ: Princeton University Press.

Freeman, Elizabeth. 2010. *Time Binds: Queer Temporalities, Queer Histories*. Durham, NC: Duke University Press.

Freeman, Elizabeth, et al. 2007. "Theorizing Queer Temporalities: A Roundtable Discussion." *GLQ* 13, nos. 2–3: 177–95.

Fusso, Susanne. 2008. *Discovering Sexuality in Dostoevsky*. Evanston, IL: Northwestern University Press.

Halberstam, Jack. 2005. *In a Queer Time in Place: Transgender Bodies, Subcultural Lives*. New York: New York University Press.

Heretz, Leonid. 2008. *Russia on the Eve of Modernity: Popular Religion and Traditional Culture under the Last Tsars*. Cambridge: Cambridge University Press.

Knapp, Liza. 2004. "Mothers and Sons in *The Brothers Karamazov*: Our Ladies of Skotoprigonevsk." In *A New Word on "The Brothers Karamazov,"* edited by Robert Louis Jackson, 31–52. Evanston, IL: Northwestern University Press.

Lane, Christel. 1978. *Christian Religion in the Soviet Union: A Sociological Study*. London: George Allen and Unwin.

Rohy, Valerie. 2006. "Ahistorical." *GLQ* 12, no. 1: 61–83.

Ruttenberg, Nancy. 2010. *Dostoevsky's Democracy*. Princeton, NJ: Princeton University Press.

Straus, Nina Pelikan. 1994. *Dostoevsky and the Woman Question*. New York: Palgrave Macmillan.

Weismantel, Mary J. 2013. "Towards a Transgender Archaeology: A Queer Rampage through Prehistory." In *Transgender Studies Reader 2*, edited by Susan Stryker and Aren Z. Aizura, 319–35. New York: Routledge.

Zaretsky, Eli. 1986. *Capitalism, the Family, and Personal Life*. New York: Harper Collins.

Naming and Claiming

Recovering Ojibwe and Plains Cree Two-Spirit Language

KAI PYLE

Abstract This article analyzes archival and oral records of Ojibwe and Plains Cree words for Two-Spirit people to show the continuity between historical and modern Two-Spirits. In the face of appropriation of historical Two-Spirits by both cisgender and transgender non-Indigenous people, as well as scholarly insistence on a disconnect between historical and modern Two-Spirits, examining the linguistic history of specific communities reveals what the author, a Two-Spirit person themself, terms "trans*temporal kinship." Referring to the ability of Two-Spirit people to establish kin relations across time, with both ancestors and descendants, the application of trans*temporal kinship and other Indigenous concepts allows Two-Spirit people to circumvent the debate in transgender studies as to whether transgender people can and should claim historical figures as "transgender ancestors." The article argues that Two-Spirit reclamation of language for people "like us" is a vital element in redressing the violence and exclusion perpetrated against Two-Spirit people today.
Keywords Two-Spirit, Ojibwe, Plains Cree, transgender history

The transgender native, the third gender, the berdache, the Two-Spirit—these figures, overlapping but not always identical, have become well-known images in both Indigenous and non-Indigenous queer and trans communities in the past thirty years. Both Indigenous and non-Indigenous people have laid claim to these figures as ancestors and queer/trans predecessors. Most of the researchers involved in "uncovering" or "rediscovering" these figures have been non-Indigenous, and many of them have had a universalist goal of shedding light on gender variance as a global phenomenon. Two-Spirit people, meanwhile, have criticized anthropologists and other scholars for this appropriation, as well as for their construction of a strict binary between "traditional/historical" and "modern" Two-Spirit people. Despite this criticism, however, Two-Spirit people have often been forced to rely on the research generated by white scholars simply to access any information about people like them from the past.

Like previous researchers and Two-Spirit laypeople, I too began my work out of a desire to find historical records of people "like me." Knowing that the

TSQ: Transgender Studies Quarterly * Volume 5, Number 4 * November 2018 **574**
DOI 10.1215/23289252-7090045   © 2018 Duke University Press

term *Two-Spirit* has been said to come from the Ojibwe term *niizh manidoowag* (popularized in the 1990s), and already involved in Ojibwe, Michif, and Cree language revitalization in my ancestral communities, I began to search for linguistic records of language for Two-Spirit people. As a Two-Spirit and transgender person, this was not just an idle curiosity of mine but a vital necessity for my continued participation in Indigenous cultural spheres: What do I call myself in my languages when speaking to others? What history can I draw on to help my community members, especially elders who speak our languages, understand who I am? These questions face nearly every Two-Spirit person who is involved with linguistic and cultural revitalization, a movement that is sweeping Indigenous communities today.

Yet in addition to the process of recovering Two-Spirit history, Two-Spirit people must also deal with the legacy of non-Indigenous claims to our Two-Spirit predecessors by both white cisgender queer people as well as white transgender people. These claims not only appropriate Two-Spirit history but also minimize the trauma of settler colonialism and heteropatriarchy that affects Two-Spirit people. Likewise, we face abundant scholarship that claims complete disconnection between historical and modern Two-Spirit people, as well as scholarship chastising transgender people of all races for attempting to claim historical figures as transgender ancestors. I argue here that examining the linguistic history of Two-Spirit people reveals the falsity of the claimed disconnect between historical and modern Two-Spirits. I also argue that by rooting ourselves in Indigenous methodologies, Two-Spirit people are able to circumvent the debate within transgender studies as to whether it is possible and desirable to claim historical figures as transgender or Two-Spirit ancestors. Despite frequent rejections within recent queer theory of ancestral claims in general, the notion of trans*historicities encourages scholars to work with the tension between recognizing similarities and situating differences, rather than simply picking a side. For Indigenous people, engaging with this concept may be an especially fruitful way to challenge assertions of a radical disconnect between the Indigenous past and present without resorting to overly romanticized or atemporal ideas about the past. Though the skepticism of reclamation work in queer and trans studies may be warranted in service of avoiding such romantic and dehistoricized portrayals of history, it can also have the effect of delegitimizing Indigenous understandings of time and kinship. Trans*historicities, then, must be flexible enough to account for Indigenous (and particularly Two-Spirit) ways of knowing and being as equally valid methods of approaching the past.

To explore what one possibility of an Indigenous trans*historical approach might look like, I have developed the term *trans*temporal kinship* to refer to the ability of transgender and Two-Spirit Indigenous people to establish kin relations across time, with both ancestors and descendants. This trans*temporal kinship, determined not by non-Indigenous scholars but by the language usage of Indigenous people themselves, is deeply rooted in Ojibwe and Cree worldviews. The term *seven generations* is common in grassroots Indigenous communities today, used to refer to an ethics that requires us to think about our impacts and responsibilities in seven-generation increments. This is reflected in the meaning of the Ojibwe word *aanikoobijigan* and the Plains Cree word *âniskotâpân*, both of which refer to great-grandparents as well as great-grandchildren, with seven generations represented between the two. These two words also refer to ancestors more broadly. Using *seven generations* and *aanikoobijigan/âniskotâpân* as a framework, it is possible to use Indigenous systems of kinships to reconceptualize what it would mean to claim Two-Spirit people as ancestors. As a form of trans*historical thinking, using the concept of trans*temporal kinship is one way to reformulate notions of what it means to claim transgender ancestors and descendants. This article will demonstrate how this trans*temporal kinship framework can be used to read linguistic sources in service of establishing relationships among Indigenous kin across time.

The form of heteropatriarchy that settler colonialism has generated in the Americas has devastated Two-Spirit people for centuries. From murder and massacre during the early periods of colonization, to abuse from church and government officials in boarding and residential schools, to the enormous rates of violence against Two-Spirits in today's world, the atrocities committed by agents of settler colonialism have long targeted Two-Spirit people because of their race, indigeneity, gender, and sexuality. Two-Spirit people inherit this intergenerational trauma as well as the abuse they face in their own lives. Despite this, however, they have continued to survive and assert unique identities and roles within their communities over a great period of time. I argue that by analyzing language used for Two-Spirit people, we can trace this survival.

This article is a survey of gender variance in Ojibwe and Plains Cree communities at the lexical level, that is, an overview of words that might refer to people today known as "transgender," "third gender," "gender variant," or "Two-Spirit." Throughout this article, I use the term *Two-Spirit* to refer to Indigenous people who fall outside the accepted boundaries of modern white or "Western" gender and sexuality, both past and present. When referring to modern Two-Spirit people, this includes those who identify as lesbian, gay, bisexual, transgender, and queer, as well as people who fit the first definition but do not identify with one of those terms. While the details of Two-Spirit identification are complex, I refer in modern-day contexts specifically to cisgender and transgender Two-Spirit people, while recognizing that these terms may not fully capture the intricacies of individual Two-Spirit people's understandings of their own gender and sexuality. I also reference the term *berdache*, a word referring to people anthropologists have theorized as a third gender in Indigenous communities, but which the Two-Spirit community has rejected because of its etymological origins as a word for a male sexual slave (Herdt 1997). I use this term only when indicating the views of nineteenth-century non-Indigenous recorders or of twentieth-century anthropologists, both of whom used the word to refer to Two-Spirit people.

The term *Two-Spirit*, which was formally adopted at the 1990 Native American/First Nations Gay and Lesbian Conference in Winnipeg, is frequently cited as being a translation of the Ojibwe phrase *niizh manitoag*, sometimes spelled *niizh manidoowag* (Anguksuar 1997). The latter is clearly inaccurate: although -*wag* is indeed a common plural ending in Ojibwe, the correct plural of *manidoo* is *manidoog*. Furthermore, *manidoog* generally refers to external spirits, rather than the spirit or soul of a person, for which the word is *ojichaagwan* (*Ojibwe People's Dictionary* 2017d, 2017e). The use of *manidoowag* suggests that someone who was only partially familiar with the language may have attempted to retranslate *Two-Spirit* into Ojibwe. Two-Spirit scholar Alexandria Wilson, on the other hand, remembers *Two-Spirit* being given to a Cree lesbian in a dream (2007). Further research may be necessary to determine the exact origins of *Two-Spirit*. Regardless, today the term is dear to many Indigenous people. In addition to being a word to refer to modern identities, *Two-Spirit* was also intended to be a replacement for the derogatory term *berdache*. Two-Spirit people attending the 1990 conference were acutely aware of anthropological work being done to "discover" historical "berdaches," and they were intent on talking back to scholars doing such work without considering or involving modern Two-Spirit people. In one of the key texts in the field of queer Indigenous studies—which has developed as another way for Two-Spirit people to talk back to scholarship about their lives and histories—the editors of the anthology *Queer Indigenous Studies* write, "As a critique of anthropological writing based in colonial and western notions of gender and sexuality, the category of Two-Spirit creates a distinct link between the histories of diversity and Indigenous GLBTQ2 people today" (Driskill et al. 2011: 11). I contend here that Indigenous language terminology for Two-Spirit people are the roots of the link between past and present as asserted by *Two-Spirit*, regardless of whether that term is of ancient or modern origin.

As the field of queer Indigenous studies has become more and more prominent in the past decade, several writers have invoked calls by Indigenous studies scholars such as Craig Womack and other Indigenous literary nationalists to investigate tribally specific histories and knowledges; the introduction to *Queer Indigenous Studies* itself spends significant space recalling this scholarly genealogy. Most notably, Qwo-Li Driskill has extensively written on the topic of Cherokee Two-Spirit people both past and present in *Asegi Stories*. This book is framed around the concept of *asegi*, which Driskill states translates as "strange" and is understood by some Cherokees to be similar to the English word *queer* (2016: 6). Driskill uses the notion of *asegi* to read various moments in Cherokee history through a queer lens, in the process demonstrating how language can be a framework for analyzing Indigenous pasts. Another excellent example of tribally specific work around Two-Spirit language is Saylesh Wesley's article "Twin-Spirited Woman: Sts'iyóye Smestíyexw Slhá:li," which recounts how Wesley's relationship with her grandmother led to the coining of a new Stó:lō word for Two-Spirit woman, which her grandmother explained can be interpreted as "'two-spirited woman,' or 'twin-soul woman,' or 'same spirit as a woman'" (2014: 343).

These groundbreaking works have guided me in choosing to examine tribally specific linguistic concepts as a way to shed light on Two-Spirit relationships with ancestral and descendant figures. I have chosen to examine Ojibwe and Plains Cree words alongside one another for several reasons. They are both part of the same language family, Algonquian, and have many linguistic similarities. In addition, Ojibwe and Cree people have a long history of connections and kinships with each other. Many bands on the Canadian prairies have both Plains Cree and Saulteaux (Plains Ojibwe) members, and many people are of mixed Cree and Ojibwe ancestry. The final reason for my choice to consider both is simply that both Cree and Ojibwe are my ancestral languages, and this project originated in my attempts to find words that have been used for Two-Spirit people in my own communities.

To accomplish this project, I examined archival written records as well as oral traditions (including those that have been received and recorded by other Indigenous people as well as oral tradition I have myself received). Archival sources are incredibly important to Indigenous people searching for words for people like them, owing to their recording of the distant past. However, such sources must be considered in light of the motives and context surrounding those who created them—primarily non-Indigenous, white men. Missionary dictionaries were created with the intent of assisting the conversion of Indigenous people to Christianity and to white "civilized" ways of life more broadly. Captivity narratives were often used as a way to demonstrate the savagery of Indigenous people to justify conquest. Ethnographies of the twentieth century were frequently intended as "salvage anthropology," hoping to record dying ways of life that were doomed to disappear. Few hoped to provide affirmation of Indigenous gender and sexual variance. Indigenous people attempting to extract knowledge from such sources face a fraught journey of interpretation.

Alongside archival sources, the other main place where records of Two-Spirit people can be found is in Indigenous oral traditions. Oral traditions come with their own set of strengths and difficulties for people trying to understand

Two-Spirit history. While oral tradition comes directly from Indigenous people without a non-Indigenous mediator, the fact that Indigenous people have for at least a century, longer in many cases, been impacted by assimilation policies must be taken into account for its potential impact on what has been passed down. This is particularly important in the case of words for Two-Spirit people because of settler colonial attempts to stamp out Indigenous gender and sexual variance.

Among the earliest written records of Ojibwe and Cree are nineteenth-century documents such as travel accounts and missionary dictionaries. While white travelers had written about the presence of "berdaches" in many Indigenous communities before this, the first appearance of a specific word for such people in Ojibwe occurs in John Tanner's 1830 captivity narrative. Tanner was an American living in Kentucky when at age nine he was captured by Ojibwe men and taken to live among the Ojibwe people in the Great Lakes and Red River regions, primarily in what is today Minnesota and Manitoba. He was sold to and adopted by an Odawa woman, Netnokwa, who thereafter raised him in the Ojibwe and Odawa cultures he was surrounded by. In 1827, he met Edwin James, who served as his amanuensis in writing his captivity narrative (Sayre 2017).

In the narrative, Tanner describes an encounter with a particular Ojibwe individual named Ozaawindib (Ozaw-wen-dib in his orthography). Ozaawindib, Tanner writes, "was one of those who make themselves women, and are called women by the Indians. There are several of this sort among most, if not all the Indian tribes. They are commonly called A-go-kwa, a word which is expressive of their condition" (1830: 105). This word, *a-go-kwa*, is the first record of an Ojibwe name for the type of person Tanner describes. The ending of the word, in modern spelling "kwe," is the ending signifying "woman," but the meaning of the rest of the word is still debated by linguists, Tanner's comment that it is "expressive of their condition" notwithstanding.

The story that Tanner tells about this *a-go-kwa* Ozaawindib is how she (the pronoun that Tanner uses) repeatedly sought his hand in marriage, which he found bothersome and even disturbing. The people around him, meanwhile, seemed to find this pursuit humorous and encouraged it. It is unclear what motivated Tanner to include this story in his narrative, and even more so, to what extent the reactions to these events can be ascribed to Ojibwe cultural norms, to his own mixed-culture background, or to an appeal to the sensibilities of his American audience. However, the ultimate effect of this story is to reinforce the image of Indigenous people as savages, who tolerate and even encourage such "disgusting" gender-variant behavior in the eyes of white Americans.

Several decades later, further northwest in Plains Cree territory, two missionaries published dictionaries of the Cree language. In 1865, Edwin Arthur Watkins published *A Dictionary of the Cree Language*, in which he recorded the word *ayākwāo* as a noun meaning "a castrated animal, a hermaphrodite" (Watkins 1865: 195). Nine years later, Francophone missionary Albert Lacombe published his *Dictionnaire de la langue des Cris*, in which he recorded what appears to be the same word, *ayekkwe, wok* (wok being the plural ending), meaning "mâle coupé, eviratus; v. g., ayekkwe-watim, cheval, ou chien coupé; ayekkwe-mustus, taureau coupé. Aussi, on appelle ainsi celui qui n'est ni mâle ni femelle, ou plutôt: qui utrumque sexum habent, Hermaphrodite" (1874: 326). Both entries record a dual meaning for this word: first, it refers to a castrated animal, and, second, to someone (not specified as to whether human or animal) who is a "hermaphrodite." Their inclusion in the dictionaries by missionaries suggests that the compilers found them to be necessary words to know for anyone interacting with Cree people. Both definitions privilege meanings that refer to physical characteristics of the body—but as later sources suggest, these may not be the only definitions of the word. As we will see below, these words, at least at one point in time, also could refer to people with seemingly unambiguously "male" physical characteristics who, like the *a-go-kwa*, took on a womanly or womanlike role in their society. Yet dictionaries compiled by white missionaries do not record this meaning.

There are several possible reasons for this absence that we can speculate on, each of which has its own interesting implications. One possibility is that missionaries simply did not see "berdaches" among Cree people and only heard these words used to refer to those with ambiguous sexual characteristics. This seems unlikely, given other records of the commonness of "berdache" figures among Indigenous people, especially plains groups—even Tanner, who would have interacted with Plains Cree groups in his travels in the Red River region, notes that "most" Indigenous groups had such figures. Still, in the 1930s Cree elder Fine-Day stated that such people were uncommon, so it is possible the missionaries did not encounter any. On the other hand, perhaps they misunderstood the *ayākwāo/ayekkwe* they saw to all be hermaphrodites, as they would not have been privy to the precise details of the bodies of every *ayākwāo/ayekkwe*. Alternatively, perhaps the missionaries fully understood the presence of "berdaches" but chose not to include them in their definitions. Why might they do this? In Lacombe's definition in particular, there is a certain amount of discomfort evident in the way that he switches from French to Latin to state that the *ayekkwe* might be an individual "who has both sexes." It is as though such a detail were so scandalous that it must be concealed from the average French-speaking audience. The presence of a gender role so far outside what was deemed acceptable by Christians would likely have been distressing to the missionaries. Despite these attempts to erase them, however, Two-Spirit people clearly existed in their communities and continued to do so despite pressure from missionaries to take up more "acceptable" gender roles.

The primary source for the presence of Two-Spirit individuals among Plains Cree people, besides these dictionaries, is David Mandelbaum's ethnographic account, *The Plains Cree* (1979). Based on the author's research among the Cree in 1934 and 1935, it attempts to reconstruct the life of Cree people during the 1800s at the height of the buffalo-hunting culture. In one section, Mandelbaum includes a recollection at length by a Cree man, Fine-Day, about a relative of his. Fine-Day states, "They were called *a·yahkwew*. It happened very seldom. But one of them was my own relative. He was a very great doctor. When he talked his voice was like a man's and he looked like a man. But he always stayed among the women and dressed like them." The preferred name of this person was *piecuwiskwew*, meaning "thunder woman" because "Thunder was a name for a man, and *iskwew* is a woman's name; half and half just like he was" (167).

The Plains Cree was published in its entirety in 1979; however, it is based on a shorter original publication from 1940. By the time Mandelbaum conducted his research in the 1930s, there was already an interest among anthropologists in the gender systems of Indigenous people and the variance among those systems. Mandelbaum refers to the "berdache" as a concept of which he assumes his readership will have prior knowledge. By 1979, interest in this topic was once again becoming strong as lesbian and gay anthropologists and other scholars were organizing to widen the extent of scholarship on gender and sexual variance (Morgensen 2011). On the one hand, this information was intended to further *global* understandings of gender and sexuality. Anthropological studies of Indigenous people at large were meant to show the great variety of potential social structures around the world at large. Mandelbaum, in his preface to the 1979 edition, recognizes both this global significance as well as the importance of this record to Plains Cree people in particular. When asked by a Cree man, "What good . . . have all your efforts among us and your writings about us done for my children and my people?" he responded that his work gave them "some record of their forefathers and of a way of life that many of them would increasingly want to know about. Together with their own oral traditions it could provide that sense of personal and social roots that most people want to have" (1979: xv–xvi). At the same time, he notes that "for an understanding of mankind generally, the studies of the Plains Cree and of other Plains Indians tell us about one general set of answers that these people developed to meet the life questions that all men and women must confront" (xvi).

Mandelbaum desired to record the ways of life that the Plains Cree people held in the time before white Canadians and Americans forced them onto reserves and reservations, and he attempted to do this by interviewing the oldest people in the community (almost entirely men). He states that at the time of his research, Cree was the primary language of the community, and the quotes in his book were recorded with the help of several interpreters (4). The effects of settler colonialism and life on the reserves between the late 1800s and the 1930s, however, should not be ignored. During this time, Canadian and American officials attempted to enforce white practices of "civilization" in Indigenous communities, suppressing, among other things, Indigenous language, religion, and gender and sexual practices. Particularly among those who had learned English, we must consider what kind of lens through which the knowledge they passed on to a white researcher was filtered. For example, the Cree language does not use gendered pronouns; the third person is nonspecific as to gender. However, Mandelbaum's record of *piecuwiskwew* uses the pronoun *he*—likely based on the usage of the interpreters (all of whom were Cree themselves). We cannot assume based on this usage that historically, Plains Cree people viewed *a·yahkwew* individuals as male, without considering the ways that white Canadian and American concepts of gender would have been transmitted to Plains Cree people by the 1930s along with the English language.

I move now from archival sources to oral tradition recorded in present-day texts, as well as oral tradition that I have received from elders myself. During an Ojibwe immersion session, I have heard Leech Lake elders use the term *ayekwe* for Two-Spirit people (pers. comm., February 25, 2017). While the elders did not give a specific definition of this term at the time, Charles J. Lippert, editor of the *Freelang Ojibwe* online dictionary, has speculated that this may be the correct spelling and pronunciation of John Tanner's *a-go-kwa*. It is notably similar in pronunciation to the Cree *ayākwāo/ayekkwe/a·yahkwew*. Unfortunately, beyond determining that the ending *kwe* likely derives from the word for woman, no one has yet come up with a clear definition for the first part of the word. Regardless, if it is the case that *ayekwe* is related to either *a-go-kwa* or *ayākwāo/ayekkwe/a·yahkwew*, the fact that elders born in the early twentieth century recall it in 2017 is a testament to an incredible survival of the word.

The word *ayākwāo/ayekkwe/a·yahkwew*, which from here I will spell in the standard modern Plains Cree orthography as *âyahkwêw*, has also survived in oral tradition to the modern day. Chelsea Vowel, a Métis author from the Plains Cree–speaking community of Lac Ste. Anne, conducted an informal research project among Plains Cree speakers and found a number of words for people who do not easily fit within modern Western standards of gender and sexuality. Among those was the word *âyahkwêw*, which speakers suggested meant "a man dressed/living/ accepted as a woman," or possibly "a 'third' gender of sorts, applied to women and men" (Vowel 2012b). Also suggesting its survival among Cree-speaking people is the frequency with which this word appears, in various folk spellings, on the public Plains Cree–language Facebook page "Nêhiyawêwin (Cree) Word/ Phrase of the Day," whenever someone asks about words for Two-Spirit people. In a comment on March 28, 2012, one person responded to a request for such words with a memory that in the 1960s, a person in his community, whom he described as "a man . . . dressed like a woman," was referred to as an *âyahkwêw* (Lin J. Oak, comment on Vowel 2012a). On a similar post on November 3, 2016, this term came up again, spelled as *hy kwew*, which another commenter deemed "offensive" and "from a different time" (Gerald M. Auger, comment on Hester 2016). Yet another person cited the phrase *âyahkwêwatim* as meaning a castrated dog, indicating that the meaning of castration that missionaries recorded in the 1800s has also survived (Mel Calaheson, comment on Hester 2016). Several users then chastised that individual, noting that *âyahkwêwatim* was an insult that should not be passed on (Gerald M. Auger, comment on Hester 2016). All of these interactions demonstrate both the survival of words for Plains Cree gender variance, as well as the complex feelings that such words evoke for modern speakers of the language who have various experiences of acculturation to white Canadian and American societies and varying levels of knowledge of traditional ways and language.

On her blog, Vowel (2012b) also recorded several other terms for Two-Spirit people that did not make it into written historical records. For "a man who dresses as a woman" and "a woman who dresses as a man," she includes the phrases *napêw iskwêwisêhot* and *iskwêw ka napêwayat*, as well as the terms *napêhkân* and *iskwêhkân*, which she writes have the meaning of "literally 'fake man[/woman],' but without negative connotations." These words are derived from the words *napêw* (man) and *iskwêw* (woman), plus the ending *-hkân*, which she states to mean "fake," but it may also be translated as something along the lines of "another kind"; adding *-hkân* to the word for a traditional chief creates the word for a modern band chief, and the ending is also related to the endings used on the words for step-parents or step-siblings (Wolfart 1979: 82). The final word she includes is *înahpîkasoht*, "a woman dressed/living/accepted as a man" or possibly "someone who fights everyone to prove they are the toughest." This is likely to be the northern or Métis Cree pronunciation of the word *ê-napêhkâsot* (northern and some Métis dialects replace *ê* with *î*), which combines the word *napêw*, meaning "man," and the ending *-hkâso*, meaning "pretend, appear to be, act like," and thus can be translated as "someone who acts like a man, appears to be a man, pretends to be a man." The range of words that Vowel has collected from Cree speakers suggests that there was and is great variation in the words used for Two-Spirit people. It would take a more in-depth study to determine the precise reasons for these variations, but we can speculate on some possibilities. Regional or community differences are a strong possibility. There may also simply have been multiple words for different kinds of people—Two-Spirit people in the past, just like in the present, are not necessarily identical to one another. An *iskwêw ka napêwayat* may not be or have been the same as a *napêhkân* or an *înahpîkasoht*, even though all three might look similar to modern white or Western-cultured eyes.

The final phrase from oral tradition that I wish to discuss is *niizhin ojijaak*, literally meaning "two spirits." This phrase is found in Ojibwe-Cree Two-Spirit elder Ma-Nee Chacaby's autobiography, *A Two-Spirit Journey*. In the book, she recalls that her grandmother, who was born in the 1860s before white settlement of the prairies, told her, "Little girl, you have *niizhin ojijaak* (two spirits) living inside you" (Chacaby 2016: 64). Chacaby interprets this as referring to her sexual and romantic preference for other girls and women, which she largely ignored until later in her life. Interestingly, Chacaby notes that her grandmother was a Plains Cree woman who spoke to her in Cree while raising Chacaby. One might expect to find the phrase in Cree, rather than in Ojibwe as the book shows it. In fact, a discussion on August 21, 2014, on the "Nêhiyawêwin (Cree) Word/Phrase of the Day" Facebook group reveals mixed opinions on whether the concept of being "Two-Spirited" could be literally translated into Cree. Some argued that interpreting this concept literally was completely foreign to Plains Cree culture. However, one woman very vehemently claimed that her grandmother, born in 1870, had used the term *kâ-nîsâcahkôwêcik*, literally, "one who has two spirits," to refer to such people (Anne Crane, comment on Wayne T. Jackson 2014). Regardless of this debate, Ma-Nee Chacaby, who is fluent in Ojibwe as well as Cree, certainly uses the term *niizhin ojijaak* when speaking Ojibwe today (pers. comm., February 25, 2017).

While in the fields of queer and transgender studies debates have raged over the extent to which historical figures who might have been "like us" can be claimed as queer and transgender ancestors, within Indigenous circles both academic and nonacademic, this has largely been a nondebate. One effect of the emergence of Indigenous studies has been a request that researchers studying Indigenous histories recognize the continuities between past and present Indigenous communities—that the people they are writing about are somebody's ancestors. Though non-Indigenous scholars have sometimes written about historical figures in a way that implies a defined break between past "berdaches" and modern Two-Spirit people (through phrases like "the last 'true' winkte who fully functioned in a traditional Two-Spirit gender role are said to have lived in the 1930s" [Lang 1997: 108], for example), the reality is much more complex. Using Indigenous languages as a guide shows how words like *winkte* (a Lakota word for Two-Spirit people) and *âyahkwêw* have been continually applied to individuals both before and after the supposed "end of the berdache." This suggests that even though modern Two-Spirit people may not be identical to historical Two-Spirits, both Two-Spirit and non-Two-Spirit Indigenous people nonetheless recognize a continuity, a kinship, between the two.

At the same time, Two-Spirit people have not entirely escaped the question of *who* gets to claim *which* ancestors. Until recently, almost all scholars writing about historical Two-Spirits have referred to them in English with pronouns deemed to match their "biological sex," rather than with pronouns in accord with their actual roles in society. While it is difficult to decide which pronouns to use to describe any historical figure who did not leave behind precise instructions, the difficulties are heightened when considering individuals who often did not even speak English and may have had vastly different gender systems in their languages. Ojibwe and Cree, for instance, refer to male or female gender only in a few specific words referring to humans and animals, and forms of speech are mostly gender nonspecific, with the exception of some exclamations. It is notable, however, that early studies of Two-Spirit history were considered studies of "homosexuality" (Morgensen 2011: 56). Both scholars and Two-Spirit activists imagined the "berdache" as a form of sexual variation that happened to emerge as a gender variation within its cultural context.

In recent years, as transgender Indigenous people have become more visible and vocal, some have contested the way that historical Two-Spirits have been claimed exclusively by cisgender gay and lesbian people, both Indigenous and non-Indigenous. Anishinaabe/Métis author Gwendolywn Benaway writes in a recent essay that "the phrase 2 Spirit is almost always applied to gay or lesbian Indigenous writers." In a claim to ancestral connection to Two-Spirit ancestors, she states that "[trans women] are the invisible descendants of the 2 Spirit women I only know through historical photographs" (2017: 126). While Benaway is careful to note that she does not mean to say that cisgender queer Indigenous people cannot claim the term *Two-Spirit*, there is nonetheless a problem when transgender Two-Spirit people are made invisible. So long as modern transgender people are oppressed within Indigenous communities and forgotten in discussions of Two-Spirit inheritance, movements for the reclamation of Two-Spirit places of belonging in Indigenous communities will remain incomplete.

In the context of Indigenous language and cultural revitalization, recovering Two-Spirit history is crucial. It is not just an exercise in finding ancestral figures who were "like us," though that is itself a worthwhile cause. In communities where language loss has been significant—which is nearly every Indigenous community in the twenty-first century—looking to Two-Spirit history offers the possibility of finding words and roles for ourselves that make us legible within the context of our own cultures and shows the continuity of our presence within our communities. As linguistic and cultural revitalization becomes ever more influential among Indigenous people, it is essential that Two-Spirit people not be left behind. While in recent years the argument that queerness and transness are colonial inventions has declined in the face of increased awareness of historical Two-Spirits, without ways to talk about Two-Spirit people in our languages we may nonetheless end up being excluded from cultural revitalization. Ceremonial activities that divide participants into strict male and female categories based on their physical characteristics, for example, can be extremely difficult for Two-Spirit people to navigate, especially for those who identify as transgender. I have personally been forced to abstain from ceremony and other cultural events because of the insistence that all people assigned female at birth wear skirts and all who are assigned male wear pants, with no space left for those of us who fall through the cracks of such a division. While there are often deeply rooted cultural logics behind these gendered divisions, they still perpetuate a system that excludes many Two-Spirit people. On the other hand, in some cases Two-Spirit people, such as DeLesslin "Roo" George-Warren, a Catawba activist profiled by NBC News (Brammer 2017), have become very active in language and cultural revitalization for this exact reason: to create (or *re*-create) space for Two-Spirit people within their culture. Either way, Two-Spirit history is a critical part of any project of Indigenous revitalization and decolonization.

While the field of transgender studies has become critical of non-Indigenous claims to Two-Spirit historical figures as legitimators of modern non-Indigenous transgender identity, it continues to discuss historical Two-Spirits as separate from living ones. As this article has shown, linguistic analyses can help demonstrate that such a division is artificial, constructed by non-Indigenous scholars in ignorance of Indigenous realities. It would be foolish, of course, to ignore the shifts in Two-Spirit identities over time, particularly those due to the impacts of settler colonialism and settler heteropatriarchy on Two-Spirit and other Indigenous people, but recognizing the continuities between historical and modern Two-Spirit people does not require us to do so. Instead, it allows us to see kinship among Two-Spirits across time.

What I am suggesting in the concept of trans*temporal kinship may look similar to ideas developed within non-Indigenous queer and transgender studies. For example, Carolyn Dinshaw writes that in her book on Medieval English sexuality, she "focused on the possibility of touching across time, collapsing time through affective contact between marginalized people now and then," and "suggested that with such queer historical touches we could form communities across time" (Dinshaw et al. 2007: 178). Trans*temporal kinship and the framework of seven generations, *aanikoobijigan*, and *âniskotâpân*, however, are firmly rooted in and intertwined with Plains Cree and Ojibwe worldviews and experiences. Within these kinship systems, we must think in both directions, to our ancestors and our descendants (literal or figurative). While "inheritance" is typically associated with ancestors and "responsibility" with descendants, the ideas of *aanikoobijigan/âniskotâpân* and trans*temporal kinship encourage us to think all of these things together. Not just what do we inherit from our ancestors, but also, what responsibilities to do we have to them? Not just what responsibilities do we have to future generations, but also, what new things will we inherit from them? These trans*historical questions may serve as a useful guide for Indigenous people as we continue to reclaim and create new places for ourselves within our communities.

Kai Pyle (Métis/Nishnaabe) is a PhD student in American studies at the University of Minnesota, Twin Cities. Their work focuses on Two-Spirit history, literature, and activism, especially in the context of language and cultural revitalization.

References

Anguksuar [Richard LaFortune]. 1997. "A Postcolonial Colonial Perspective on Western [Mis] Conceptions of the Cosmos and the Restoration of Indigenous Taxonomies." In *Two-Spirit People: Native American Gender Identity, Sexuality, and Spirituality*, edited by Sue-Ellen Jacobs, Wesley Thomas, and Sabine Lang, 217–22. Urbana: University of Illinois Press.

Benaway, Gwendolywn. 2017. "Ahkii: A Woman Is a Sovereign Land." *Transmotion* 3, no. 2: 109–38.

Brammer, John Paul. 2017. "Native American Two Spirit Fights to Keep Tribe's Language Alive." NBC News, May 8. www.nbcnews.com/feature/nbc-out/native-american-two-spirit-fights-keep -tribe-s-language-alive-n755471.

Chacaby, Ma-Nee, with Mary Louisa Plummer. 2016. *A Two-Spirit Journey: The Autobiography of a Lesbian Ojibwa-Cree Elder*. Winnipeg: University of Manitoba Press.

Dinshaw, Carolyn, et al. 2007. "Theorizing Queer Temporalities: A Roundtable Discussion." *GLQ* 13, nos. 2–3: 177–95.

Driskill, Qwo-Li. 2016. *Asegi Stories*. Tucson: University of Arizona Press.

Driskill, Qwo Li, et al., eds. 2011. *Queer Indigenous Studies: Critical Interventions in Theory, Politics, and Literature*. Tucson: University of Arizona Press.

Herdt, Gilbert. 1997. "The Dilemmas of Desire: From 'Berdache' to Two-Spirit." In *Two Spirit People: Native American Gender Identity, Sexuality, and Spirituality*, edited by Sue-Ellen Jacobs, Wesley Thomas, and Sabine Lang, 276–83. Urbana: University of Illinois Press.

Hester, Ernest. 2016. "How do you say 'homosexual' in your dialect?" Nêhiyawêwin (Cree) Word/ Phrase of the Day. Facebook, November 3. www.facebook.com/groups/18414147673 /permalink/10154563170807674/.

Jackson, Wayne T. 2014. "kâ-nîsâcahkôwêcik?? Those who are two-spirited?" Nêhiyawêwin (Cree) Word/Phrase of the Day. Facebook, August 20. www.facebook.com/groups/18414147673 /permalink/10152620864617674.

Lacombe, Albert. 1874. *Dictionnaire de la langue des Cris*. Montreal: C. O. Beauchemin and Valois.

Lang, Sabine. 1997. "Various Kinds of People: Gender Variance and Homosexuality in Native American Communities." In *Two Spirit People: Native American Gender Identity, Sexuality, and Spirituality*, edited by Sue-Ellen Jacobs, Wesley Thomas, and Sabine Lang, 100–18. Urbana: University of Illinois Press.

Mandelbaum, David. 1979. *The Plains Cree: An Ethnographic, Historical, and Comparative Study*. Regina, SK: Canadian Plains Research Center.

Morgensen, Scott Lauria. 2011. *Spaces between Us: Queer Settler Colonialism and Indigenous Decolonization*. Minneapolis: University of Minnesota Press.

Ojibwe People's Dictionary. 2017a. s.v. "/-aad-/." ojibwe.lib.umn.edu/word-part/aad-medial (accessed May 21, 2017).

Ojibwe People's Dictionary. 2017b. s.v. "ikwekaazo." ojibwe.lib.umn.edu/main-entry/ikwekaazo-vai (accessed May 21, 2017).

Ojibwe People's Dictionary. 2017c. s.v. "ininiikaazo." ojibwe.lib.umn.edu/main-entry/ininiikaazo-vai (accessed May 21, 2017).

Ojibwe People's Dictionary. 2017d. s.v. "manidoo." ojibwe.lib.umn.edu/main-entry/manidoo-na (accessed May 21, 2017).

Ojibwe People's Dictionary. 2017e. s.v. "=jichaag." ojibwe.lib.umn.edu/main-entry/jichaag-nad (accessed May 21, 2017).

Sayre, Gordon. 2017. "Tanner, John." *American National Biography Online.* www.anb.org/articles/16/16–03525.html (accessed May 25, 2017).

Tanner, John. 1830. *A Narrative of the Captivity and Adventures of John Tanner, (U.S. Interpreter at the Saut de Ste. Marie,) during Thirty Years Residence among the Indians in the Interior of North America.* New York: G. and C. and H. Carvill.

Vowel, Chelsea. 2012a. "I have a question about terminology for two-spirited people, particularly those who are transgendered." Nêhiyawêwin (Cree) Word/Phrase of the Day. Facebook, March 10. www.facebook.com/groups/18414147673/permalink/10150729217552674/.

———. 2012b. "Language, Culture, and Two-Spirit Identity." *Âpihtawikosisân*, March 29. apihtawikosisan.com/2012/03/language-culture-and-two-spirit-identity/.

Watkins, Edwin Arthur. 1865. *A Dictionary of the Cree Language.* London: Society for Promoting Christian Knowledge.

Wesley, Saylesh. 2014. "Twin-Spirited Woman: Sts'iyóye Smestíyexw Slhá:li." *TSQ* 1, no. 3: 338–51.

Wilson, Alexandria M. 2007. "N'tacimowin inna nah': Coming in to Two-Spirit Identities." EdD diss., Harvard University.

Wolfart, H. Christoph. 1979. *Plains Cree: A Grammatical Study.* Philadelphia: American Philosophical Society.

Glands, Eugenics, and Rejuvenation in *Man into Woman*

A Biopolitical Genealogy of Transsexuality

KADJI AMIN

Abstract This article argues that Lili Elbe has been misrecognized as transsexual, just as *Man into Woman* (1933) has been misread as a transsexual autobiography. It proposes instead that we understand those who sought transition during the first decades of the twentieth century according to early endocrinological understandings of ovarian or testicular grafting as a means of rejuvenation, or of intersex conditions as the origins of both homosexuality and gender variance, as belonging to the prehistory of transsexuality. The article understands "prehistory" not as the stable foundation of contemporary transsexuality or transgender identity but as the crystallization, in a different form, of something whose various elements will eventually shift, be rejected, and/or fuse with new particles to compose what we now know as "transgender." Prehistory is thus genealogical in the Foucauldian sense. Exploring a disturbing genealogy of transgender that is implicated in eugenics, rather than recovering transgender figures in history, broadens understandings of what medical transition meant in the recent past. More importantly, it centers for transgender history the intertwined biopolitical genealogies of transgender and homosexuality alike.
Keywords sexology, Magnus Hirschfeld, Eugen Steinach, intersex, sexual inversion

Tom Hooper's film *The Danish Girl* (2015) ends with the death of its heroine, Lili, after complications from an experimental early twentieth-century gender-affirming surgery. Her death is presented as hopeful rather than senseless or tragic. When she awakens after surgery, Lili's first words are "I am entirely myself." Later, lying in a garden, she recounts "the most beautiful dream" to her wife, Gerda: "I dreamed I was a baby in my mother's arms. She looked down at me, and she called me, 'Lili.'" These are Lili's last words. After Lili's death, Gerda and Lili's childhood friend Hans revisit the Danish landscapes beloved by Lili's male former self, a landscape painter. Gerda is wearing a scarf she shared with Lili. A gust of wind unwinds and wafts it far above their heads. As Hans moves to catch it, Gerda instructs him to "let it fly." The camera follows the scarf sailing high in an ethereal

TSQ: Transgender Studies Quarterly ★ Volume 5, Number 4 ★ November 2018 **589**
DOI 10.1215/23289252-7090059 © 2018 Duke University Press

sky, intercut with shots of Gerda's face, at once laughing and tearful. In the manner of historical fictions, we next see a black screen with white words telling us a few choice, supposedly factual details. Crucially, we are informed that Lili's "bravery and pioneering spirit remain an inspiration for today's transgender movement."

The film's ending reassures viewers that Lili died happy, having become entirely herself, a woman, and attained a wholeness of identity that reparatively extends, in dream, even to infancy. Beyond fulfilling her own desires, the film suggests, in a gesture of "emotional rescue" (Love 2007: 31–52), that Lili helped us attain what *we* desire. With the evocatively hopeful image of the ascending scarf and the didactic affirmation, at the end, of Lili's contribution to the transgender movement, *The Danish Girl* implies that Lili died so that trans people in the present might have access to gender-affirming surgeries that would never have been developed had brave "pioneers" like her not been willing to risk their lives to undergo them. The film emphasizes the utter historical novelty of Lili's condition, which is misdiagnosed by a parade of doctors as a glandular imbalance, homosexuality, and schizophrenia. The single sympathetic doctor who promises to make her the woman she believes herself to be simultaneously warns, "The surgery has never been attempted before, never." In short, Lili is presented as *the first transsexual*—the first person to undergo the gender-affirming genital surgeries available to trans women today. As such, her death and suffering are implicitly redeemed by a present in which (some) trans women are able to safely medically transition and to be recognized, not as mad, but as women.

History telling, particularly within popular mass-media genres, is the first sign that a new movement has gained an established presence. The mainstream "arrival" of the transgender movement is signaled by the current mini-explosion of films depicting key origin points in transgender history. *The Danish Girl* is part of a newfound interest in marking foundational moments in transgender history and in honoring, and claiming, trans ancestors. The stakes are high for which stories, which origin points, and which ancestors can be claimed for transgender history. Arguably, Lili Elbe is the wrong figure to be honored as a foremother for today's transgender movement. *The Danish Girl*'s very visibility relies on the hierarchical structures of value and silent modes of normativity that render a relatively privileged white woman with access to doctors and surgery an appealing mainstream heroine. Equally important to the film's appeal to cisgender audiences is what makes Lili[1] anything but a heroine for the transgender movement—her lack of significant involvement with communities of sex and gender variants, and her disgust, in Elbe's multiply authored "memoir" *Man into Woman*, at the inverts and transvestites she encounters (in her male form as Andreas) at Dr. Hardenfeld's clinic (Hoyer 1933: 51). Lili's story, at least in its published form, is not one of community, solidarity, or social transformation; it is the romance of an individual with modern medical science.

In this article, however, I am less concerned with the issue of who constitutes a politically enabling ancestor for transgender history than I am with the very structure of historical narratives that seek origin figures for the transgender movement today. Whether overtly politicized or mainstream, such narratives tend to be overwhelmingly linear. To be plucked from the past and made a historical figure too often means being identified as the origin for a future that is known in advance. Elbe is significant today because she had been rendered newly familiar in light of contemporary certainties about what "transgender" means. Given the political significance of transgender history in the contemporary moment, transgender scholarship could benefit from critiques of recuperative and presentist histories that have been flourishing for the last decade or so within postcolonial and queer studies. Heather Love (2007) has argued, for instance, that the "emotional rescue" of figures from a presumably tragic queer past does more to console queer critics and readers in the present than to attend to the pain of that past. Anjali Arondekar (2009) has critiqued the propulsion of the history of sexuality by a "recuperative hermeneutics" bent on recovering queer figures from the archive, despite the fragmentary condition of that archive. Ironically, a recuperative hermeneutics dovetails with sexological and colonial forms of knowledge-power based on the diagnosis and classification of racial-sexual deviance. Such critiques are particularly crucial at the contemporary moment in which "transgender" is being rapidly institutionalized in public policy, academia, and activism (Valentine 2007). In the academy, this rapid institutionalization may goad scholars to avidly seek transgender figures across history and geography, potentially erasing, in the process, the inseparability of gender variance from complex conditions including political economy, religion, colonialism, and state formation (Reddy 2005; Arondekar 2009: 91).

The history of the adaptation of *Man into Woman*—first into David Eberhoff's novel *The Danish Girl* (2000), then into Hooper's film by the same name—provides scholarship with an object lesson in how historical difference is straightened into recognizability and divested of what gave it meaning in its own time. Whereas, in Hooper's film, Lili is the first transsexual, in *Man into Woman*, she is almost unrecognizable according to the grid of transsexuality. *Man into Woman* (*Lili Elbe: Ein Mensch wechselt sein Geschlecht*) was based on Elbe's and her wife Gerta's letters and diaries and included as many as six author/editors, including Elbe's surgeon Kurt Warnekros, the journalist Loulou Lassen, and her friend Ernst Ludwig Hathorn Jacobson who, under the pseudonym Neils Hoyer, is the sole legally recognized author. Warnekros and Jacobson may have increased the emphasis on medical science, which is further buttressed in an introduction by the sexologist Norman Haire. Rather than an "authentic" autobiographical narrative, *Man into Woman* is best regarded as a multiply authored, semifictional text (Meyer 2015: 79–221). Though its empirical truth-value is questionable and the extent to which it represents Lili Elbe's subjectivity remains uncertain, it does offer an important window into the frameworks that could have made sense of Lili's gendered difference, and the sex-altering surgeries she underwent, in 1920s–30s Europe. In *Man into Woman*, Lili is less transsexual than she is intersexed. She seeks surgery less to affirm the woman she always knew herself to be than to kill off Andreas—the male personality, diametrically opposed in temperament, tastes, and gender from her own—who cohabits the gender-variant body they both share. Whereas, in the film, Lili undergoes two surgeries, the first "to remove the male organs entirely" and the second "to construct a vagina," in *Man into Woman*, her surgeries include the transplantation of ovaries and, later, a uterus. These surgeries, moreover, are as much about *rejuvenatio*n as they are a means of changing the markers of Lili's bodily sex: by obtaining the ovaries of a woman in her twenties, Lili becomes young again. These plot elements had to be significantly distorted so that Lili might become a transsexual ancestor for the present.

To make sense of all the ways *Man into Woman* does not fit the model of later transsexual narratives, this article reconstitutes its links to the once cutting-edge science of glandular rejuvenation. This is the interest, during the early twentieth century, in the glands—particularly the testicles and ovaries—as the origins, not only of sex, gender, and sexuality but also of vitality and, therefore, youth itself. Rooted in eugenic thought, rejuvenation was a "wrong turn" in the history of science and a false start in the history of transsexuality. The availability of synthetic testosterone and estrogen would later render ovarian and testicular grafting obsolete as sex transition surgeries, just as the ascendance of the "trapped in the wrong body" trope would take precedence over alternate explanations for gender variance, including the action of internal ovaries or testes or the sense of having multiple differently gendered personalities. This does not mean that now that we understand the "true" nature of Elbe's being, we can dispel the falsified theories of glandular science to retell her narrative as one of transsexuality. What it does mean is that we must devise alternate historical methods for attending to bad objects from the past that fall out of present understandings of transgender; for parsing the inchoate conditions of the emergence of what will become transgender and transsexuality but that, at its origins, is barely recognizable as such; for accounting for scientific dead ends that appeared charged, in the moment, with futurity, but that are now discredited; and for assessing the residues of such disturbing histories in the present.

This article argues that Lili Elbe has been misrecognized as transsexual, just as *Man into Woman* has been misread as a transsexual autobiography. It proposes instead that we understand those who sought transition during the first decades of the twentieth century according to early endocrinological understandings of ovarian or testicular grafting as a means of rejuvenation, or of intersex conditions as the origins of *both* homosexuality *and* gender variance, as belonging to the *prehistory* of transsexuality. I understand "prehistory" not as the stable foundation of contemporary transsexuality or transgender identity but rather as the crystallization, in a different form, of a network whose nodes eventually shifted, were rejected, and fused with new elements to compose what we now know as "transgender." Prehistory, thus understood, is genealogical in the Foucauldian sense. Genealogy, Michel Foucault writes, "is not the erecting of foundations: on the contrary, it disturbs what was previously considered immobile; it fragments what was thought unified; it shows the heterogeneity of what was imagined consistent with itself" (1984: 82). I follow transgender studies scholar Henry Rubin (2013) in developing genealogy as a method for understanding the relation between this past and contemporary transgender politics. Exploring a disturbing genealogy of transgender that is implicated in eugenics, rather than recovering transgender figures in history, broadens understandings of what medical transition meant in the recent past. More importantly, it centers for transgender history the intertwined *biopolitical* genealogies of transgender *and* homosexuality alike.

Against *Endochronology*

During the 1990s, scholars sought to bolster the establishment of transgender studies as a discrete field by correcting what they saw as the prior miscategorization of transgender subjects as homosexual. Pivotal to this process was a return to late nineteenth- and early twentieth-century European sexology. In contrast to the then-established interpretation of the "invert" as a diagnosis, however homophobic and distorted, of homosexuality, scholars reread sexual inversion as a figure of gendered difference rather than of deviant sexual desire. Jay Prosser was a trailblazer in foregrounding the transgendered and even transsexual aspects of early sexological theories and case studies that had been distorted or ignored so that inversion might be read, and more often than not, critiqued, as a medical figure for homosexuality. He affirms the identity of the plot elements of sexological case studies of the past with those of transsexual autobiographies of the present. Of British sexologist Havelock Ellis's case studies, for example, Prosser emphasizes, "The features that make these life-stories read as classical transsexual plots make up a long, almost formulaic list. What is remarkable is the incredible *stability* of these narrative features, the *consistence* with which they reappear in contemporary transsexual autobiographies" (1998: 125; my emphasis). Within this history of continuities, endocrinology plays a starring role. Whereas psychiatry and psychoanalysis pathologized transgender identification as delusional and even psychotic, the endocrinological orientation of early sexologists led them to relate it, instead, to a glandular anomaly in embodied sex, and thus, to logically entertain the possibility of surgical and, eventually, hormonal treatments.

At the time of Prosser's writing, this reading of inversion as transsexual amounted to a strong affirmation of the historical and material reality of transgender desires for reembodiment in an intellectual and popular climate in which such desires were most often regarded with suspicion and disbelief. In tracing continuities and affirming an orderly, linear progression from the sexology of inversion to that of transsexuality, however, Prosser had to minimize the ways in which early sexological endocrinology birthed subjectivities, politics, and imagined futures wildly aslant of those now associated with transsexuality.

The reclamation of sexological inversion as transgender or transsexual is paradigmatic of the sometimes uneven traffic between transgender studies and the history of science. I borrow Jordy Rosenberg's term *endochronology* to index such a linear and selective approach to endocrinological sexology (Rosenberg 2018: 301). Endochronology creates an orderly and causal narrative of chronological development—*toward* gay, lesbian, or transgender identity—out of the strange conditions of early endocrinological science. To do so, it is necessarily selective. While key transgender studies scholars and historians of science have noted the imbrication of early European sexology with glandular rejuvenation and eugenics (Gill-Peterson 2014; Meyerowitz 2002; Rubin 2013, Sengoopta 2000; Stryker 2008), endochronology must bypass or deemphasize this ontology. We might discern an endochronological impulse behind any effort to claim, as transgender, historical figures who argued that they had a glandular imbalance or harbored the sex glands of their desired gender within their abdominal cavity in order to seek access to medical transition. While it compellingly connects such figures to the transgender present, endochronology does so at the cost of investigating their links to a more disorienting history in which medical transition is a linchpin for biopolitical eugenics and the seizure of bio-matter by capital.

To counter the endochronological reflex, we need an arsenal of methods that would allow us to think historical temporality otherwise. In what follows, I attend to the arrested futures (Stoler 2013: 21–22) of a superseded episode in the history of science. This episode is, nonetheless, crucial, for it provided the theoretical backbone for the first comprehensive medical theories of homosexuality and transsexuality alike. If, at some points, the prehistory I sketch here seems to threaten the aspirations of contemporary transgender politics, this is the sign that it is *effectively* genealogical. For, a genealogical approach "permits the dissociation of the self, its recognition and displacement as an empty synthesis, in liberating a profusion of lost events" (Foucault 1984: 81).

Man into Woman as Rejuvenation Narrative

Man into Woman has been read as a bad transsexual text. For Tim Armstrong (1998) it reiterates the male fantasy of "making" a woman while lending credence to Janice Raymond's transmisogynist screed (1994) against transsexual women's surface "appropriation" of the material signs of femininity. For Sandy Stone (1992), it exemplifies the purism of a transsexual autobiography that would repudiate any possibility of gender ambiguity, bow to male medical authority as to God himself, and fail utterly to develop a transsexual "counter-discourse" to that of medicine. To be sure, *Man into Woman* is not the place to go for either a feminist text that upends gender norms or a transgender text that contests medical authority; however, critics are beginning to acknowledge that it is also a more complex and contradictory text than previously recognized (Meyer 2015; Steinbock 2009). It may be time, then, to reevaluate *Man into Woman*, beginning with its status as a transsexual autobiography. For, most critics take for granted that it *is* a transsexual narrative, even when they note that it employs older sexological categories, such as inversion, and was written decades before the emergence of later transsexual autobiographies (Armstrong 1998; Steinbock 2009). However, *Man into Woman* was not only published prior to other transsexual autobiographies; it was written *before transsexuality*. Not enough attention has been paid to *trans* historicity*, that is, to the specific ways in which subjects have made sense of the desire to transform their sexed bodies before the medical diagnosis of transsexuality, and thus the Euro–North American tropes that define transgender being, had solidified. Lili does not so much transition from man into woman as she undergoes surgery to strengthen, through the transplantation of fresh, young ovaries, the stunted ovaries both she and her doctor believe she bears within her and remove the male organs that are interfering with her female development. Her "transition" is from a mixed-sex being to one that is unequivocally female.

This is not to say that *Man into Woman* is an intersex, as opposed to a transsexual, text. During the glandular era, intersexuality was the go-to explanation for both inversion and transvestitism. At the moment in which medicine was crediting the glands with the ability to control sex, gender, sexuality, development, vitality, intelligence, and even character, sexologists were identifying the testes and ovaries as the necessary seat of "disorders" of gender and sexuality. Hermaphroditic gonads, the presence of stunted internal testes or ovaries, or an imbalance in glandular secretions were thought to cause both same-sex desire and cross-gender expression. Eugen Steinach (1861–1944)—whose sensational experiments with the cross-sex transplantation of ovaries and testicles in rats were the prototype for Elbe's experimental procedure—proposed that male homosexuality was caused by a failure of the gonads to achieve full sexual differentiation. These hermaphroditic gonads could produce female secretions, altering the sex drive in a "female" direction—that is, toward men (Steinach 1940: 91). The German sex-ologist and homosexual emancipation leader Magnus Hirschfeld (1868–1935) enthusiastically embraced Steinach's theory of homosexuality, which accorded well with his own theory of "sexual intermediaries" and politicized bid to prove homosexuality entirely congenital. He proposed that homosexual men's brains were feminized by their female testicular secretions (Sengoopta 1998: 105) and speculated that sperm might be found in the urethra of female homosexuals and periodic blood in that of male homosexuals (Hirschfeld 2000: 171). Male homo-sexuals, he believed, were prone to cyclical menstrual symptoms—such as blood flow from the nose, mouth, or rectum, nervousness, and moodiness—as well as symptoms of menopause in middle age (170). Elbe visited Hirschfeld's Institute for Sexual Science, and the authors of *Man into Woman* were clearly familiar with his theories. The fact that Lili suffers "at almost regular intervals these mysterious fits of depression, accompanied by severe haemorrhages and violent pains," (Hoyer 1933: 99) and understands them as indicative of the presence of internal ovaries exemplifies how early demands for sex alteration were often based on the inter-sexual physiology of inversion (see also Meyerowitz 2002; Rubin 2003).

According to Michael Pettit (2013), early endocrinology had subjectivizing effects. The glands and their secretions were thought to influence not only one's physical features, but also one's entire personality. *Man into Woman* carries this glandular conception of selfhood to its logical limits. Given that the main char-acter has both testicles and ovaries, s/he is "in fact, two beings: a man, Andreas, and a girl, Lili. They might even be called twins who had both taken possession of one body at the same time" (Hoyer 1933: 20). Andreas, the product of testicular secretions, is a typically masculine man, with tastes, thoughts, and talents entirely opposed to those of Lili, a product of ovarian secretions. By this logic, and contrary to Stone (1992) and Caughie's (2013) readings and Hooper's adaptation (2015), *Man into Woman* is not a transsexual "wrong body" narrative. In the film, panting with desperation, Lili strips before a mirror, tucking her penis and squeezing her arms to her chest to create the appearance of breasts. By contrast, in *Man into Woman*, Andreas, on looking at his reflection, thinks of a phrase he had uttered that evening, "I am like one who only owns the façade of his house. The mirror in front of him showed him the façade. It was the unblemished body of a man" (Hoyer 1933: 115). Far from hating or rejecting his male body, Andreas calls on tropes of bourgeois possessive individualism to understand it, at this point in the narrative, as his sole remaining possession, and one that Lili increasingly occupies at that. For her part, Lili's overwhelming desire is less to be rid of a "wrong body" than it is to stop sharing this body with Andreas, her usurper. *Man into Woman* calls on "Jekyll and Hyde" tropes to frame Lili/Andreas not as a single androgynous or transsexual person but as a set of warring personalities secreted by polarized gonads.

For proponents of glandular rejuvenation, the ovaries and testicles were not merely the origin of sex, gender, and sexuality. They were the fount of life itself. Sex, Eugen Steinach (1861–1944) proclaimed,

> is the root of life. Just as it produces physical and psychic maturity, induces and preserves the period of flowering, shorter or longer, here richer, there poorer, so it is also responsible for the withering of the body and gradual loss of vitality. Sex is therefore the obvious means for natural stimulation or "activation" in youth, and also the instrument for methodical "reactivation" in old age. Sex is not only the measure for the rise, peak, and fall of the currents of life, but also, up to a point, for their restitution. (1940, 11)

Sex is the vitality of life itself. As the root of life, sex *debilitates* and *capacitates* (Puar 2017). Its government of growth, maturation, reproduction, and withering is but a one aspect of its modulation of all those distinctions of race, fitness, and ability that served, in the moment of eugenic modernity, to adjudicate who should live, thrive, and reproduce and who should be sterilized, let die, or serve as biocapital and vital labor for lives more worthy. Rather than an axis of difference that "intersects" with race and (dis)ability, sex is the very principle that drives racialized biopolitics and eugenics.[2]

In *Man into Woman*, the battle of Andreas and Lili over a single body will be decided by a eugenicist commitment to the most vital of the two lives. Although Andreas, as a man and a celebrated painter, might seem likely to hold that title, the narrative has him sliding to the very brink of physiological degeneracy. Andreas's increasing lassitude, weakness, and ill health (which, in Elbe, may have been the result of debilitating x-ray treatments) are inversely proportionate to Lili's growing vitality: "Whereas he felt tired and seemed to welcome death, Lili was joyous and in the freshness of youth" (Hoyer 1933: 21). In the eugenicist imaginary that animates the narrative, the right to life belongs to the young and healthy. When Lili first meets Dr. Werner Kreutz (modeled on Elbe's surgeon Dr. Kurt Warnekros), he offers her "a new life and a new youth" (25). He means this quite literally. "A man is as old as his endocrine glands," declared Steinach (1940: 130). If sex is the principle of life and the endocrine glands are the site of sex, then, logically, a person's age and vitality would be determined by that of their ovaries or testicles. Elbe was forty-seven at the time of her first surgery. In *Man into Woman*, when Lili learns that her donor ovaries are barely twenty-seven years old, she asks with excitement, "Is it really true, Matron, that the age of a woman is determined by her ovaries? Is that really the decisive factor for a woman?" (172). After this surgery, she affirms to Kreutz, "I feel I am getting younger and younger every day" (244).

To read *Man into Woman* as a transsexual autobiography separates it from a genre of writing, in full force at the time, with which some of its readers would have closely associated it: rejuvenation narratives, in which gland transplantations, or the ingestion or injection of organ slurries and secretions, promise regeneration and a second youth (McLaren 2012: 81–108). So literal are the rejuvenating effects of Lili's new ovaries that they are understood to have legal consequences. Just as Lili (successfully) petitions to legally use her new name and have Andreas's marriage to Gerta annulled, she (unsuccessfully) seeks to legally change her age to accurately reflect her "biological age," that is, the age of her new ovaries (Hoyer 1933: 244). Lili's efforts to legally change her age after a transition-related surgery demonstrate just how inseparable from regenerative life is the version of sex at play in *Man into Woman*. But *Man into Woman*'s focus on the regenerative effects of Lili's surgeries might also be intended to deflate assumptions that, as an intersexed person, Lili must be degenerate. This possibility is raised only to be triumphantly dismissed. A general practitioner admits that, while he initially thought Lili "a pitiful, degenerate, unfortunate creature," he can now pronounce her "a healthy and vigorous *woman*" (259; my emphasis). In the glandular era, health, vigor, and clearly dimorphic gender are inseparable from bio-racial fitness. While an invert might be a degenerate, and sickly Andreas is pronounced better off dead, Lili, as an exemplar of youthful, vigorous, feminine European womanhood, is worthy of medical enhancement and the right to reproduce. Indeed, the surgery from which she eventually dies, which is strongly implied to be the transplantation of a uterus, was intended to allow her "to become a mother" (viii).

Rejuvenation and Eugenics in Sexology

Man into Woman's positioning of sex-altering surgeries as a means of rejuvenation is not astonishing if we consider that the surgery credited with making Lili a woman—the transplantation of ovaries—was initially developed not as a method of transition, but rather as an experimental rejuvenation treatment (Steinach 1940: 187–88). Rejuvenation cannot be thought apart from a modernist eugenic imaginary that combined glandular therapies, whose effects some thought heritable (Pettit 2013; Serlin 2004), with efforts to direct reproduction. The centrality of rejuvenation's eugenicist imaginary to both sexology and the German homosexual emancipation movement, however, risks falling out of endochronological accounts of homosexual or transgender history. In what follows, I briefly sketch this genealogy through the figures of Hirschfeld, whose Institute of Sexual Research in Berlin offered some of the earliest sex transition surgeries before it was raided by the Nazis in 1933, and Harry Benjamin, who met with and learned from leading early twentieth-century sexologists and endocrinologists before going on to develop "transsexualism" as a treatable clinical entity in 1953.

As we have seen, Hirschfeld was an ardent proponent of Steinach's theory that homosexuality was caused by "female" testicular secretions. Hirschfeld's enthusiasm was motivated by his conviction that the best hope for decriminalizing male homosexuality in Germany was to prove it entirely congenital, not "spread" by the contact of immoral adult men with innocent adolescents. Locating an organic cause for homosexuality, however, implied the possibility of "curing" it. This is precisely what Steinach set out to do in supervising testicular experiments on homosexual men. If homosexuality was caused by testicles that produced the "wrong" sexed secretions, then, Steinach reasoned, it could be "cured" by surgically replacing a homosexual man's faulty testicle with a "healthy" testicle from a heterosexual man (Sengoopta 1998). Far from decrying such homosexual-eradicating experiments, Hirschfeld praised them, even in the face of the scientific community's skepticism, referring some of his own unhappy patients to surgeons for the procedure. In Chandak Sengoopta's (1998: 455) analysis, this favorable attitude was indicative of the inconsistencies within Hirschfeld's understanding of homosexuality. Hirschfeld claimed that, though homosexuality was congenital, it was a benign variation rather than either a disease or a symptom of degeneration. At the same time, he pathologized homosexuality in relation to racial fitness by theorizing it as a "disorder of evolution" (Hirschfeld 2000: 433). He simultaneously speculated that homosexuality might have evolved as a "preventative means" against degeneration, ensuring that a degenerate family line would die out. In this eugenic line of reasoning, homosexuality ought *not* be cured, because that would permit the reproduction of a degenerate family line (451). While surgically, Elbe's case may have been exceptional, it aligned well with parallel attempts, applauded by homosexual emancipationists and progressive sexologists alike, to convert effeminate inverts into healthy heterosexual men through testicular transplants. In both cases, gland transplantation was intended to "fix" an intersexual condition that caused disorders in sex, restoring, in the process, "healthy" sex polarity.

Hirschfeld has largely been remembered as a progressive Jewish sexologist and early homosexual emancipationist who was repeatedly physically assaulted by anti-Semites and eventually forced into exile, his Institute for Sexual Science shuttered by the Nazis. We should not allow this memory, however, to blot out the fact that, like many sexologists—including Norman Haire, author of the introduction to *Man into Woman* and likewise Jewish and homosexual—he was an ardent believer in the beneficial social effects of eugenic policies to guide reproduction, revitalize the worthy, cure sexual abnormalities, and grade individuals on the basis of their evolutionary fitness.[3] Indeed, the upstart field of sexology claimed scientific legitimacy by positioning itself as a eugenic science, one that was of scientific and social import precisely because it was concerned with the motor of the evolution and fitness of the race—that is, sex—and with disorders of sex that threatened bio-racial fitness.[4] As Hirschfeld wrote from exile to an old friend, "No doubt the purification process which is now being carried out in Germany is in many respects just what we had wanted for a long time, but the costs of this procedure, the violent behavior and particularly the intolerance, are too high a price to pay" (quoted in Grossman 1995: 145). While they may not have agreed with the *methods* of the Nazis, progressive sexologists like Hirschfeld and Haire embraced eugenic thought as the very foundation of their dreams of progressive social change.

The Eugenic Prehistory of Transsexuality

The medical genealogy of transsexuality is firmly entrenched in early endocrinology's investment of glandular sex with regenerative meaning. Benjamin's position as both the "father" of transsexuality and a living link (with a life span of more than a century, from 1885 to 1986) between early endocrinology and sexology and the later clinical treatment of transsexuality is well-known. However, a selective endochronology tends to govern how this link is narrated. In this way, Benjamin's significant work with "reactivation" therapies can be made to seem inessential to his better-known development of a treatment for transsexuality.

Benjamin was, in fact, Steinach's "American disciple" (Person 2008: 267). Highly influenced by Steinach and early endocrinologists, he had a thriving practice revitalizing men in the United States, became a leader in the smaller practice of reactivating women, and innovated "gerontotheraphy"—a term he coined. What was unique about Benjamin is that, rather than retiring after decades as a celebrity reactivation doctor, he shifted his focus in middle age to defining "transsexualism" and devising a medical protocol for its treatment. The fact that he was able to imagine medical transition as a legitimate "treatment" for transsexualism during the 1950s stemmed from his intellectual formation by 1920s and 1930s endocrinology and sexology, as well as his skeptical distance from mid-century psychiatry. Declaring, "actually, we are all 'intersexes,' anatomically as well as endocrinologically," Benjamin builds his theory of transsexuality from an updated version of Hirschfeld's theory of sexual intermediaries (Benjamin 1966: 21). Despite a lack of evidence, he entertains the possibility that transsexuality might be caused by an endocrine imbalance, referencing one case in which large amounts of estrogen were found in the testes of someone he presumed to be a trans woman (98). Thus, Benjamin's "work in offering sex reassignment to transsexuals was a natural progression from this work in rejuvenation" (Person 2008: 272). Rejuvenation itself, however, was part of a eugenicist imaginary focused on enhancing the fittest forms of life. Though even manual workers would be able to work longer and harder when rejuvenated, the principle social argument for the benefit of rejuvenation was bound up with restoring the vitality of "great men"—white businessmen, politicians, artists, and scientists whose old age was considered an immense loss for society. Benjamin himself wished that all "aging intellectual, political and industrial leaders would be 'Steinached'" (quoted in McLaren 2012: 93–94). This stops short of eugenics proper, since the Steinach procedure of vasoligature enhanced the sexual and physical vigor of aging men to the detriment or destruction of their reproductive potency. However, it is entirely apiece with a broader modernist eugenic imaginary that sought civilizational regeneration through biological means (Sengoopta 2000: 465).

There is one particularly concrete and material connection to eugenic practice in Elbe's story: Warnekros, Elbe's surgeon and one of the editors of *Man into Woman*, went on to join the Nazi party and perform involuntary eugenic sterilizations. Warnekros's later career as a Nazi eugenicist gynecologist raises the question of the origins of Elbe's transplanted ovaries and uterus. In 1930–31 Germany, before the ascent of National Socialism, there were any number of medical reasons for which a healthy uterus or ovaries might have been removed (Sengoopta 2000). It is not out of the question, however, that Elbe's transplants could have been obtained as the result of sterilization procedures.[5] Warnekros's later work for the Nazis may also cast *Man into Woman*'s much-critiqued emphasis on Lili's normative femininity in a different light. At a time in which absolutely heterosexual and dimorphic sex was, in conjunction with whiteness, one of the foremost indicators of biological fitness and evolutionary superiority, to subvert or challenge conventional femininity would have marked Lili as degenerate and, therefore, unworthy of glandular rejuvenation in the guise of sex transition therapy. Lili's portrayal as a biologically fit, youthful, and normatively feminine woman, in implicit contrast to sex degenerates, the disabled and ill, and the racially inferior, is required by *Man into Woman*'s subscription to the imaginary of eugenic modernity. While they disagreed vociferously over both theories and methods, European scientists and political progressives alike put their faith in biology as cause of and cure for social ills during the 1920s and 1930s. This overarching eugenic modernity is what would have permitted a surgeon like Warnekros to go from performing an experimental sex-altering surgery during the Weimar Republic to conducting eugenic sterilizations under National Socialism. While the Nazis surely would not have approved of the former, within the broader imaginary of eugenic modernity, both qualified as methods of social hygiene and eugenics. In *Man into Woman*, sex-altering rejuvenation surgery converts Andreas/ Lili from an ill, aging, hermaphroditic, possibly sterile "creature" to a healthy, young, feminine, possibly fertile, *woman*.

With its fixation on the unique potencies of the ovaries and testicles, early endocrinology envisioned sex as at once the *sign* of racial (un)fitness and the easily manipulable *means* of improving the race. We must not forget, however, that colonial necropolitics was the flip side of this biopolitical enhancement of European life (Mbembe 2003). The German colonial genocide of the Herero and Nama peoples in southwest Africa must be remembered as the counterpart to the racial "improvement" of those of European stock through glandular manipulation. Eugenic thought was the theoretical backbone and flexible rationale—differentially applied across geography and race—for colonial necropolitics, glandular eugenics, and rejuvenating sex alteration alike.

Biopolitical Genealogies of the Present

To what extent is transsexuality implicated within early endocrinology's eugenic imaginary? My intent is hardly to replace an affirmative endochronology that severs sexological sex from eugenics with a negative endochronology that indicts contemporary transsexuality as rooted in eugenic thought. Both versions are equally endo*chronological*: both are linear narratives that emphasize continuity and locate the "truth" of the present in a singular historical origin point. The version of genealogy I advocate, however, recognizes not one but multiple ramifying and often contradictory origins. After all, while endocrinology is *one* significant sexological root of transsexuality, there are assuredly others, including some that do not originate in Euro–North American science at all, as well as others that take up its technologies to capacitate understandings of sex and transition that originate elsewhere. Historical roots may be better conceived as a spreading rhizomatic system without an arboreal center: they send up new shoots from any node, each of which is both root and stem (Deleuze and Guattari 1987). Genealogy acknowledges multiple, contingent origins rather than a singular, determining one; it understands historical time not as a causal, straight line but as a fragmented and tangled network of ruptures, continuities, reversals, and reconfigurations. In a genealogical approach, that which persists through an epistemic shift is less reassuring than uncanny, like seeing a strange face in a reflection and realizing it is your own. Glandular rejuvenation was abandoned with the leap in endocrinology that occurred once testosterone, estrogen, and progesterone were chemically isolated and their interactions with genes, the brain, and other hormones empirically studied. Nevertheless, elements of this bygone form of thought persist, albeit in novel configurations in which they are partially unhinged from their original significance.

Any biopolitics of transgender life must contend with the ways in which, in the contemporary moment, multiple systems of oppression and privilege conspire to drastically reduce the life chances of trans people, particularly trans women of color. But the genealogy of transsexuality and, with it, of the medical technologies many trans people seek to access also emerges from the older biopolitics of rejuvenation, biosocial regeneration, and eugenics I have sketched in this article. Across ruptures in the history of science, the bio- and geopolitics of transgender, and even the understanding of "sex" itself, the strands of vitality, race, and (dis)ability twist and extend, fuse and separate. Contemporary issues—such as that of the differential life chances of trans people diversely positioned within social hierarchies of race, class, geography, and gender; the role of law, social services, and medicine in capacitating some versions of "transgender" and debilitating others; the legitimation of medical and legal transition through assurances of their positive impact on trans peoples' productivity and mental health; and the politics of transgender sterilization versus the right to reproduce—take up transsexuality's biopolitical genealogy within novel configurations. Tracing genealogical continuities across epistemological ruptures demonstrates that there is nothing presumptively "innocent" about the trans subject across time and place, that access to the medical technologies of transition is always also access to the medical management of populations and rationalization of health and productivity, and that transgender identity is never a sufficient container or teleology for the histories, technologies, and institutional networks of transgender biopolitics.

Kadji Amin is assistant professor of women's, gender, and sexuality studies at Emory University. Previously, he was a Mellon Postdoctoral Fellow in "Sex" at the University of Pennsylvania Humanities Forum (2015–16) and a faculty fellow at the Humanities Institute at Stony Brook (2015). He is the author of *Disturbing Attachments: Genet, Modern Pederasty, and Queer History* (2017). He is working on a second book project that traces critical genealogies of key ways in which "transgender" is being institutionalized in the global North.

Acknowledgments

I would like to thank Alex Greenberg for his help with German-language research. I am indebted to the crucial feedback of Jordy Rosenberg, Durba Mitra, and two anonymous readers.

Notes

1.   I follow the conventions of literary criticism in referring to the historical figure, Lili Elbe, by her last name, and the character, Lili, by her first name.
2.   On biopolitics, see Foucault 1990.
3.   For a new study that critiques heroic accounts of Hirschfeld's legacy, frankly acknowledges his eugenic views, and situates his work for sexual emancipation in relation to German colonialism and racism, see Bauer 2017.
4.   Hirschfeld's Institute for Sexual Science offered eugenic marriage counseling on a voluntary basis, and the Medical Society for Sexology he cofounded was soon renamed the Medical Society for Sexology *and Eugenics*. He defended eugenic science even after the rise of Nazism in Germany, proposing in his critique of Nazi racism that only a eugenics

"freed of the traditions of caste, of slavery, and of colonialism can be a thoroughgoing and a true eugenics" (1938: 174).

5.   Though sterilization and abortion were both technically illegal in Weimar Germany, sterilization had a higher medical status than abortion and was sometimes covered by insurance. Atina Grossman notes that one Dresden doctor sterilized minors and "incompetents" with parental consent (1995: 72–74).

References

Armstrong, Tim. 1998. *Modernism, Technology, and the Body: A Cultural Study*. Cambridge: Cambridge University Press.

Arondekar, Anjali. 2009. *For the Record: On Sexuality and the Colonial Archive in India*. Durham, NC: Duke University Press.

Bauer, Heike. 2017. *The Hirschfeld Archives: Violence, Death, and Modern Queer Culture*. Philadelphia: Temple University Press.

Benjamin, Harry. 1966. *The Transsexual Phenomenon*. New York: Warner.

Deleuze, Gilles, and Félix Guattari. 1987. *A Thousand Plateaus: Capitalism and Schizophrenia*. Minneapolis: University of Minnesota Press.

Foucault, Michel. 1984. "Nietzsche, Genealogy, History." In *The Foucault Reader*, edited by Paul Rabinow, 76–100. New York: Pantheon.

——. 1990. *The History of Sexuality: An Introduction*. New York: Vintage.

Gill-Peterson, Julian. 2014. "The Technical Capacities of the Body: Assembling Race, Technology, and Transgender." *TSQ* 1, no. 3: 402–18.

Grossmann, Atina. 1995. *Reforming Sex: The German Movement for Birth Control and Abortion Reform, 1920–1950*. Oxford: Oxford University Press.

Hirschfeld, Magnus. 1938. *Racism*. Translated and edited by Eden Paul and Cedar Paul. London: Victor Gollancz.

——. 2000. *The Homosexuality of Men and Women*. Translated by Michael Lombardi-Nash. New York: Prometheus.

Hoyer, Niels, ed. 1933. *Man into Woman: An Authentic Record of a Change of Sex*. Translated by H. J. Stenning. London: Jarrolds.

Love, Heather. 2007. *Feeling Backward: Loss and the Politics of Queer History*. Cambridge, MA: Harvard University Press.

Mbembe, Achille. 2003. "Necropolitics." *Public Culture* 15, no. 1: 11–40.

McLaren, Angus. 2012. *Reproduction by Design: Sex, Robots, Trees, and Test-Tube Babies in Interwar Britain*. Chicago: The University of Chicago Press.

Meyer, Sabine. 2015. *"Wie Lili Zu Einem Richtigen Mädchen Wurde" Lili Elbe: Zur Konstruktion von Geschlecht Und Identität Zwischen Medialisierung, Regulierung Und Subjektivierung*. Bielefeld, Germany: Transcript Verlag.

Meyerowitz, Joanne. 2002. *How Sex Changed: A History of Transsexuality in the United States*. Cambridge, MA: Harvard University Press.

Person, Ethel. 2008. "Harry Benjamin: Creative Maverick." *Journal of Gay and Lesbian Mental Health* 12, no. 3: 259–75.

Pettit, Michael. 2013. "Becoming Glandular: Endocrinology, Mass Culture, and Experimental Lives in the Interwar Age." *American Historical Review* 118, no. 4: 1052–76.

Preciado, Beatriz. 2013. *Testo Junkie: Sex, Drugs, and Biopolitics in the Pharmacopornographic Era*. Translated by Bruce Benderson. New York: Feminist Press.

Prosser, Jay. 1998. "Transsexuals and Transsexologists: Inversion and the Emergence of Trans-sexual Subjectivity." In *Sexology in Culture: Labelling Bodies and Desires*, edited by Lucy Bland and Laura Doan, 116–32. Chicago: University of Chicago Press.

Puar, Jasbir. 2017. *The Right to Maim: Debility, Capacity, Disability*. Durham, NC: Duke University Press.

Raymond, Janice. 1994. *The Transsexual Empire: The Making of the She-Male*. New York: Teachers College Press.

Reddy, Gayatri. 2005. *With Respect to Sex: Negotiating Hijra Identity in South Asia*. Chicago: University of Chicago Press.

Rosenberg, Jordy. 2018. *Confessions of the Fox*. New York: Random House.

Rubin, Henry. 2003. *Self-Made Men: Identity and Embodiment among Transsexual Men*. Nashville: Vanderbilt University Press.

Sengoopta, Chandak. 1998. "Glandular Politics: Experimental Biology, Clinical Medicine, and Homosexual Emancipation in Fin-de-Siecle Central Europe." *Isis: A Journal of the History of Science Society* 89, no. 3: 445–73.

———. 2000. "The Modern Ovary: Constructions, Meanings, Uses." *History of Science* 38, no. 4: 425–88.

Serlin, David. 2004. *Replaceable You: Engineering the Body in Postwar America*. Chicago: University of Chicago Press.

Steinach, Eugen. 1940. *Sex and Life: Forty Years of Biological and Medical Experiments*. New York: The Viking Press.

Steinbock, Eliza. 2009. "Speaking Transsexuality in the Cinematic Tongue." In *Somatechnics: Queering the Technologisation of Bodies*, edited by Nikki Sullivan and Samantha Murray, 127–52. Farnham, UK: Ashgate.

Stoler, Ann Laura. 2013. "'The Rot Remains': From Ruins to Ruination." In *Imperial Debris: On Ruins and Ruination*, edited by Ann Laura Stoler, 1–36. Durham, NC: Duke University Press.

Stone, Sandy. 1992. "The *Empire* Strikes Back: A Posttranssexual Manifesto." *Camera Obscura*, no. 29: 150–76.

Stryker, Susan. 2008. *Transgender History*. Berkeley: Seal Press.

Valentine, David. 2007. *Imagining Transgender: An Ethnography of a Category*. Durham, NC: Duke University Press.

Trans of Color Critique
before Transsexuality

JULIAN GILL-PETERSON

Abstract How has a reliance on the medical archive distorted the intelligibility of trans of color life in the past? This essay interrogates the limit points of black trans and trans of color life in the early twentieth century. Examining a case at the Johns Hopkins Hospital from the 1930s where medical protocol was confounded by a black trans patient's refusal to cooperate, the author asks what the silence and unknowability produced around this person's life might do in the service of trans of color studies. Complicated by the fact that federal privacy regulations governing the medical archive actually serve to protect the doctor, not the patient in this case, prohibiting disclosure of the contents of the archive, the author works to transform the impossibility of recuperating a black trans or trans of color subject into a positive condition for the advancement of a trans of color critique that undermines medicine's reason.
Keywords medicine, blackness, trans of color, intersex, archive

> The appearance of the patient in street dress . . . was that of a "snappy" young
> negro woman.
> —Hugh Hampton Young, *Genital Abnormalities, Hermaphroditism, and Related*
> *Adrenal Diseases*

T he Medical Records Office of the Johns Hopkins Hospital in Baltimore is responsible for providing current and recent medical records to patients, but it also stores some of the historical files of the hospital. When I first visited the office, I was there to look at early twentieth-century records from the Harriet Lane Home, the first pediatric clinic in the United States attached to a medical school. With its sizeable Endocrine Clinic, and in concert with the neighboring Brady Urological Institute, the home's records contained several hundred cases falling under the ambiguous catch-all "Hermaphrodism [*sic*]" from the 1910s to 1950s, a complex discursive field that touched on trans life in a period before the terms *transvestism* and *transsexuality* came into widespread usage in the United States.

TSQ: Transgender Studies Quarterly ★ Volume 5, Number 4 ★ November 2018 **606**
DOI 10.1215/23289252-7090073 © 2018 Duke University Press

Because the office's digital microfilm machine was not working the day I arrived, I set up shop on an analog machine in the middle of a room where staff were fielding phone calls and subpoenas for medical records. As the day went on, we got to talking. I asked about the apparent scarcity of resources for such an important office and in return was asked about what I was looking for in such old records. I explained that I was researching medical sex reassignment in the era before transsexuality. I added that I was looking at the racial divide in medicalization to grasp how persistent racial logics inform the later emergence of transsexuality and medicine's claim to know trans life. While we were chatting, a woman next to whom I was working asked if there were any experiments performed on black patients among the cases I was looking at. That prompted a conversation about the long history at Hopkins of nontherapeutic and coercive medical violence perpetrated on black people, from more famous cases like Henrietta Lacks to less well-known but systemic violations of personhood and care (see Washington 2006; Skloot 2010). In an office administered overwhelmingly by black women there was no shortage of stories about warnings from family and friends that African Americans—whether patients or staff—needed to remain vigilant at Hopkins. My cubicle neighbor mentioned that an older relative of hers used to avoid walking alone at night in East Baltimore, having heard enough rumors about "night doctors" (see Skloot 2010: 158–69) to know that she might be abducted off the street for medical experimentation.

As I read through the archive of "hermaphroditic" patient files from the 1910s–1950s, including those marked "Colored," the weight of my conversation with the staff prompted a question whose epistemological limits this essay pursues. How has the overexposure of medicine as an available archive of transgender history produced an incalculable deflation of trans of color life's intelligibility, especially black trans life? If many black residents of Baltimore have, since the opening of Hopkins, been wary of being medicalized out of legitimate fear of the nontherapeutic violence underwriting "modern" medicine, what effects have practices of self-protection, strategic invisibility, and escape had on the hospital's archive? In other words, how does the use of the medical archive distort the very historicity of black trans and trans of color life through the recording of differing types of absence, silence, or opacity? And, as C. Riley Snorton puts it in *Black on Both Sides* (2017: 57), under such conditions how might we see the "fugitive moments in the hollow of fungibility's embrace"?

If historical practices of illegibility and invisibility inform the limitations of the medical archive from one side, on the other stands not only the racialized logics of medical discourse but also newer limits imposed by the governance of the archive. Contemporary federal health privacy regulations epistemically repeat the historical erasure of black trans and trans of color life at Hopkins.[1]

While doctors carefully compose published medical discourse, the heterogeneous unpublished accounts found in medical records that would undermine that discourse cannot always be made public, for reasons that will be explored later in this essay. Having spent time with these records, I am convinced that the account of black trans life in the archive of Hopkins, despite its dehumanizing and profoundly racist context, is much richer than published medical discourse from the era would lead us to believe. Yet the collision of historical, medical, and privacy ethics prohibits me from describing much of that richness. Ensnared in the position of an enforced ignorance that conspires with and extends the objectifying logic of medical discourse in favor of the privacy of doctors, not patients, this essay works to transform the resulting impossibility of recuperating a clear black trans or trans of color subject into a positive condition for trans of color historiography. Confronting the limits of a "case study" caught at the crossroads of what can be known through the medical archive, I ask what trans of color studies can (and cannot) do to address the continued underappreciation of trans of color knowledge and practice as the disavowed source of the "modernity" of transsexuality and gender.

As a contribution to trans of color historiography, this essay's trans of color critique before transsexuality explores one alternate history of the intersectionality of race and transness by investigating the disavowed reliance of discourses of gender and transsexuality on the embodied knowledge of black trans and trans of color people, asking us to understand more sharply what it means to say that gender and transgender have "always" been racial categories.

The Archiving of Early Twentieth-Century Black Trans Life

Hugh Hampton Young helmed the Brady Urological Institute, which along with the Harriet Lane Home saw patients diagnosed with "hermaphroditism" at Hopkins in the early twentieth century. Young established many of the foundational diagnostic and therapeutic procedures that made American urology modern. In invoking the word *modern*, I mean to resignify it as a result of dehumanizing, violent processes through which the human body was abstracted into distinct parts and systems out of experimental research on living and dead people who were then largely excluded from its supposed universalism. Like gynecology, as Snorton shows in the case of J. Marion Sims's violent experiments on enslaved black women (2017: 18–20), urology constituted itself through the availability of dehumanized bodies for experimental research that was frequently nontherapeutic, dangerous, and ineffective. Black bodies, disabled bodies, women's bodies, and children's bodies, particularly in their overlap with queer, intersex, and trans forms, were frequently those that urology made available to itself at the Brady Institute. The resulting "objectivity" produced by doctors like Young covered over and disavowed its own conditions of production, promising modernizing access to parts of the body long considered unreachable precisely by obscuring the material ways that knowledge was produced through painfully destructive techniques.

During the 1920s and 1930s Young developed a specific expertise for assigning sex to nonbinary infants, children, and adolescents, as well as adults medicalized for various intersex conditions. In 1937 he published a landmark textbook, *Genital Abnormalities, Hermaphroditism, and Related Adrenal Diseases*. Laying out a general nosology and etiological theory with detailed guidelines for clinical and surgical procedures, Young based the book on what Hopkins prided itself on as a "modern" research hospital: extensive case histories. Young pulled the case files of patients he had treated in the 1920s and 1930s to illustrate his methodology for determining sex and making medical reassignments through plastic operations he developed. Although this was the "Age of the Gonads," as Alice Dreger (1998) puts it, during which the presence of ovaries or testes were given by far the greatest weight in producing a "true" sex, the technical means for assessing sex were as disorganized as they were invasive. In these decades before synthetic hormones became standardized and commonly available, Young prioritized visual anatomical evidence. Extensive physical examination preceded diagnoses of hermaphroditism. Cystoscopy and x-ray procedures to picture the inside of the body were, like the physical exam, preludes to exploratory laparotomy, an invasive surgical procedure whose logic was to cut open the body and look inside for gonads or other ostensibly sexed organs. Disqualified from scientificity under this paradigm were a patient's self-identity and embodied self-knowledge.[2]

As trans and intersex studies scholars have noted (Preves 2001; Rubin 2012; and Repo 2013), the surgical episteme that grew up around the medical management of nonbinary and intersex patients diagnosed as "hermaphrodites" or "pseudo-hermaphrodites"—which were expansive categories covering dozens, if not more, genetic, hormonal, anatomical, and other forms of embodiment—directly prefaces the emergence of American transsexual medicine. The basic protocols of medical transition were first standardized to transform the bodies of infants, young children, and teenagers into a binary sex, while any lingering evidence of an "intermediate" or "mixed" sex was considered pathological, a form of arrested development or atavistic evolutionary regression.

While this field of medical practice was not designed with trans people in mind, it nonetheless began to attract their attention long before the first trans medicine clinics opened in the United States. Doctors like Young exercised an aggressive gatekeeping role around the new protocol of transition and sex reassignment, refusing requests from trans people who began to seek out the services of the Brady Institute in the 1930s. Many of these trans people strategically adopted intersex rhetoric to describe themselves, hoping that would legitimate their requests

(5014.10, 5014.11, BUI Records). In this, they reflected a much broader trend: from Lili Elbe ([1933] 2004) in the 1930s to Christine Jorgensen (1968) in the 1960s, many public trans figures claimed to be vaguely intersex so that their transitions could be described as a kind of correction of a mistake made by nature.

Intersex medicine prefaces transsexuality chronologically and conceptually because intersex bodies were framed by medicine as the fullest expression of a concept of sexed plasticity that was central to the medical alterability of the human body in the twentieth century. The broader theory in the biomedical sciences that all human life was to a degree "naturally" mixed in sex in its embryonic and infantile forms was at its height at the time Young was most involved in this work. In its intersex form, this plasticity represented a supposedly arrested or atavistic capacity of the sexed body to take on multiple forms that had not properly waned in early infancy, and it was also racialized in the eugenic and evolutionist paradigms of the era. Sex became in places like Hopkins a phenotype that could be surgically manipulated through its plasticity, leveraged precisely in order to push it into a binary form. The surgical (and, later, hormonal) project of normalizing the intersex body carried a great deal of racial meaning informing the "modernity" of human sex as alterable but binary.[3]

While the medical transformation of intersex plasticity into binary form resulted in the racialization of sex as a pliable phenotype, making it signify through whiteness, this brought other hypervisible forms of race and antiblackness into play. The standard patient forms at Hopkins contained a field not just for sex but also race and "national stock." As a result it is easy to see in the archive that the overwhelming majority of people diagnosed with hermaphroditism at the Brady Institute in this era were white. That is not surprising, for several reasons. First, the institute was not in the habit of providing free treatment nearly as often as the "charitable" mission of Hopkins suggested. Patients were expected to pay for many services and procedures, even if their data were being used as part of research. Unless a local charity or social-work organization was able to sponsor medical treatment, costs for the many procedures and hospital stays were prohibitive for working-class black residents of Baltimore (see 1005.1 BUI Records and 2001.6 Edwards Park Collection).

What's more, the racial discourse of plasticity was synonymous with the calculation of which bodies were worthy of what forms of medicalization. Precisely because of the longer history in American medicine "in which captive flesh functions as malleable matter for mediating and remaking sex and gender as matters of human categorization" (Snorton 2017: 20), black and brown bodies were consistently read as less plastic, as less evolved sexually, and thereby less worthy of medical care now that a universalizing modernity was attached to plasticity as the capacity to remake the white body into a binary form.[4] Moreover, the many ways in which African Americans, in particular, practiced wariness and distance in relation to

Hopkins made some people less likely to willingly visit the Brady Institute. For Young, blackness signified both as a devalued fungibility and a kind of super-humanity of the flesh, a combination he saw as desirable for research despite the relative rarity of black patients at the Brady Institute (see Jackson 2016 and Harvey 2016). Young was interested in a presumed exceptional pathology he imagined residing somewhere in black bodies, including in those patients who visited the institute in the 1930s who may have been trans rather than intersex. Contrary to his objectifying motivations, however, black trans life could just as much confound as enable the production of racial knowledge about sex.

One of Young's cases in *Genital Abnormalities* in which no medical sex was assigned ignites the paradoxical space occupied by black trans life in this early twentieth-century framework of racial plasticity. Indeed, none of Young's "modern" medical procedures were undertaken. Instead of a rehearsal of surgical laparotomy or plastic surgeries, Young published a short biography of this person's life, including an abridged interview. While the dialogue is paraphrased and highly edited from notes, the archiving of this person's ostensible voice raises a number of interesting challenges to the medical discourse of sex and the intelligibility of black and trans of color life in the era before transsexuality.

The patient, whom I will refer to by the pseudonym "Billie,"[5] was in their[6] mid-twenties when they entered Young's ward. Now in Baltimore, they had pre-viously lived in various places throughout the South and Midwest. In taking Billie's history, Young (1937: 139) emphasized that although they had been raised a girl, they had always been "stronger than the girls" at school, excelling at sports. As a teenager, Billie's mother had taken them to the doctor because they had yet to menstruate. Apparently the doctor, after making an examination, prescribed "medicine to take by mouth" but said "nothing about her condition" (139). As a teenager Billie also began to date girls. Young fixated on their "taking an active male part during sex," something from which, according to him, "the patient derived great pleasure, as did her partner" (139). Still, as a young adult Billie also married a man. The marriage was far from amiable, and Billie continued to see women as well. After less than a year Billie decided to leave their husband and return home to their parents. After trying and failing to reconcile some months later, Billie moved to St. Louis, worked in a factory, and pursued a relationship with a woman, eventually securing a divorce. A second attempt at marriage with another man led to similar conflicts, spurring the move to Baltimore to live with relatives (140).

Young performed a physical exam at admission. As was common with many of his patients, he arranged for nude photographs of Billie's body and genitals to be published in *Genital Abnormalities*, with only a minute censoring of the eyes serving as the slightest gesture at privacy. He also published a photograph of Billie in their clothes, which was more unusual. "The appearance of the patient in street dress," he commented, "was that of a 'snappy' young negro woman with a good figure" (141). A very brief description of a cystoscopy procedure follows, before the case study ends not with the usual laparotomy and sex assignment but with Young's interview. I quote this in its entirety because its public, published status, compared to the unpublished documents from Billie's records in the archive, will become important:

> The patient was asked if she were satisfied with her present life.
>
> "No," she said, "I feel, sometimes, as if I should like to be a man. I have wondered why my passions always have been directed towards women. I have derived great pleasure from many sexual affairs with women, and never with my two husbands."
>
> "Would you like to be made into a man?" "Could you do that?"
>
> When assured that this would be quite easy, that it would only be necessary to remove the vagina, and do a few plastics to carry the urethra to the end of the penis the patient said, "Would you have to remove the vagina? I don't know about that because that's my meal ticket. If you did that I would have to quit my husband and go to work, so I think I'll keep it and stay as I am. My husband supports me well, and even though I don't have any sexual pleasure with him, I do have lots with my girl friends." (142)

The case history abruptly ends here without any comment from Young.

Billie's apparent reaction to Young's proposal for sex assignment as a man raises a set of interesting questions. Why did Young publish a summary of a case that involved neither a surgical procedure nor a complete diagnosis? And what does the abrupt ending suggest about Billie's embodied knowledge? Valuable in Young's eyes as a case of presumed exceptional pathology, the photograph of Billie in their clothing and the extensive quoted dialogue suggest Young's desire for racialized knowledge to add to his body of research on hermaphroditism. The impression that Young is also sanitizing his account by omitting the reason for which no laparotomy or sex reassignment was carried out is also glaring. Billie does not seem to reject a masculine identity or the possibility of sex reassignment but instead interrogates the surgical premise of the epistemology of sex to which Young is attached. Billie seems to reject the proposal to remove their vagina on the grounds of knowledge gained through lived experience. For someone sometimes hailed as a black woman in the 1930s, marriage to a man seems to represent to Billie a financial and social situation that was in some way worth the emotional and sexual dissatisfaction it entailed. Billie seems to have been willing to live as a masculine person with a penis and a vagina, knowing that their livelihood was secure in an important way. Billie's ease in imagining a life married to a man for practical reasons, while pursuing meaningful relationships with women, is a pointed indictment of the medical model in which Young worked, in which the production and enforcement of heterosexuality was as important as visibly binary sex (Redick 2004: 28–38). Billie assents to no contradiction, no need for a binary sex or heterosexuality in order to live.

Whether Billie's feeling that "sometimes" they "should like to be a man" articulates as clearly trans is, similarly, unknowable. While it would be hasty to claim Billie as trans in the contemporary sense of that term, their lack of conformity to the intersex medical model and the absence of any archival evidence of a lesbian identity makes the entanglement of trans and intersex categories here worth pursuing. Indeed, what interests me in this published case history is precisely the opacity of Billie's self-knowledge. The dominant categories of 1930s urology lose their traction in the partiality and unintelligibility of this account. Billie is fairly invisible throughout, but that position is quite powerful in undermining Young's medical authority. What is at hand in reading this text is not the recovery of a clearly black trans person from the past but a situation more like that described by Snorton (2017: 2) in which "trans . . . finds expression and continuous circulation within blackness, and blackness is transected by embodied procedures that fall under the sign of gender."

I say with great care, then, that Billie "seems to reject" Young's medical discourse because there isn't much reason to take the published account in *Genital Abnormalities* at face value. Indeed, that is precisely why I went to Hopkins to locate Billie's and other medical records of people discussed in *Genital Abnormalities*. I suspected that Billie probably wielded much greater leverage in their encounter with medicine than Young wanted readers to think. I also suspected that Billie's refusal to be given a binary sex and undergo medical reassignment might testify to the ways in which the social heterogeneity of black trans life in this era sought escape or strategic unintelligibility from the reach of medical science. Billie's refusal of categorization also frustrates any impulse to recuperate a legibly black trans subject in this era. Instead, in this short text transgender history is confronted by the limits of its investment in Western forms of knowledge about gender that are archived as meaningfully historical because they emanate from "modern" discourses like urology that squander the intelligibility of trans of color life they nonetheless rely on to produce knowledge.

I suspected that Billie's unpublished records would yield an account in which, despite the epistemic and material violence of medicine, we might read an irruptive heterogeneity of black trans life that could serve as a source for building an alternate account of their experience at Hopkins. And what I read in the archive more than confirmed that hunch. However, here federal privacy regulations collude with Young after the fact, and I cannot disclose what I read. The Health

Insurance Portability and Accountability Act (HIPAA) includes regulations that are ostensibly meant to protect the privacy of patients in medical research. Unless a person's death is confirmed or individual permission is secured (the latter being almost always impossible in researching trans history), a presumption of privacy is applied to records containing personal health information (PHI) (see Lawrence 2016). To access these materials, researchers are required to undergo review by their home institutional review board (IRB), as well as the Johns Hopkins Hospital's Privacy Board. In the case of Billie's files, however, an additional ethical problem comes into play. In *Genital Abnormalities* Young published the patient file numbers used by the Brady Institute for the cases he discusses. The consequence of Young's casual approach is that patients like Billie have already had their privacy and confidentiality breached since 1937 under the retrospective criteria of HIPAA. To mitigate that damage, no information in the archive can be disclosed that exceeds what is already public.

HIPAA regulations are supposed to "protect" patients by preserving their privacy. In this case they work much more effectively to protect the privacy of Hugh Hampton Young. Billie's records, which contain unredacted and unabridged sources of information, are disqualified from public circulation, and their possible contradictions of Young's published work are kept unsaid. HIPAA prohibits any further examination of why Billie refused Young's medical model, or evaluation of the honesty of his account in *Genital Abnormalities*. For instance, the full notes from which Billie's quoted speech and interview are derived are archived in these records. An explanation of how Billie was referred to the Brady Institute is also contained there, whereas Young chooses not to disclose that. And while Billie's voice is presented as written by Young in *Genital Abnormalities*, in their medical records there is a handwritten letter from Billie to Young in which they speak through their own voice. Although I can reference the mere existence of these types of documents, that is as far as I can go. The ways that published discourse rely on the deletion or suppression of knowledge generated by patients are left intact. Given how freighted the relation to Hopkins has been for black residents of Baltimore, this continuing silence bears a real magnitude. The use of the medical archive to examine black trans and trans of color life from the early twentieth century may in and of itself reinforce illegibility, but the governance of the archive also constricts and actively antagonizes attempts to pursue a trans of color critique of medicine.

Billie's life is archived in such a way that they are restrained, even after the fact, from challenging the whiteness of the history of transsexuality and the underestimation of the ways in which medicine made sex and gender modern through the simultaneous objectification and devaluation of black life. If Billie is not a visible black trans subject, if Billie's life is besieged by limitations on and limitations of knowledge, then what does the fragmentary evidence of their life in the archive contribute to a trans of color critique of medicine?

Opacity in Trans of Color Critique

Part of why Billie's life matters so much is that their interruption of ordered medical knowledge places blackness in an opaque position to transness at a moment prior to the erasures engendered by transsexuality in the mid-century, proliferating the historical meanings that attach to the sign "trans." Once "the newly-spectacularized medico-juridical discourse of transsexuality" had established itself in the mid-century, as Susan Stryker (2009: 79) puts it, it also got away with making its constitutive racialization scandalously invisible. This is the specifically abstract effect of transsexuality's whiteness that Stryker describes in the case of Christine Jorgensen's global circulation as a marker of modernity in the 1960s. "It is not Jorgensen's pale skin or Scandinavian-American cultural heritage that made her white," argues Stryker, "but rather the processes through which her presence racializes others while rendering opaque her own racialization" (81–82). Transsexuality became exportable as a technology of modernization in the mid-century by activating its whiteness to racialize its others as less than human, making itself innocent of race and transforming itself into a universal category. For that reason, trans of color historicity from the early twentieth century plays a particularly important role in destabilizing the racial innocence of transsexuality and exploring, as Snorton (2017), Elias Vitulli (2016), Kadji Amin (2017), and Emma Heaney (2017) have, the many disavowed racial histories of transness that precede it. The unique task of early twentieth-century trans of color historiography is both to center black trans and trans of color life in contexts that differ from the established narratives of trans history in that moment, while simultaneously pulling the mid-century advent of transsexuality out of joint with itself, showing how its whiteness is built on the forgetting of the black trans and trans of color historicity that directly precedes and exceeds it.

In calling on "trans of color studies," less a fait accompli than a growing horizon of thought and practice, I also draw especially on work by Snorton and Jin Haritaworn (2013), micha cárdenas (2016a and 2016b), Trish Salah (2014), and Kale Fajardo (2016). Trans of color studies exposes how the whiteness of transsexuality actively interferes with the intelligibility and material viability of black, brown, indigenous, and other trans of color and nonbinary lives, making them more invisible, marginal, or exceptional than they otherwise would be in the field of transgender studies. Transgender studies has to an important extent magnified the whiteness of transsexuality by its reliance on its medical archive, for that archive is an artifact of the science of transsexuality, which is to say that it pretends to speak for and grant total access to trans life while obscuring the racial conditions of subjection under which it produces that knowledge as universal.

What is at stake in a trans of color critique of medicine is not only the dehumanization of trans of color life through which medicine emerged but also the undermining of the rationality of medicine and its racialization of knowledge about gender. I argue that before there is a "transsexuality" to hoard attention away from trans of color life it might be easier to see what has for too long remained its penumbra: the fungibility of blackness to the modernity of sex, on one hand, and what Robert F. Reid-Pharr (2017) calls the "announcement of black life," on the other. Following Reid-Pharr's (2016: 9) call for a "post-humanist archival practice" that does not frame Western humanism in rigid terms as a domineering metaphysical force, but seeks out the heterogeneity of sociality in the "archive of flesh" of historically lived blackness, the limits of intelligibility in this archive can serve as grounds for the production of alternate forms of knowledge that affirm opacity and heterogeneity. Billie's life was both postwar trans medicine's disavowed predicate and the limit point of its own diminished epistemology. Billie gives lie to the way that medicine's antiblackness is not only a vehicle of material domination but also simultaneously a profound restraint on what it can know. Billie's blackness and transness take irruptive form as a puncture of medical modernity, coming decades before the discourse of transsexuality. The racialized impasse over their sex in the archive might be read as productive, bringing forth not a subject of the black trans or trans of color past but an invitation to read into the opaque interiority of trans of color life without judging it by the severely partial perspective of the medical science of human sex.

This move toward opacity, interiority, and illegibility, largely driven by broader work in black studies (Ellison et al. 2017), critically responds to the recent turn to biopolitical analysis in transgender studies (see Stryker and Currah 2014: 303). While immensely productive in diagramming how gender and, now, transgender, have become vital domains of administrative regulation and partial normalization for the state, the law, and medicine, trans of color and black trans studies offer conceptual tools for avoiding the pitfalls in Michel Foucault's biopolitical rendering of race and racism, in which colonialism and transatlantic slavery are displaced from modernity, emptying race of its historicity (Weheliye 2014). While the very alterability of sex and gender condensed into the concept of racial plasticity is exemplary of a biopolitical grammar, Billie's blackness and transness also gesture to a more opaque relation to biopolitics, in which the interiority of their embodied knowledge escapes capture by Young and, much later, transgender studies. While it makes sense, then, to insist on seeing the twentieth-century development of trans medicine as part of a broader biopolitical regulation of the sexed and gendered body (see, for example, Preciado 2013), Billie's life places black trans historicity and the question of their opacity in relation to biopolitics at the heart of that historical endeavor.

Trans of color critique can push transgender studies to take up its relationship to the limits of knowledge archived in historical sources like Billie's medical records, not in the hopes of finding a salvageable trans of color subject but to author desubjectivating accounts of the trans of color past.[7] Billie appears in the archive forcibly desubjectified, in the sense of having been deprived of personhood by Young's diagnostic model and its safeguarding by HIPAA. Instead of taking that desubjectification as proof of the unintelligibility of black trans life, however, it can be read as a partial escape from the biopolitical form of subjectivity into which transness was being increasingly confined over the twentieth century. Hardly a triumph or scene of clear-cut resistance, given the partiality of our perspective within a compromised archive, Billie's life registers more akin to what Kevin Quashie (2012: 24–26) calls "the sovereignty of quiet," an expressive form of human interiority that lacks the publicness associated with resistance or subversion. There is a certain risk to this move, as it relies, precisely, on the very opacity of the relation of trans of color life to institutions of capture like medicine, but the potential reward is a kind of counterhistory of privacy that evaded the normative history of concepts of gender, a situation in which, as Snorton puts it, "silence becomes countermythological" (2017: 151).[8]

The call is not to abandon medicine as an archive because of its epistemic bankruptcy (although we need nonmedical archives to supplant its rationality, too). The call, instead, is for forms of archival reading attuned to the unanticipated significance of historical desubjectification. Billie's life may have been highly distorted by medical discourse and further diminished by HIPAA regulations, legally proscribing access to unpublished archived sources of their personhood. Yet the dynamic interplay between the horrific publication of photographs of Billie's naked body and the photo of them in their everyday clothing also announces this black trans person's life as socially meaningful outside the parameters of medicine. From his partial and limited perspective, Young reads Billie as "a snappy young negro woman" in "street dress." The challenge for trans of color critique is to produce out of the surplus of his ignorance saturating that description a different form of knowledge, to take the weakness of medicine in this moment to affirm the rich but opaque interiority of blackness and transness preserved in the archive. That, I would argue, constitutes one distinction between early twentieth-century trans historicity in general and black trans, or trans of color historicity.

This essay has worked to identify and open up this problem for further study. It has not, nor could it, pretend to provide a single model for how to do so. Still, imagine what it might mean for the silence produced through Billie's medicalization to generate insight into black trans historicity not only in a negative sense but also in a move toward the undoing of the genealogy of transsexuality by privileging practices of black trans fugitivity as the reference point for the era "before" transsexuality. If medicine's modernity buries its reliance on racialized knowledge, then we should place black trans and trans of color knowledge in the center of the frame to produce counterhistories of life and embodiment without deference to medicine. Billie's mostly private and opaque embodied knowledge, lavishly lacking scientificity, points the way to another form of trans historiography, just as it points toward another way of life.

Julian Gill-Peterson is assistant professor of English at the University of Pittsburgh. They are the author of *Histories of the Transgender Child* (2018) and coeditor of "The Child Now," a special issue of *GLQ*.

Acknowledgment
I am grateful to Kadji Amin, Emma Heaney, and Jennifer Nash for their feedback on this project.

Notes

1. I use this phrase because flattening blackness and other forms of racialization into a single "trans of color" denotation would be a reduction of the complexity at hand in this essay, which is about a black trans person in particular.

2. See 5009.7, 5009.8, and 5009.11, BUI Records, Alan Chesney Mason Medical Archives, Baltimore. Due to privacy restrictions on materials at the Alan Mason Chesney Medical Archives and Medical Records Office of the Johns Hopkins Hospital, these numeric codes stand in place of bibliographic citation for certain unpublished documents. A copy of the code's key is stored at the archives, available for access to anyone who applies to the Johns Hopkins Privacy Board. I say "mostly," because in some cases with intersex children Young would wait to see how the sexed body grew into puberty before making a declaration of sex, not out of deference to patient autonomy per se but because he had no predictive model or effective way to override the body's plasticity without synthetic hormones. I look at this issue in detail in my book *Histories of the Transgender Child* (Gill-Peterson 2018).

3. I outline the racialization of modern sex through plasticity in much greater detail in Gill-Peterson 2017.

4. For example, see Edwards A. Park to Hugh Hampton Young, June 19, 1935. Edwards Park Collection, Alan Mason Chesney Medical Archives, Baltimore. In this letter, Parks, who was head of the Harriet Lane Home, analogizes a young black infant diagnosed with an intersex condition to what he construes as less evolved "mammals."

5. This pseudonym is meant to anonymize this person and minimize any implication that I know their actual gender identity (I do not). In *Genital Abnormalities* Young published the ostensible first names and initials for many patients, although these do not necessarily correspond to their actual legal or preferred names. I choose not to use the name that Young ascribes to this person to emphasize my refusal of his ethics.

6. To avoid implying that I know this person's preferred gender marker, I am deliberately using the singular *they/them/their*.

7.   In calling for attention to processes of desubjectification I am drawing on Foucault's rendering of that concept in his work on ethics, particularly as developed by Lynne Huffer (2009); but, following Alexander Weheliye (2014), I am also calling for a reckoning with the concept through black feminist work on the desubjectification wrought by the Middle Passage and slavery, most famously in the production of "flesh" (Spillers 1987).

8.   I am grateful to Jennifer Nash for raising this point.

References

Amin, Kadji. 2017. "Transing Intersectionality: Race, Species, and the Emergence of Transsexuality, 1890–1960." Paper presented at National Women's Studies Association Annual Meeting, Baltimore, MD.

cárdenas, micha. 2016a. "Pregnancy: Reproductive Futures in Trans of Color Feminism." *TSQ* 3, nos. 1–2: 48–57.

———. 2016b. "Trans of Color Poetics: Stitching Bodies, Concepts, and Algorithms." *Scholar and Feminist Online* 13, no. 3–14, no. 1. sfonline.barnard.edu/traversing-technologies/micha-cardenas-trans-of-color-poetics-stitching-bodies-concepts-and-algorithms.

Dreger, Alice. 1998. "A History of Intersexuality, from the Age of Gonads to the Age of Consent." *Journal of Clinical Ethics* 9, no. 4: 345–55.

Elbe, Lili. (1933) 2004. *Man into Woman: The First Sex Change.* Edited by Niels Hoyer. London: Blue Boat Books.

Ellison, Treva, et al. 2017. "We Got Issues: Toward a Black Trans*/Studies." *TSQ* 4, no. 2: 162–69.

Fajardo, Kale. 2016. "Queer/Asian Filipinos in Oregon: A Trans*Colonial Approach." Lecture, University of Pittsburgh, February 29.

Gill-Peterson, Julian. 2017. "Implanting Plasticity into Sex and Trans/Gender: Animal and Child Metaphors in the History of Endocrinology." *Angelaki: Journal of the Theoretical Humanities* 22, no. 2: 47–60.

———. 2018. *Histories of the Transgender Child.* Minneapolis: University of Minnesota Press.

Harvey, Sandra. 2016. "The HeLa Bomb and the Science of Unveiling." *Catalyst: Feminism, Theory, Technoscience* 2, no. 2: 1–30.

Heaney, Emma. 2017. *The New Woman: Literary Modernism, Queer Theory, and the Trans Feminine Allegory.* Chicago: Northwestern University Press.

Huffer, Lynne. 2009. *Mad for Foucault: Rethinking the Foundations of Queer Theory.* New York: Columbia University Press.

Jackson, Zakiyyah Iman. 2016. "Losing Manhood: Animality and Plasticity in the (Neo)Slave Narrative. *Qui Parle* 25, nos. 1–2: 95–136.

Jorgensen, Christine. 1968. *Christine Jorgensen: A Personal Autobiography.* New York: Bantam.

Lawrence, Susan. 2016. *Privacy and the Past: Research, Law, Archives, Ethics.* New Brunswick, NJ: Rutgers University Press.

Preciado, Paul B. 2013. *Testo Junkie: Sex, Drugs, and Biopolitics in the Pharmacopornographic Era.* Translated by Bruce Benderson. New York: Feminist Press.

Preves, Sharon E. 2001."Sexing the Intersexed: An Analysis of Sociocultural Responses to Intersexuality." *Signs* 27, no. 2: 523–56.

Quashie, Kevin. 2012. *The Sovereignty of Quiet: Beyond Resistance in Black Culture.* New Brunswick, NJ: Rutgers University Press.

Redick, Alison. 2004. "American History XY: The Medical Treatment of Intersex, 1916–1955." PhD diss., New York University.

Reid-Pharr, Robert F. 2016. *Archives of Flesh: African America, Spain, and Post-humanist Critique.* New York: New York University Press.

———. 2017. "Effective/Defective James Baldwin." Lecture, University of Pittsburgh, February 2.

Repo, Jemima. 2013. "The Biopolitical Birth of Gender: Social Control, Hermaphroditism, and the New Sexual Apparatus." *Alternatives: Global, Local, Political* 38, no. 3: 228–44.

Rubin, David A. 2012. "'An Unnamed Blank That Craved a Name': A Genealogy of Intersex as Gender." *Signs* 37, no. 4: 883–908.

Salah, Trish. 2014. *Lyric Sexology.* Vol. 1. Berkeley, CA: Roof.

Skloot, Rebecca. 2010. *The Immortal Life of Henrietta Lacks.* New York: Broadway.

Snorton, C. Riley. 2017. *Black on Both Sides: A Racial History of Trans Identity.* Minneapolis: University of Minnesota Press.

Snorton, C. Riley, and Jin Haritaworn. 2013. "Trans Necropolitics: A Transnational Reflection on Violence, Death, and the Trans of Color Afterlife." In *Transgender Studies Reader 2,* edited by Susan Stryker and Aren Z. Aizura, 66–76. New York: Routledge.

Spillers, Hortense. 1987. "Mama's Baby, Papa's Maybe: An American Grammar Book." *Diacritics* 17, no. 2: 64–81.

Stryker, Susan. 2009. "We Who Are Sexy: Christine Jorgensen's Transsexual Whiteness in the Postcolonial Philippines." *Social Semiotics* 19, no. 1: 79–91.

Stryker, Susan, and Paisley Currah. 2014. "General Editors' Introduction." *TSQ* 1, no. 3: 303–7.

Vitulli, Elias. 2016. "Trans*Disability Scholarship Roundtable." Paper presented at "Trans* Studies: An International Transdisciplinary Conference on Gender, Embodiment, and Sexuality," September 9, University of Arizona.

Washington, Harriet. 2006. *Medical Apartheid: The Dark History of Medical Experimentation on Black Americans from Colonial Times to the Present.* New York: Doubleday.

Weheliye, Alexander. 2014. *Habeas Viscus: Racializing Assemblages, Biopolitics, and Black Feminist Theories of the Human.* Durham, NC: Duke University Press.

Young, Hugh Hampton. 1937. *Genital Abnormalities, Hermaphroditism, and Related Adrenal Diseases.* Baltimore, MD: Williams and Wilkins.

Image Politics and Disturbing Temporalities

On "Sex Change" Operations
in the Early Chilean Dictatorship

FERNANDA CARVAJAL

Abstract This article analyzes the use of images in the press coverage on the first trans woman in Chile who managed to successfully change her legal gender in 1974, under the dictatorship of Augusto Pinochet, and who identified herself with the name of Marcia Alejandra. First, the author explains how sex change worked as a device in Chile during that period. Then, the author discusses a leaflet with photographs of Marcia Alejandra, configured according to the rhetoric of "before" and "after" her gender reassignment surgery, in order to analyze how these images published in the press disrupt our understanding of the political and medical narratives on the body that encode trans historicities, and even of a progressive temporality itself.

Keywords "sex change," image politics, Chilean dictatorship, disturbed temporalities

T his article is part of a larger research project that explores the conditions that made possible the development of legal and medical procedures that gave trans women access to "sex change" operations under the dictatorship of Augusto Pinochet in Chile (1973–90). During that period, gender reassignment surgeries were carried out in several health establishments without judicial mediation. In other Latin American countries also under military dictatorships—such as Argentina (1976–83) and Brazil (1964–85)—laws prohibiting such surgeries were often subsumed under other laws that criminalized any "mutilation" of the body (López Bolado 1981; Cardozo and Rodriguez 2016; Braga 2016). In Chile, however, there was no specific legislation regulating such surgeries. Not only were genital modification surgeries *not* penalized, but they even came to be discreetly offered in some public hospitals and private clinics in Santiago, starting in 1973, and as a free service for beneficiaries of the public health system in the Hospital van Buren of Valparaíso, starting in 1976. In this context, appealing to Law 17,344, which authorizes the change of names and family names, some trans women[1] obtained legal changes of name and sex. In this way, during the military dictatorship, a crucial chapter in the history of the relations between the state and the demands of the trans population began.

Here, I use the formulation "sex change" enclosed in quotes both to mark my own distance from the term and as a way of highlighting the epistemological (and temporal) tension that arises from using the available categories of the recent historical past. The formula "sex change" can be problematic because it might presuppose a linear and irreversible trajectory, one that marks an original departure point that, following the biological sex assigned at birth, is more "real" and "true" than what precedes it. This is certainly how the press covered (and visually rendered) Marcia Alejandra, the first trans woman to successfully change her legal gender, under the dictatorship of Augusto Pinochet, in 1974. As we will see, for press discourse Marcia Alejandra's operation marks a temporal point of arrival, which becomes the teleological product of the surgical techniques of genital modification.[2]

One of the distinguishing characteristics of Pinochet's dictatorship was the relationship between the systematic application of policies of torture, the execution and "disappearance" of individuals, and the simultaneous (though not subsequent) establishment of economic policies that promoted an indiscriminate openness to international trade, the reduction of public spending, and financial liberalization. These economic policies made Chile, according to some, the first neoliberal laboratory on the planet (Harvey 2007; Gárate 2015).[3] As the Chilean philosopher Willy Thayer (2006: 20–21) points out, "The coup did not happen *in* Chilean history, it happened *to* Chilean history." In this sense, the dictatorship inaugurated a new mode of hegemonic time. But that does not imply that the military coup must be considered an interruption of "national" history or that it implies its end. On the one hand, what the dictatorship does in its self-proclaimed *estado de excepción*, or "state of emergency," is confirm the exceptionalism of Chilean history—its more than two hundred years of republican political violence (since 1810) in the name of the law. On the other hand, the dictatorship perpetuated this violence as a transition from the state to the market as the main regulator of social relations. In the name of progress and achievement—that is, modernization as a historical and chronopolitical norm—the dictatorship governed both state and market according to the binary of repression/consent, which is based partly on the state monopoly over violence, torture, and the ideological instruments of persuasion. The dictatorship also promoted certain economic freedoms, self-entrepreneurship, and the production of inequality and indebtedness, which served to undermine the reconstitution of collective ties.

In this article, I argue that this characteristic of dictatorial governance has a correlate in different sex-gender technologies that emerged during the same period, through which a disciplinary regime of sex began—in an incomplete, fragmentary, and contradictory manner—to make way for a more flexible model of identity and sex, or what Paul B. Preciado has called "pharmacopornographic" technologies (2014: 63–73) of body production.[4] This does not imply, however, a clear, straight trajectory of any supposed "sexual modernization," which would leave behind all disciplinarian characteristics. On the contrary, I am interested in observing the interplay of tense, turbulent, and overlapping body technologies (and temporalities) that become clear when we juxtapose the visual imagery of the "before" and "after" of a "sex change" and that of the military coup in Chile.

It is not difficult to see how the dictatorship reinforced a disciplinary (and temporal) regime of sex by intensifying the propagation of the heterosexual family as the main model for masculine and feminine sexual and social identities, according to conservative Catholic values (Grau et al. 1997). The dictatorship imposed a militarist-patriarchal discourse that exacerbated virile identifications with the rhetoric of command (Richard 1993). It also promoted the traditional figure of motherhood, which placed women in the role of the moral guardians of society and depositories of national traditions and perhaps of "history" itself (Junta Nacional de Gobierno 1974: 191–200). During this period, Penal Code Article 365 (which criminalized the practice of sodomy, specifically, male homosexuality, since 1875) and Article 373 (which criminalized "affronts to decency" and was used to penalize transvestism and street prostitution) were also in effect. It is important to note that these articles were applied before, during, and after the dictatorial period—consensual sex between two same-sex adults was not decriminalized until 1999. However, as is the case in other Latin American countries under military dictatorships, there are no records of a repressive policy devised by the military with the purpose of directly persecuting sexual diversity.[5]

Anyway, from the earliest years of the dictatorship, there were signs of the gradual emergence of pharmacopornographic techniques for the control of bodies that reveal more diffuse power mechanics involving the modulation of subjective desire, the diversification of the sexual market, and the medicalization of sexuality. Beginning in the late 1970s, traditional brothels were replaced by individual, discreet services that took place in strip clubs, saunas, and cabarets (Salazar and Pinto 1999); meanwhile, the first gay clubs (Contardo 2011), associated with the strengthening of nightlife and sexual markets, began to emerge in this period. Also, instead of framing the medical-legal path to sex change in a prohibitive manner, endowing the state with authority over the bodies of trans individuals, as in the Argentine and Brazilian dictatorships, the Chilean dictatorship opened a discreet space where "sex change" surgeries could be carried out in public hospitals and private clinics, and in some cases, civil rectifications of name and sex were managed and left up to the discretion of a judge.[6] In effect, this ultimately formalized the admissibility of the surgeries and a judicialization of civil name and sex change. This implied that, once the surgery was performed, the person requesting the civil sex change had to undergo a medical examination that gave rise to potentially abusive procedures and to forms of physical and moral punishment, which revealed the other face of this permissive legal framework: the vulnerability of the trans population to state-sponsored institutional violence. This coexistence of permissiveness and abuse at play in the judicialization of "sex change" in Chile reflects neoliberal modes of governance, which, in a society just beginning to accommodate multiplicity and difference, confront and undermine the legitimacy of disciplinary-style interventions and state planning. It also promoted a proliferation of legal arbitration that introduced more sophisticated forms of violence against the trans population (Carvajal 2016).

In the absence of LGBT rights organizations, which in Chile were formed only after 1991, in the postdictatorial period, members of the Sociedad Chilena de Sexología Antropológica (the Chilean Society of Anthropological Sexology, or the SChSA),[7] along with doctors and lawyers, helped launch an array of medical-legal actions around access to "sex change" operations. Indeed, the sexological discourse of the 1960s is an essential precedent for understanding how "sex change" functioned as a device during the early years of the dictatorship. In 1967, the doctors of the SChSA decided to discuss the feasibility of introducing a medical-legal path for "sex change" in the country, as a way to provide a solution to the criminalization of trans women. The doctors discussed a case that was well covered in the press, which reported the arrest of a waitress at her place of work under Article 373 of the Penal Code because her official documents did not match her gender expression.[8] The doctors presented genital modification surgery as the solution that would "define" sex and thus grant entry to citizenship. An inextricable link between class, work, the criminalization of trans people, medical power, and sex-gendered normalization technologies was thus put forward by the medical profession and, eventually, the state.[9] In this discussion, "sex change" surgery was presented under a humanitarian, modernizing discourse and through a temporality inextricably linked to progress, as one way to guarantee "rights" and make possible the "desires" of people to define themselves in one sex (Quijada 1968).[10]

In the space that remains here, I analyze how the press covered the image of the first transsexual woman to successfully change her legal gender, in 1974, who identified herself as Marcia Alejandra. I argue that this case inaugurates a particular construction of transsexuality in the press, and it shows how "sex change" was configured as a temporal and political device in the early years of the dictatorship. At the same time, the media construction of the story of Marcia Alejandra has characteristics that do not appear in later press coverage, particularly the superimposition of elements from the political context in the story of the "before" and "after" her transition. What can a perspective from the global South reveal about the narration of Marcia Alejandra's transition, and how does it offer us another way of thinking trans-historically from a geographical perspective outside the framework of the North American context?

The way in which the story of Marcia Alejandra was constructed in the media shows how the sensationalist press in the early years of the dictatorship used medical-sexological discourse to present genital modification operations as a technology of bodily and moral correction, codified in terms of technological-moral-temporal progress.[11] Several contemporaneous newspaper and magazine articles suggest that Marcia Alejandra's life—marked by suffering and police harassment (by the application of Article 373)—was something that surgery could solve. Here, we can observe a contrast to what was happening at the same time in the North American context where, as David Valentine (2007: 57–65) has pointed out, the depathologization of homosexuality and the pathologization of trans-genderism was followed by a process of gay and lesbian inclusion, which some sectors have understood as a path toward the normalization of homosexuality. Valentine warns that the differentiation between homosexuality and transsexuality led to a separation between gender and sexuality that, instead of being presented as a historically produced distinction, was institutionalized as a question of ontology and as a sign of both progress and modernization. In Chile, on the other hand, the decoupling of transsexuality as a diagnostic category coexisted with the criminalization of homosexuality, thus implying a divergence between the notions of "progress" that the differentiation of categories carried with it in each context. The Chilean press constructed an account of Marcia Alejandra's "sex change," establishing a distinction between homosexuality and transsexuality in terms of the temporal and medical passage from illegality to the legality of an identity. Indeed, from then on, the sensationalist press of the early dictatorship placed stories of transvestism and prostitution-related homosexuality in the crime sections and transsexual women in the entertainment chronicles of magazines and newspapers (even though, of course, the transsexual women who engaged in the sex trade or other work related to nocturnal commerce were also exposed to the application of Article 373).

Here, I focus on the only images of Marcia Alejandra published in the press, configured according to the rhetoric of "before" and "after" surgery, in order to ask how time is being reconfigured by (and through) the juxtaposition of the two images below. The story of Marcia's transition exemplifies a standard narrative to which, as Emma Huston (2015) has pointed out, trans people are often reduced. This narrative is characterized by the logic of the medical criteria for diagnosing transsexuality, the confessional discourses of the press, and the conventions of autobiography, which make transgender subjects intelligible by imposing a linear, teleological, and irreversible narrative that seeks to award sexual and biographical coherence. These characteristics are clearly present in how the story of Marcia Alejandra was publicized. But, at the same time, that story was part of a broader sociopolitical narrative, which provides points of departure from any such linear temporality. I am interested in how the images of Marcia Alejandra published in the press disrupt our understanding of political and medical narratives of the body, and, in doing so, challenge notions of progressive temporality. The seemingly linear modification of Marcia's body—or at least how such a corporeal shift came to be represented in the press—offered a striking parallel to the temporal progression of the years before and after the inauguration of the Chilean dictatorship led by Pinochet (that is, the "yesterday" and the "today" of the Chilean coup of September 11, 1973, in which the Armed Forces ousted progressive president Salvador Allende from power).

Images and Reports of Marcia Alejandra's "Sex Change" in the Press

Historically, the sensationalist press has been a space in which segregated and marginalized identities may gain access to public visibility—a documentary base through which trans histories are sometimes constructed and narrated. One of its distinctive features is the more prominent presence of images over stories. This access to visibility is always mediated and paradoxical, as the sensationalist press resorts to distortion, stereotypes, and stigmas to shed light on marginal and otherwise anonymous subjects, enshrouding them in scandal and crime and capturing them as information commodities. During the first years of the Chilean dictatorship, such sensationalist narratives were used by the press to exploit a series of stories about transsexual women, as in the case of Marcia Alejandra. Marcia Alejandra was a trans woman who was able to undergo surgery in May 1973 during the Unidad Popular (Popular Unity) government, and in May of 1974, with the nation already under dictatorship, she was the first trans woman to obtain a legal change of name and sex. Her identity transition—exploited by the press when her case came to light—was thus marked by the historical event of the coup d'état.

It is possible to identify an affinity between the media coverage of Marcia Alejandra's "sex change" and the official campaign by the dictatorship of Pinochet called "*Ayer hoy*" (Yesterday Today), which sought to legitimize the 1973 coup that overthrew Allende and his party, Unidad Popular. As Cora Gamarnik (2012) points out, this propaganda campaign was one of the psychological operations devised by civil servants of the Chilean dictatorship. The propaganda campaign took the form of leaflets and a book, *Chile ayer hoy* (*Chile Yesterday Today*), which circulated internationally and was disseminated nationally in various print media. Its main objective was to generate popular support for the coup d'état and to associate the Marxist past of the Unidad Popular government with lies, betrayal, and corruption, as well as unrest and social disorder. The methodology and objectives of these campaigns (recorded in recently declassified secret documents) included the repeated use of simple images and direct messages. Using leaflets that included photographs, a series of "rhetorical units" of dictatorial discourse enunciated a "refounding" of the nation, which was supported by the national security doctrine (Berríos 2009). More specifically, the leaflet consisted of a montage of two side-by-side images (fig. 1) that illustrated, on the left, images of "*ayer*" (yesterday) representing the "chaos" of the Unidad Popular (demonstrations, scenes of violence, empty businesses, dirty streets), and, on the right, images of "*hoy*" (today) pertaining to "order" (people walking peacefully on the street, looking at store displays, shopping in packed businesses, reading in parks, images of a "happy" and heterosexual family life).

One of the questions that structure this article is how to read the "trans" bodies of the past in relation to the (political) present, at the points of rupture that have the potential to frustrate linear, progressive, and modernizing stories. I thus propose that the story of Marcia Alejandra was portrayed in media as a sexed and gendered recoding of the ideological distinction between (yesterday's) chaos of Unidad Popular and (today's) order of the dictatorship embedded in the

Figure 1. Cover of the book *Chile ayer hoy* (*Chile Yesterday Today*), Editorial Nacional Gabriela Mistral, 1975

Yesterday Today campaign. Thus, Marcia Alejandra's biography was temporally divided into a "before" of being an offender, associated with sexual "indefinition," homosexuality, and the criminalization of nonnormative sexualities (as per Article 373 of the Penal Code) and an "after" that was associated with her sexual "definition" as a woman, granting her a coherent legal status. It is this post-transition Marcia Alejandra who now more comfortably fits the image of the heteronormative family of "today."

To support these claims, it is necessary to analyze a series of contemporary articles published on Marcia Alejandra. In recounting her past life, several press releases recall that Marcia Alejandra had been arrested during a police raid on the clandestine gay bar El Anillo Rojo (The Red Ring) that took place on March 1973 and also in the "Escándalo de la calle Huanchaca" (Huanchaca Street scandal; *La estrella* 1969) that occurred on June 1969, due to the application of Article 373 of the Penal Code. One article, for example, indicates that "on both occasions, Alberto Arturo Torres, known [at the time] as Marcela, was among the detainees" (*Revista vea* 1974). The reference to the Huanchaca Street scandal is significant, as it refers to the arrest of a group of homosexuals and transvestites while they were having a party where, according to the press, there were also political activities linked to leftist groups (*La estrella* 1969). Thus, the press constructed a temporal association between homosexuality/transvestism, subversion of the state, and Chile's precoup political reality. These discourses constructed Marcia Alejandra's past in relation to a position of illegality and lawlessness, reinforced by the fact that some press releases explicitly linked the doctors who had performed the operation on her with Unidad Popular, saying that they had been "detained in [the prison of] Chacabuco" (*La tercera* 1974).[12]

In contrast, when the articles refer to Marcia Alejandra's life after her surgery and the civil rectification of her name and sex, they construct a future-oriented present that promises the beginning of a new life. In doing so, the press simultaneously reconciles familial heterosexuality with Marcia's career as a *vedette* or a showgirl, and also connects her figure and persona to the military world. In August 1974, the dictatorship issued a decree authorizing female recruits be required to enter the Escuela de Servicios Auxiliares del Ejército (the Army School of Auxiliary Services, or the ESAFE), thereby incorporating women into the Armed Forces for the first time.[13] One report from that period reads, "The young woman [Marcia Alejandra] points out that even though she did complete her military service as a man, she would like to do it now in the ESAFE and that, as she said, 'hopefully they will assign me an artillery weapon'" (*Revista vea* 1975b). The statement, which can be read as a sexual joke and an eroticization of artillery weapons, lets us note that discourse on transsexuality in the sensationalist press allowed the coexistence of notions that in other official contexts were incompatible: the admissibility of corporal transformation[14] (with "corrective" purposes) with military rituals and practices, and the image of an erotic and sexually active femininity in the figure of the decent wife. This juxtaposition exhibits the many folds and textures of the regime's patriarchal discourse, which explicitly contradicts the rhetoric of the patriotic woman, the family, and Catholic fundamentalist values that the dictatorship officially promoted.

However, the linearity and irreversibility between the "yesterday" and "today" in the press stories are constantly interrupted by moments of return and regression to the past. One of the aspects of "sex change" that generated significant social anxiety was the way in which a change in gender identity could affect an understanding of sexual practices. When the press published the news in 1974 that Marcia Alejandra was then living with a man who was her partner, the media called into question any distinction between transsexuality, homosexuality, and sodomy, stating that she could now be prosecuted under Article 365 for the crime of sodomy. In this case, it was the legal discourse that was responsible for differentiating and separating transsexuality from homosexuality, separating Marcia Alejandra from her offending past: faced with the possibility that Marcia Alejandra could be arrested and prosecuted for sodomy while living with a man, attorney Abogado Hugo Soto explained that sexual relations between people with different sexual organs did not constitute a crime, even if one of the subject's genitalia was "artificial" (*El Mercurio de Antofagasta* 1973). Attorney Soto, who in this article talks about "laboratory" men and women, removes the imagery of the hermaphrodite that persisted in some medical discourses of the period, showing instead a certain optimism about the "scientific" and "modern" aspect of such surgical technologies, and admitting that the body should not be understood as strictly natural but as coconstituted by and through technical intervention. This argument coincides with legal discourses at the time that reasoned that the juridical logic behind the crime of sodomy is the principle that any copulation must take place between people of different sexes (which, in fact, implies male and female genitals), even when the sexual act is not intended for procreation (Arancibia 1966).

Among the press accounts that mention Marcia Alejandra published between 1974 and 1975, we observe that her image was regularly exploited on the covers of newspapers and magazines, and that photographs were used to portray her both in everyday scenes and in her role as a showgirl. The diptych format of the photo spread, used to visualize the "before" and "after" of the surgery, was used only once (fig. 2), in an article published in October 1975 in *Revista vea* (1975a), a tabloid magazine of broad national circulation that was supportive of the military regime.

Figure 2. "Confesiones de un transexual," *Revista vea*, October 9, 1975, 2–3

In these images and their accompanying captions, one visual feature immediately stands out: the discrepancy between the large size of the image on the left, which occupies half of the page (with no context) and shows Marcia Alejandra looking at the camera half-naked and coyly placing her finger in her mouth, and the small photograph on the upper-right, which shows her emerging from a police van. The captions for these photographs read, "Marcia Alejandra after the operation (left). Above, when she was still a man and was arrested in Antofagasta's 'Red Circle.'" What trajectory might we trace between the surgery's "before" and "after" (or between the "yesterday" and the "today" of the body represented in the images)? How is this trajectory related to the narrative of the precoup chaos and the postcoup order promoted by the dictatorship to present itself as a therapeutic factor for society? The captions attempt to establish a linear, progressive narrative that subscribes to the discourse that surgery presents as a bodily, moral, and legal correction. But that temporality and this historicity (which is also expressed in the use of both masculine and feminine pronouns to refer to Marcia Alejandra) are visually and conceptually disturbed on the plane of the image.

The caption of the police van photograph seeks to restore the masculine identity of Marcia Alejandra, but the image does not show a male body. We do not know the extent to which Marcia Alejandra managed the circulation of her own image, or if indeed she was able to at all. But the postoperative photography of Marcia Alejandra is confronted with an image of her past as a "transvestite" (which also appears in press releases that reported that before surgery Marcia Alejandra identified herself as "Marcela"). The bodies exhibited in the images are not rendered equally "feminine." Neither do they help trace a clear path between a clearly masculine past and a clearly feminine present. Although the "before" of Marcia Alejandra being arrested by the police, due to her nonnormative expression of gender and her work in the night trade, corresponds with the images of chaos and social disorder that sought to codify the past of the Unidad Popular, the photo of the present is stereotyped and continues to point to the scandal of "yesterday" through the sexualized pose. Furthermore, in the photograph on the left, Marcia's muscular arm places a masculine trait in the visual foreground, making reference to some of the estrangements of "sex change." Although press coverage and medical discourse attempt to establish surgery as a decisive point that makes Marcia Alejandra's biographical narrative temporally coherent, they ultimately reveal that a clear distinction between before and after cannot be reduced to a single event.

The cis-hetero-phonocentric form of writing and reading, to invoke Jacques Derrida's notion of phonocentrism, is organized according to a linear norm with a straight orientation and an irreversible temporalized event (like the "sex change").[15] Such norms, however, can never be totally imposed, since they are limited from the inside by spacing and interval (Derrida 1998). From this perspective, if the images illustrate the linear sequence dictated by the captions to present a past to which we should not return, it seems most logical that the photograph depicting the scene of police repression should be on the left side (where reading begins), and that the postoperative image of Marcia Alejandra would be on the right. Nevertheless, the placement of the photographs is reversed, as if the inversion and the disproportionate size of both photographs could convert a temporal axis into a spatial axis, turning the "before" and the "after" into a forward and a behind. What if we read the queer arrangement of these two images to indicate that, far from mere linear trajectory and progressive change, a temporality of the repressed instead incessantly returns? This return then also points to forms of historical violence that return, and indeed that never fully disappear. Does the coexistence of what lies ahead, and what remains behind, signal that the identity of the trans subject—now marked by its legality—is always on the verge of falling back into illegality?

The spatial axis visually arranges the images in terms of the near and the distant, opening up a tactile dimension that diagrams a criminal, untouchable body (that must stay behind, in the past) and a future body (that must move forward, and to which a greater proximity is possible). But the photograph of Marcia Alejandra as a *vedette* along with her "criminal" image can also be seen as a cis-hetero-patriarchal resource that has the effect of "cooling" and distancing the postoperative image of Marcia Alejandra in order to protect the public from her eroticism. What proximity—and what frictions—are admissible here in relation to trans bodies?

These images allow us to reflect on the multidirectionality of the temporal and spatial narratives presented here, because the perturbations on the time line before and after the "sex change" are also present in the images of Marcia's past and future body. For medical narratives, as well as those used to characterize Marcia in the press, these two temporal locations are articulated as stable and producing a coherent relationship between old and new. On the other hand, as Atalia Israeli-Nevo (2017: 39) points out, the temporal space of such a transition can be understood as an opportunity to "decelerate" time, distorting "a trans linear temporality, sending it back and forth." For Israeli-Nevo, "this slowing moves trans time, exposing the lines that link normative trans narratives and cisgender temporality" (Fisher, Phillips, and Katri 2017: 9). This photo spread allows us to reflect on a temporality that transgresses progress, and what these images show is how the background becomes the foreground: between Marcia Alejandra's photograph (today) as a showgirl and the (past) one of her police arrest, a spatial estrangement moves away and brings closer both images, producing the return and the proximity of the repressive time that wants to be left behind.

According to the normative temporality of the press, genital modification surgery is presented as a means to eliminate conflicts with the law in people who were marked from a police perspective as being of an "indeterminate sex." However, placing transgender people in a position where they violate the law was not (and is not) a scene that we have left behind us, especially when it is possible to undergo a genital modification surgery, but civil sex and name changes were not (and are not) legally protected. While in the 1970s there were juridical procedures that permitted some changes of sex and name, this depended entirely on the judge in question. This was, however, a precarious situation, and laws in the 1970s did not guarantee the right to identity of trans individuals writ large. To this day, despite the legality of sex-change operations, Chile does not have a gender identity law (such as Argentina's 2012 Gender Identity Law) to facilitate the civil modification of name and sex. If the before and after of Marcia Alejandra's sex-gender transition that the photo spread sought to make visible was haunted by the yesterday and today that the dictatorship sought to establish to move on from the Unidad Popular past, is it possible, using these images, to think that the affirmation of progress as a historical norm constitutes a euphemism for naming violence as a historical norm?

Conclusion

What do these images have to say to those who look at them decades after they were produced? It is indeed possible to imagine that Marcia Alejandra's photographs operate as an interruption, a suspension of temporalities in which we might expect to view a passage forward, a transition of body, form, desire, and time.

During the Chilean dictatorship, there was an attempt to decriminalize (and heterosexualize) the trans body through the mechanism of surgery, which was even practiced in public hospitals, as a sign of technical-moral progress. However, the trans body exists in a space of rupture. It unleashes a more complicated series of temporary breaks that take place both inside and outside the images I have presented here. Indeed, if we return to the cover of the book *Chile Yesterday Today*, it is possible to observe an affinity between the photograph of the barricade (on the left) and that of Marcia Alejandra emerging from the police van (on the right) that seeks to produce an image of the "chaos" of "yesterday" that must be left behind. But the same does not hold true for the image of the present. The photograph of the white nuclear family, happy in the image of "today," remains in conflict with the sexualized pose of Marcia Alejandra that continues to point to the scandals of yesterday—scandals that become visible in part because of the eroticism of the image.

The images composed by the sensationalist press to narrate Marcia Alejandra's transition in a linear and unidirectional manner ruins the progressive logic between the before and after of dictatorship—between "chaos" and "order," "yesterday" and "today"—causing a confrontation of temporalities and a confusion of political affinities. The media images of Marcia Alejandra are a photographic residue, a set of images discarded by historiographical narrations, lost in the sensationalist pages of newspapers that are rarely reread as historical evidence (or for their queer potential). But these are residual images that return, producing different forms of distance and proximity. Does not the reappearance of the image of Marcia Alejandra emerging from the police van, originally published before the coup d'état in March 1973,[16] remind us that, at least for some of us, the state of emergency is the rule, even in a supposed democracy? These images allow us to reflect on how the foundational, progressive, and modernizing discourse of the state, through which the dictatorship sought to legitimize the coup d'état to "normalize" society, is interrupted when the trans body reintroduces a moment of repression prior to the coup. For this is a moment that repeatedly returns—one that is never to be left behind. The trans body inhabits a rupture that disturbs such simple binaries between the past and present, "yesterday" and "today." By exhibiting the violence of state security forces, the trans body disrupts the safe and comfortable boundary between the before and after of the dictatorship, showing the return of a repressive time from whence we can never truly escape. Perhaps these images of Marcia Alejandra's trans*historical body show that, just as gender has no established physical, legal, or metaphorical destiny, nor are progress and modernization the only destinies of historical time.

Fernanda Carvajal is a sociologist, teacher, and researcher at the Universidad de Buenos Aires and a postdoctoral fellow at the National Scientific and Technical Research Council (Consejo Nacional de Investigaciones Científicas y Técnicas, CONICET). She holds a master's in communication and culture and a PhD in social sciences. She resides in Buenos Aires and works on crossings between art, politics, and sexuality since the 1970s in Chile. She is a member of the groups "Art, Culture and Politics in Argentina," directed by Ana Longoni, and "Micropolitics of Sexual Disobedience in Contemporary Argentine Art," directed by Fernando Davis. She coordinates the Southern Conceptualisms Network, from which she formed the curatorial team of the exhibition *Losing the Human Form: A Seismic Image of the 1980s in Latin America* at Reina Sofia Museum in Madrid (2012), Lima (2013), and Buenos Aires (2014). She is working together with Alejandro de la Fuente on the compilation of the Mares of the Apocalypse Archive.

Notes

1. Throughout this article I use contemporary categories such as "trans woman" or "trans femininities," although these terms were not used yet in the studied period—itself a willful anachronism.

2. The strong preponderance of genitality in the definition of sex, which crystallizes the formula "sex change" in the social imaginary, leaves in the shadows the fact that there are not one but multiple sex-gender techniques of corporal modification, from the use of hormones and other type of surgeries such as mammoplasty, up to clothing or haircuts, which can produce the self-perceived sex.

3. It should be noted that the liberalization of the Chilean economy was executed not only by the Ministry of Economy but also by the Central Planning Office (ODEPLAN), staffed by a second generation of economists trained in Chicago and politicians linked to right-wing politics and fundamentalist Catholicism.

4. Preciado distinguishes the disciplinary sex regime, based on a dichotomous logic (man/woman) and organized around the heterosexuality/homosexuality dyad, from the pharmacopornographic regime, according to which body-control techniques do not attempt to punish or correct deviations from the norm from outside but to modulate the bodies using synthetic materials, prostheses, or the consumption of hormones, which infiltrate the inside of the individual body and modify the way of conceiving the body, in order to artificially produce a standard corporality, but in such a way that each organ no longer corresponds "to a single function or even a single location" (2014: 154).

5.   An exception is the dictatorship of Alfredo Stroessner in Paraguay, where it is possible to identify a repressive policy aimed against male homosexuality (Carbone 2016).

6.   It is important to clarify that, although the medical-legal procedures surrounding "sex change" did not take place behind the backs of dictatorial institutions, the information gathered so far does not suggest an official policy in relation to genital modification surgery. See Carvajal 2016.

7.   A significant fact to mention is that the members of the SChSA were sympathizers of the left wing, and Dr. Osvaldo Quijada had been close to the Chilean Communist Party. During the government of Salvador Allende, the SChSA played an active role in the development of sex education policies (Barón and Lagos 1997).

8.   This discussion has been recorded in Quijada et al. 1968.

9.   This same argument is later taken up by Dr. Guillermo MacMillan, the doctor who developed the clinical path for genital modification surgeries at the Van Buren Hospital in Valparaíso, since 1976, who in a 1988 article stated that after surgery the applicant is then "rehabilitated" and "ends his conflict with the law due to conduct judged as immoral or dishonest" (1988: 95).

10.   The members of the Chilean Society of Sexology proposed this discourse on guarantees to what in those years in Chile was called "the right to personality" (González Berendique 1968).

11.   This article is part of a larger study that included the review of sixty-five articles on transsexuality and "sex change" in different newspapers of three cities: Santiago, Valparaíso, and Antofagasta (*La estrella del norte, El mercurio de Antofagasta, La estrella de Valparaíso, Las últimas noticias, La tercera*), and in the magazine *Revista vea*.

12.   The Chacabuco Prisoners Camp was located at the Chacabuco Saltpeter Office, one hundred kilometers from the city of Antofagasta. It was used from the beginning of November 1973 until April 1975, with more than one thousand political prisoners.

13.   In 1978, the dictatorship officially expanded military service to both men and women.

14.   The nuance between correction and transformation refers to the fact that, during this period, unlike the medical and legal discourse, the Chilean Catholic Church accepted what it called a correction of the "malformed sex" but rejected "sex change," the genital modification, in "healthy" bodies (Torres in Quijada et al. 1968).

15.   I return to Derrida's notion of phonocentrism understood, quickly and succinctly, as the belief that writing is merely a derived method of capturing speech, which underlies the "metaphysics of presence." Phonocentrism presupposes an irreversible and linear temporality, proper to speech and orality, an argument that, following Derrida's perspective, I want to call into question.

16.   This image, with different frames, appeared at different times in newspapers and magazines of the period in May 1974, when the case of Marcia Alejandra came to light. In October 1975, when the leaflet we analyzed was published, it was the first time that the figure of the policeman was shown alongside Marcia Alejandra.

References

Arancibia, Armando. 1966. *La figura delictiva del artículo 365 del código penal (The Criminal Figure of Article 365 of the Penal Code)*. Santiago de Chile: Editorial Jurídica de Chile.

Barón Irma, and Tulio Lagos. 1997. *Educación sexual en Chile (Sexual Education in Chile)*. Santiago de Chile: Contempo Gráfica.

Berríos, Lorena. 2009. "En busca de un nuevo rostro: Fotografías de un discurso dictatorial. Chile, 1973–1976" ("Searching a New Face: Photographs of a Dictatorial Speech. Chile, 1973–1976"). *Revista comunicación y medios,* no. 20: 16–40.

Braga de Almeida Neves, Benjamin. 2016. "Transmasculinidades no ambiente escolar: Laicidade e resistências" ("Transmasculinities in the School Environment: Laicity and Resistances"). In *A política no corpo gêneros e sexualidade em disputa (Body Politics: Genres and Sexuality in Dispute),* edited by Alexsandro Rodriguez, Gustavo Monzeli, and Sergio da Silva, 161–78. Vitoria: Edufes.

Carbone, Rocco. 2016. *Putos de fuga: Diversamente deseante en Paraguay (Vanishing Points/Leaky Fags: Diversely Desiring in Paraguay).* Los Polvorines: Universidad Nacional de General Sarmiento.

Cardozo, Pablo, and Alexsandro Rodriguez. 2016. "Fundamentalismo Religioso E a Saúde Trans No Brasil" ("Religious Fundamentalism and Trans Health In Brazil"). In *A política no corpo gêneros e sexualidade em disputa (Body Politics: Genres and Sexuality in Dispute),* edited by Alexsandro Rodriguez, Gustavo Monzeli, and Sergio da Silva, 237–58. Vitoria: Edufes.

Carvajal, Fernanda. 2016. "Regulaciones y contra-regulaciones del género y la sexualidad durante el terrorismo de Estado en Chile (1973–1990). El 'cambio de sexo' como dispositivo en el discurso médico legal, la prensa oficialista y el arte anti-dictatorial" ("Regulations and Counterregulations of Fender and Sexuality during State Terrorism in Chile [1973–1990]. The 'Sex Change' as a Device in the Legal Medical Discourse, Official Press, and Anti-dictatorial Art"). PhD diss., Universidad de Buenos Aires.

Contardo, Óscar. 2011. *Raro: Una historia gay de Chile (A Gay History of Chile).* Santiago de Chile: Planeta.

Derrida, Jacques. 1998. *De la gramatología (Of Grammatology).* Mexico City: Siglo Veintiuno.

La estrella del norte. 1969. "¿Tres delitos un escándalo?" ("Three Crimes One Scandal?"). June 17.

Fisher, Simon Elin, Rasheedah Phillips, and Ido Katri. 2017. "Trans Temporalities." *Somatechnics 7,* no. 1: 1–15.

Gamarnik, Cora. 2012. "Fotografía y dictaduras: Estrategias comparadas entre Chile, Uruguay y Argentina" ("Photography and Dictatorships: Comparative Strategies between Chile, Uruguay, and Argentina"). *Nuevo mundo mundos nuevos (New World New Worlds),* June 10. nuevomundo.revues.org/63127.

Gárate, Manuel. 2015. *La revolución capitalista de Chile (1973–2003) (The Capitalist Revolution of Chile [1973–2003]).* Santiago de Chile: Editorial Universidad Alberto Hurtado.

González Berendique, M. A. 1968. "Justificación jurídica" ("Legal Justification"). In Quijada et al. 1968: 89–97.

Grau, Olga, et al. 1997. *Discurso, género, poder: Discursos públicos. Chile 1978–1993 (Speech, Gender, Power: Public Speeches. Chile 1978–1993).* Santiago de Chile: Arcis/Lom/La Morada.

Harvey, David. 2007. *Breve historia del neoliberalismo (A Brief History of Neoliberalism).* Madrid: Akal.

Huston, Emma, 2015. "Passing: Beyond the Single Story Narrative." Paper presented at the Trans Studies Now conference, Sussex Centre for Cultural Studies, Brighton, England. www.academia.edu/13447243/Passing_Beyond_the_Single_Story_Narrative.

Israeli-Nevo, Atalia. 2017. "Taking (My) Time: Temporality in Transition, Queer Delays, and Being (in the) Present." *Somatechnics 7,* no. 1: 34–49.

Junta Nacional de Gobierno. 1974. "La Junta de Gobierno se dirige a las mujeres de la República de Chile" ("The Governing Board Addresses Women of Chilean Republic"). In *1974 Primer año de la Reconstrucción Nacional* (*1974 First Year of the National Reconstruction*), 191–200. Santiago de Chile: Gabriela Mistral.

López Bolado, Jorge. 1981. *Los médicos y el código penal* (*The Doctors and the Penal Code*). Buenos Aires: Editorial Universidad.

MacMillan, Guillermo. 1988. "El urólogo y el transexualismo" ("The Urologist and Transsexualism"). *Revista Chilena de urología* 51: 94–95.

El mercurio de Antofagasta. 1973. "Abogado Hugo Soto: En Chile debe legislarse sobre el cambio de sexo" ("Attorney Hugo Soto: Chile Must Legislate on Sex Change"). May 14.

Preciado, Paul B. 2014. *Testo yonki: Sexo, drogas y biopolítica* (*Testo Junkie: Sex, Drugs, and Biopolitics in the Pharmacopornographic Era*). Buenos Aires: Paidós.

Quijada, Osvaldo. 1968. "El cambio de sexo y su justificación antropológica" ("Sex Change and Its Anthropological Justification"). In Quijada et al. 1968: 17–31.

Quijada, Osvaldo, et al. 1968. *Cambio de sexo: Puntos de vista antropológico, biológico, embriológico, genético, clínico endocrinológico, psiquiátrico, religioso católico y jurídico* (*Sex Change: Anthropological, Biological, Embryological, Genetic, Clinical Endocrinological, Psychiatric, Religious, Catholic, and Legal Points of View*). Buenos Aires: Joaquín Almendros.

Revista vea. 1974. "El Hombre que se convirtió en mujer" ("The Man Who Became a Woman"). May 10, 16–17.

———. 1975a. "Confesiones de un transexual" ("Confessions of a Transexual"). October 9, 2–3.

———. 1975b. "Marcia Alejandra a la conquista de la capital" ("Marcia Alejandra to the Conquest of the Capital"). March 27, 23.

Richard, Nelly. 1993. *Masculino/Femenino: Políticas de la diferencia y cultura democrática* (*Masculine/Feminine: Policies of Difference and Democratic Culture*). Santiago de Chile: Francisco Zegers Editor.

Salazar, Gabriel, and Julio Pinto. 1999. *Historia contemporánea de Chile IV: Hombría y feminidad* (*Contemporary History of Chile IV: Manliness and Femininity*). Santiago de Chile: Lom Ediciones.

La tercera de la hora. 1974. "¡Desapareció Marcia Alejandra!" ("Marcia Alejandra Disappeared!"). July 5.

Thayer, Willy. 2006. *El fragmento repetido: Escritos en estado de excepción* (*The Repeated Fragment: Writings in a State of Exception*). Santiago de Chile: Ediciones/Metales Pesados.

Valentine, David. 2007. *Imagining Transgender: An Ethnography of a Category*. Durham, NC: Duke University Press.

Curating *A Third Gender: Beautiful Youths in Japanese Prints*

ASATO IKEDA

Abstract Should we discuss practices around sex and sexuality in early modern Japan as a distinct, foreign phenomenon entirely unique to the period and culture, or can we somehow draw a genealogy and create a trans-historical narrative that ends with today's LGBTQ+ culture? These questions were central to the process of organizing the exhibition *A Third Gender: Beautiful Youths in Japanese Prints* at the Royal Ontario Museum (ROM) in Toronto in 2016. The exhibition focused on visual representations of male youths, called *wakashu* in Japanese, who were the object of sexual desire for both women and adult men in Edo-era Japan. Presented in the form of an exhibition, the project necessitated engaging the past with the present and the general public with scholarship. In this short reflection essay, the author and curator explains how the *Third Gender* project approached the question of Edo-era Japan's trans-historicity.
Keywords Japan, third gender, exhibition, museum, LGBTQ+ community

How do we—and can we at all—talk about sex, gender, and sexuality in early modern Japan without imposing contemporary North American values and preconceptions? This became a recurring question during the process of organizing the exhibition *A Third Gender: Beautiful Youths in Japanese Prints* at the Royal Ontario Museum (ROM) in Toronto in 2016, which I curated as a specialist in a different field (modern Japanese art) in the capacity of a postdoctoral fellow at the museum, in collaboration with Joshua S. Mostow, a scholar in this field who provided his expertise to the curatorial project (Mostow and Ikeda 2016). The exhibition focused on visual representations of male youths—called *wakashu* in Japanese—who were the object of sexual desire for both women and adult men in the Edo period (1601–1868), and some of whom engaged in male same-sex relations and cross-dressing (fig. 1). Since *A Third Gender* was a museum exhibition, the project required engagement between scholarship and the public, and we had to take seriously the question of how to convey information about the past in a way that would be meaningful, relevant, and accessible to the general audiences.

TSQ: Transgender Studies Quarterly ∗ Volume 5, Number 4 ∗ November 2018 **638**
DOI 10.1215/23289252-7090101 © 2018 Duke University Press

Figure 1. *A Third Gender* installation shot. Royal Ontario Museum, Toronto

This in turn necessitated the exploration of how we might approach the relationship, if any, between gender practices in early modern Japan and contemporary North America.

The reason this exhibition project received sizable attention (first, internally at the museum—since I initially proposed this to be a much smaller show—and, second, externally from the general public) was without question related to the urban North American population that was increasingly aware and accepting of diverse models of sexual and gender relations. It was natural, then, that the museum tried to capitalize on this opportunity to cater to the historically marginalized LGBTQ+ communities who might be interested, it was supposed, in the unique gender relations the exhibition would deal with. The museum's desire to cultivate a relationship with the LGBTQ+ population through *A Third Gender* grew even stronger after the exhibition team held workshops with some members of the community about the show: it was confirmed that indeed the LGBTQ groups consulted would enthusiastically support the project, yet they also raised some questions about it. Because the ROM was an academic research institution, the exhibition team had to ensure that the show was grounded in solid scholarship and research, and that it would not make a simplistic equation between Edo-period gender practices and today's LGBTQ+ culture. The museum team agreed that it would be essential to highlight historical specificity and carefully contextualize the subject.

In this essay, I discuss how the museum sought to reconcile what we considered ethical responsibilities to minority communities in the present and to scholarly and academic integrity with respect to the past. After briefly explaining the exhibition itself, I discuss the process in which we engaged with Toronto's

LGBTQ+ communities, encountered questions and problems, and made efforts to resolve them.

  A Third Gender displayed approximately eighty Japanese artworks from the collection of the Royal Ontario Museum. The main focus of the exhibition was the images of male youths who were visually distinguished by their shaven pates, as well as forelocks and side locks (which they would have to shave off once they reached adulthood; fig. 2). "Third gender" is admittedly a contentious concept, heavily entrenched in nineteenth-century Victorian ideals and Western colonialism; nevertheless, we used the term specifically as theorized by Mostow in his chapter "The Gender of *Wakashu* and the Grammar of Desire," in the edited volume *Gender and Power in the Japanese Visual Field* (Mostow 2003). Mostow develops a distinct theory that considers gender along grammatical lines: he makes the point that, in some languages that have gender categories (masculine, feminine, and neuter), the classificatory pattern of nouns has no relation to their biological sex, and he proposes that we look at Edo-period sexual relations in terms of who can select whom and who "agrees" with whom. His theory illuminates the structural nature of Edo-period sexual practices wherein both women and adult men compete for wakashu, but adult men were always in the end the active, desiring subject (and the penetrator) of their sexual object (wakashu and women). Building on this logic, *gender* was defined in the exhibition as a composite of biological sex, age, appearance, and role in the sexual hierarchy. The term *third gender*—as opposed to, for instance, *wakashu*—in the title was also meant to attract audiences who would not otherwise be interested in a show about Japan by making it clear that the show engaged with gender issues. The introductory section of the exhibition explained how to visually identify wakashu and contextualized the male youth in Edo-period Japan by explaining two important aspects of the society: (1) Confucianism, the ancient Chinese philos-ophy that advocates a harmonious society based on hierarchical relations and that places a division between samurai, farmers, merchants, and artisans, and (2) the commoditized sex culture as exemplified by the popularity of pleasure quarters and the production of erotic prints.

  The subsequent sections of the exhibition illumi-nated the relationships some wakashu had with adult men, as well as women. *Nanshoku* (male-male eroticism) was widely practiced among samurai prior to the Edo period and has been categorized by several scholars as "homosexuality." Among the samurai class, the rela-tionship between a wakashu and an adult man was pedagogical in nature, but it sometimes, if not always,

Figure 2. *Wakashu with a Shoulder-Drum,* Hosoda Eisui (active 1790–1823). Royal Ontario Museum

included a romantic and sexual element (Screech 1993; Leupp 1997; Pflugfelder 1999). Once the wakashu himself became an adult, sexual relationships with other adult men were no longer considered appropriate. No longer a wakashu, he was expected to direct his attention toward a possible wakashu partner. In the Edo period, nanshoku also came to be practiced by merchants—not just by samurai—and was popularized and commercialized. It was practiced alongside *joshoku* (male-female eroticism), in what Mostow calls "phallocentric pansexuality," in which "bisexuality" was common and organized around the adult male, who had power over both wakashu and women (2003: 69–70). An illustration from a book by Kitao Shigemasa from the 1770s titled *Kai-zukushi* (*A Compendium of Shells*) shows the wakashu on the far left embraced by an adult man while two women gossip about them on a street (fig. 3). The exhibition in this context displayed portraits of *onnagata* (female impersonators) from the all-male kabuki theater, which was initially strongly associated with prostitution and cross-dressing wakashu (Matsuba 2016; Morinaga 2002; Mezur 2005).

The popularity of wakashu was not limited to adult men, and the third section of the exhibition focused on prints showing romantic attraction between wakashu and young women (*musume* in Japanese). Kitagawa Utamaro's print, included in his series *Twelve Forms of Women's Handiwork*, for example, portrays

Figure 3. *Kai-zukushi* (*A Compendium of Shells*), unknown artist, attributed to Kan'ei period (1624–44). Private collection

a young male-female couple. A wakashu with two swords—indicating his status as a samurai—has just purchased tooth powder at Asakusa Kannon Temple. A woman with a *tenugui* scarf covering her hair looks at him admiringly. The exhibition ended with images of *haori geisha*—female prostitutes of the early nineteenth century who cross-dressed as wakashu and affected the wakashu's shaven pate (Mostow 2008: 397). The images of *haori geisha* attested to the constructed and performative nature of the "gender" of wakashu.

As an exhibition, *A Third Gender* sought to deliver scholarly content to a general audience, and this required thinking about how to convey information about the historical figures (and concept) of wakashu to contemporary viewers in North America. As an institution that takes community response sincerely and seriously, the museum wanted to ensure that their project would be favorably received by—and would not "offend," to quote an actual term used at a staff meeting—the local communities, especially the LGBTQ+ audiences. One might reasonably wonder why a show about Edo-period Japan has anything to do with contemporary North American LGBTQ+ audiences, but the museum's view was not groundless. The connection between the male-male practices in early modern Japan and contemporary LGBTQ+ cultures has been made in the past by scholars and the general public alike. In those cases, however, the open acceptance of male same-sex love in premodern Japan seemed to have empowered, rather than offend, contemporary LGBTQ+ members both inside and outside Japan. From *Barazoku*, the first Japanese gay magazine in the 1970s, through art historian Tan'o Yasunori's 2008 book *Nanshoku no fūkei* (*Landscape of Male Love*), to Richard B. Parkinson's *A Little Gay History* (2013), there has been a long-standing effort to locate the origin of gay identity in nanshoku practice and to create a genealogy of male same-sex love. These preexisting studies brought up a series of questions: Should we ourselves approach our exhibition of wakashu in a similarly genealogical manner? Should the museum conduct outreach to Toronto's LGBTQ+ community, for instance, by teaming up with pride-related organizations and events? Or did we want to resist the very tendency to draw transhistorical comparisons? What would LGBTQ+ audiences in Toronto (and elsewhere) think of the show?

To ascertain the LGBTQ+ community's response to the show prior to the opening, with help from the Mark S. Bonham Centre for Sexual Diversity Studies at the University of Toronto, the museum held two workshops about the exhibition in 2016: one for members of the transgender community, and the other for the gay, lesbian, and bisexual communities, inviting social workers, political activists, and scholars who work in those fields. At the workshops where I gave a preliminary presentation about the exhibition, the fact that it was being put on by a large public museum was enthusiastically welcomed. However, some important and pertinent questions were raised by the participants. These issues were largely about the use (and politics) of language—pronouns in particular—regarding wakashu and onnagata. Some asked, for example, whether wakashu should be referred to as "he" if they were indeed a "third gender." Participants were especially cautious about using the pronoun *he* for the female impersonators, who had strong connections with wakashu in the early history of kabuki. Onnagata, some argued, should perhaps be considered women, if these performers behaved like women both onstage and off, rather than as men "impersonating" women. The workshop participants generally concurred that even though the show was about Edo-period Japan, it should somehow invite audiences to reflect on today's gender politics.

These workshops helped us understand that some LGBTQ+ members identify with historical figures and therefore project their identity onto them: some transgender participants seemed to understand wakashu and onnagata as "trans," as they viewed themselves. Part of this identification process was no doubt related to our perceptions about the erasure of the voices of the powerless in the past and the recuperative power of history: one important goal of historical projects is to identify powerless or subaltern subjects and to insist on their explicit presence within historical narratives. A perennial problem in documenting such subjects, however, is the archival silences that surround them: we do not know much about their lives, and while this gives us much room for interpretation, it also raises ethical questions about our obligations to historical subjects who left few, if any, indications of how they might speak for themselves. Although, theoretically, adult men could have written about their experiences of being wakashu in their youth, there are few records that tell us how wakashu understood their roles in relation to adult men and women. It is difficult to find a "memoir" of a wakashu or an onnagata. How, then, do we fill in what is absent from archival accounts without imposing our own categories and language, some of which are de facto ahistorical or anachronistic? To what extent should we consider contemporary communities' requests for particular language or other interpretive gestures, especially when we consider these communities' temporal and geocultural distance from Edo-era Japan?

Of course, individual visitors to the exhibition have autonomy and freedom to identify or not identify with images of Japanese wakashu from centuries ago. At the same time, however, as scholars, Mostow and I felt responsible for carefully historicizing and contextualizing the Edo-period gender system and clarifying the fundamentally different social structures and realities of Edo Japan and our contemporary society. As scholars whose argument needs to be grounded in research and historical evidence, we would not and could not, for example, label wakashu or onnagata as "gay" or "transgender," as these are modern terms and identities. It is important, in other words, to acknowledge that Japanese society in the 1600s to 1800s was considerably different from Canadian society in 2016. To begin with, Edo society, in which neo-Confucianism prevailed, was a patriarchal one structured on strict hierarchies of class, biological sex, and age, in which adult men had real power over both wakashu and women. The priority and focus was on the desire and pleasure of the adult men. Accordingly, it was largely the social structure, not individual preference or orientation, that determined people's gender roles and sexual behaviors. Nanshoku was practiced only between wakashu and adult men, and it was predicated on a power hierarchy; at the same time, sexual relationships between adult men, or between women, were not socially accepted. There are examples of gender-crossing (such as wakashu or kabuki actors dressing as women, or women dressing as wakashu), but not everybody could dress as they wished (Walthall 2009; Robertson 1992). Edo-era Japan was not a modern, democratic, individualistic society in which one could freely proclaim one's gender "expression" or "identity" in the manner so important to participants in our contemporary workshops. In the Edo period, what one "felt like" largely did not matter: gender and sexual roles were in principle assigned and imposed based on biological sex, age, marital status, and profession. Highlighting the fundamental difference between Edo society and our contemporary world is in fact essential to communicating the role of wakashu to the general public. Without careful historical contextualization, for instance, nanshoku might be understood as a form of pedophilia. Also, images that show wakashu having sex could be considered child pornography, which is defined as images that depict sexually explicit activities involving a child under the age eighteen (Ikeda 2016: 9). In these cases, drawing ahistorical equivalencies between past and present or relying on modern assumptions about sexual categories would have resulted in a grave misunderstanding of Edo-era sexual practices and could have even made the display of art illegal.

While the exhibition catalog conceived as a purely scholarly endeavor and coauthored by Mostow and myself remained exclusively historical, for the exhibition, the museum team did incorporate feedback received from Toronto's LGBTQ+ members at the workshops. Reflecting the current sensitivity around gender pronouns, the exhibition text did not include the words *he* or *she* and simply referred to wakashu as "wakashu" (or "the figure," or "the youth"). The text also made it clear that wakashu, as male youths, occupied a marginal social position and that their voices were for the most part unrepresented. While the exhibition mainly focused on Edo Japan, the last section of the show was devoted to gender/sexuality issues in contemporary North American society. Right before exiting the exhibition, visitors were invited to provide feedback on the show on a comment board and participate in an interactive panel that asked them to choose their gender/sexual identity from eighteen options: among them were "female," "male," "heterosexual," "asexual," "cisgender," "trans*," "not even close," "uncategorizable," and "questioning." Reflecting one particular workshop attendee's proposal to include a global map and history, the museum placed a panel that showed examples of gender or sexual variance, such as ancient Greek pederasty, India's *hijras*, and Two-Spirit people in some North American indigenous cultures. This last panel was meant to introduce to the viewers varying cultural systems that do not fit the model of gender binaries and heteronormative sexuality—a model that is heavily entrenched in nineteenth-century Victorian ideals and Western colonialism. The museum's exhibition program, supported by and jointly organized with the Mark S. Bonham Centre for Sexual Diversity Studies, followed this initiative to investigate diverse sexual and gender practices beyond Japan by featuring the roundtable discussion "Lost in Translation? Gender and Sexuality across Time and Cultures" with Richard Parkinson from the University of Oxford (formerly of the British Museum), who discussed homoerotic poems from ancient Egypt; and PhD candidate at York University Andrew Gayed, who presented on the issue of homosociality in the work of contemporary Egyptian photographer Youssef Nabil. The museum installed all-gender washrooms next to the *Third Gender* exhibition space, the timing of which coincided with the news coverage around North Carolina's new law to ban transgender people from using public bathrooms according to their gender identity. ROM's initiative therefore received national media coverage for its decision to opt for inclusive bathrooms (Jones 2016). My intern, Josiah Ariyama, who belongs to Toronto's LGBTQ community, conducted a workshop to educate docents—consisting almost exclusively of white, heterosexual seniors—about terms and concepts (such as *trans* or *cisgender*) and prepared them for possible questions from audiences.

In conclusion, I would like to return to the question I posed at the beginning. How do we—and can we at all—talk about sex, gender, and sexuality in early modern Japan without imposing contemporary North American values and preconceptions? The way in which the public received *A Third Gender* might provide us a clue. A number of exhibition and catalog reviews came out, notably when the show traveled to and opened at the Japan Society in New York in March 2017 (Kingston 2016; Lyons 2016; Whyte 2016; Buruma 2017; Chira 2017; Frank 2017). Some reviewers were more intently focused on the critical differences between early modern Japan and contemporary North American gender issues/LGBTQ+ culture, but others clearly showed a desire to see the Edo-period culture in trans-historical—and trans-cultural—ways. Some described wakashu with precisely the words Mostow and I had refrained from using—such as *gay, homosexual,* or *transgender*—and understood the Edo culture as being about "gender fluidity," "gender expression," or "gender identity." While Mostow and I considered scholarly fidelity to the language and categories (and to the historical evidence) of Edo

Japan as essential to the *Third Gender* project, we also, after all, realized that scholars could not control its reception or its audiences' interpretations. For me, however, it was the process of keeping asking questions and grappling with them with other staffs at the ROM and with Toronto's LGBTQ+ communities that was most meaningful and heartening. While I would still personally insist, as a scholar, that wakashu were not "trans," through the process of this exhibition project, as I witnessed, the museum underwent significant transformation with respect to its handling of trans issues. The installation of gender-neutral washrooms (and the media attention to it) visibly increased the museum staff's awareness and sensitivity around the subjects of gender and sexuality. The museum has begun to build networks with LGBTQ+ communities that, one would hope, will continue into the future. In this sense, despite—or, actually, thanks to—the complex issues of representation that arose from our dual ethical obligations mentioned above, the exhibition provided an important opportunity for discursive dialogue about the diversity of sex, gender, and sexuality in a public sphere that involves the past, the present, and, possibly, the future.

Asato Ikeda is an assistant professor of art history at Fordham University and the author of *The Politics of Paintings: Fascism and Japanese Art during the Second World War* (2018).

Acknowledgments
I would like to express my sincere thanks to Joshua S. Mostow, Sascha Priewe, Sharalyn Orbaugh, Nick Hall, James Walker, Joshua M. Ferguson, Michael Chagnon, Brenda Cossman, Mark Bonham, Toronto's LGBTQ+ members who attended the ROM workshops, and the Mark S. Bonham Centre for Sexual Diversity Studies at the University of Toronto.

References
Buruma, Ian. 2017. "The 'Indescribable Fragrance' of Youths." *New York Review of Books*, May 11. www.nybooks.com/articles/2017/05/11/japanese-edo-indescribable-fragrance-youths.

Chira, Susan. 2017. "When Japan Had a Third Gender." *New York Times*, March 10. www.nytimes.com/2017/03/10/arts/design/when-japan-had-a-third-gender.html.

Frank, Priscilla. 2017. "The Androgynous 'Third Gender' of Seventeenth-Century Japan." *Huffington Post*, April 13. www.huffingtonpost.com/entry/third-gender-japanese-art_us_58e6 a18ce4b0585892c9c078.

Ikeda, Asato. 2016. Introduction to Mostow and Ikeda 2016: 11–18.

Jones, Sian. 2016. "Gender-Neutral Washrooms at the Royal Ontario Museum Reflect Changing Times: Museum Rethinks Public Washrooms to Become More Inclusive." *CBC News*, May 25. www.cbc.ca/news/entertainment/rom-gender-neutral-washrooms-1.3589399.

Kingston, Jeff. 2016. "Is Japan Ready for the LGBTQ Revolution?" *Japan Times*, July 30. www.japantimes.co.jp/opinion/2016/07/30/commentary/japan-ready-lgbtq-revolution/.

Leupp, Gary P. 1997. *Male Colors: The Construction of Homosexuality in Tokugawa Japan*. Berkeley: University of California Press.

Lyons, Michael. 2016. "Art and Port in Edo Period Japan." *Xtra*, May 3. www.dailyxtra.com /toronto/blogs-and-columns/history-boys/art-and-porn-in-edo-period-japan-191968.

Matsuba, Ryoko. 2016. "*Fleurs du mal*: Onnagata (Female-Role Specialists) and *Nanshoku* (Male-Male Sex) in Edo-Period Kabuki." In Mostow and Ikeda 2016: 40–51.

Mezur, Katherine. 2005. *Beautiful Boys/Outlaw Bodies: Devising Kabuki Female-Likeness*. New York: Palgrave Macmillan.

Morinaga, Maki Isaka. 2002. "The Gender of Onnagata as the Imitating Imitated: Its Historicity, Performativity, and Involvement in the Circulation of Femininity." *positions* 10, no. 2: 245–84.

Mostow, Joshua S. 2003. "The Gender of Wakashu and the Grammar of Desire in Late Seventeenth-Century Edo." In *Gender and Power in the Japanese Visual Field*, edited by Joshua S. Mostow, Norman Bryson, and Maribeth Graybill, 49–70. Honolulu: University of Hawai'i Press.

———. 2008. "Utagawa Shunga, Kuki's 'Chic,' and the Construction of a National Erotics in Japan." In *Performing Nation: Gender Politics in Literature, Theater, and the Visual Arts of China and Japan, 1880–1940*, edited by Joshua Mostow, Doris Croissant, and Catherine Vance Yeh, 383–424. Leiden: Brill.

Mostow, Joshua S., and Asato Ikeda. 2016. *A Third Gender: Beautiful Youths in Japanese Edo-Period Prints and Paintings (1600–1868)*. Toronto: Royal Ontario Museum Press.

Parkinson, Richard B. 2013. *A Little Gay History: Desire and Diversity across the World*. New York: Columbia University Press.

Pflugfelder, Gregory M. 1999. *Cartographies of Desire: Male-Male Sexuality in Japanese Discourse, 1600–1950*. Berkeley: University of California Press.

Robertson, Jennifer. 1992. "The Politics of Androgyny in Japan: Sexuality and Subversion in the Theater and Beyond." *American Ethnologist* 1, no. 3: 419–42.

Screech, Timon. 1993. "Race and Gender? Human Categorisation in Japan." In *Disrupted Borders: An Intervention in Definitions and Boundaries*, edited by Sunil Gupta, 133–43. London: Rivers Oram.

Tan'o, Yasunori. 2008. *Nanshoku no fūkei (Landscape of Male Love)*. Tokyo: Shinchōsha.

Walthall, Anne. 2009. "Masturbation and Discourse on Female Sexual Practices in Early Modern Japan." *Gender and History* 21, no. 1: 1–18.

Whyte, Murray. 2016. "At the ROM, an Ancient Third Gender Informs the Present." *Toronto Star*, May 16. www.thestar.com/entertainment/2016/05/16/at-the-rom-an-ancient-third-gender -informs-the-present.html.

Interview with Maya Mikdashi
and Carlos Motta on *Deseos* / رغبات

LEAH DEVUN and ZEB TORTORICI

Abstract Special issue editors Leah DeVun and Zeb Tortorici interview Maya Mikdashi and Carlos Motta about their collaborative film, *Deseos* / رغبات (*Desires*, 2015), which places queer and gender-variant historical characters within a fluid chronological framework. In this interview, Mikdashi and Motta discuss issues such as imperial and colonial temporality, queer networks of community, and a desire for happy endings in history.
Keywords decoloniality, queer temporality, film and video art, Ottoman Empire, Spanish Empire, transgender studies, imagination, historical narration

This interview with Maya Mikdashi, an anthropologist and assistant professor in the Department of Women's and Gender Studies at Rutgers University, and Carlos Motta, a multidisciplinary artist based in New York, emerges from an event on "Trans*historicities" held at the Fales Library and Special Collections at New York University in November of 2017. For that event, the editors of this special issue invited several artists, activists, and scholars to discuss how their work engages with history and notions of time. Among them, Maya Mikdashi and Carlos Motta discussed their thirty-three-minute film, *Deseos* / رغبات (*Desires*, 2015), which exposes the ways in which medicine, law, religion, and cultural tradition shaped dominant discourses of the gendered and sexed body through the narration of two parallel stories: that of Martina, who lived in Colombia during the late colonial period of the early nineteenth century and that of Nour, who lived in Beirut during the late Ottoman Empire. Part documentary and part fiction, the film presents an imaginary correspondence between these individuals. The criminal court of colonial New Granada prosecuted Martina in 1803 for being a "hermaphrodite" after being accused by her female lover of having a body that was "against nature." Martina was tried in a court of law and ultimately set free after medical doctors appointed by the court were unable to find evidence of her lover's accusation. This story is

TSQ: Transgender Studies Quarterly * Volume 5, Number 4 * November 2018
DOI 10.1215/23289252-7090115   © 2018 Duke University Press

documented in the 1803 legal case found in the Archivo General de la Nación in Bogotá, Colombia. Meanwhile in Beirut, Nour married her female lover's brother after her mother found them making love. Although Nour's story does not occur in a courtroom, nor is it found in an extant legal case, notions of Islamic and late Ottoman laws, cultures, and histories condition her narrative. We posed a series of questions to the filmmakers following the event.

Leah DeVun and Zeb Tortorici: Deseos / رغبات *(2015) engages questions of history, moving across disciplines and boundaries, bodies and desires. Could you discuss how your work plays with time, especially nonlinear notions of chronology, to consider overlapping colonial legacies, decolonial praxis, or other kinds of dislocations?*

Maya Mikdashi: When we began writing *Deseos* / رغبات, one of our guiding questions was how to imagine the cacophony of imperial and colonial temporality, a temporality that our current lives—living in a settler colony that is also the world's imperial hegemon—are also unfolding within. The most striking temporal dissonance in our film is between the script and the visual image. While the script and the characters are written as nineteenth century, the visuals are contemporary and filmed on location in Lebanon and Colombia. This dissonance points to a rupture in the epistemological barriers between the past and the present, between archives and the future (it should be noted that the ordering of experience into discrete categories of past, present, and future—the production of "history"—was also very much a colonial technology). The dissonance also highlights, or points to some of the tensions that emerge when thinking and researching sexuality and gender systems in a trans-temporal framework, in terms of how our desire *for* particular histories and records chafes against our theoretical training and commitments (Freeman 2010; Fuentes 2016; Gordon 2008). I have to say, for me personally it was very interesting to write from this particular time period (early nineteenth century) precisely because of the different imperial networks, and their attendant legal regimes, that are (re)making the world at that time. Legal regimes are citational over time, and many aspects of the legal ideologies and practices discussed in our film live on robustly in current legal systems. For us, part of thinking about ways of making and regulating life and the category of the human, particularly life that may today be considered "queer," occurs at the intersections of criminality, personal status, religiosity, secularism, and imperial law. In my academic work, an ethnography of the contemporary Lebanese legal system and its regulation of sexual difference and secularism during the US-led international war on terror, the intersections are strikingly similar, though the actors have to a large extent changed.

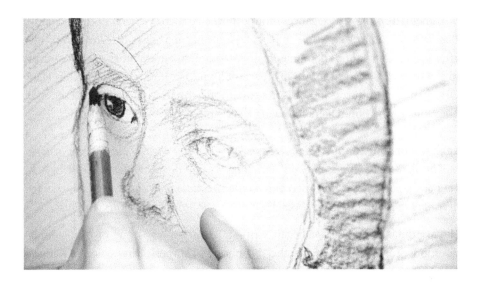

Carlos Motta: *Deseos* / رغبات is an experiment in translocations of time. Our characters are separated by geography, language, culture, class, ethnicity, political context, and by the impossibility to ever have really met. Yet they share the experience of secrecy and silence, and they correspond lovingly—as best friends—by writing letters to each other. Today, the Internet has made (some of) these boundaries easier to bypass and has created networks of queer relationality and kinship. Nineteenth-century queers, however, lived in isolation by contemporary standards. Even though it is known that queers may have had certain networks of connectivity, international relations seem unlikely. This film plays with time to reflect on the creation of the language of oppression and queers' strategies of liberation and survival.

LD and ZT: *Your film reimagines past images and narratives, finding inspiration in the colonial archives of Nueva Granada (in present-day Colombia) and in the imaginative and speculative histories of the Ottoman Empire (in present-day Lebanon and Syria). How does history operate imaginatively in your work, either as a vehicle for what might have happened, or as a set of aspirations for the future? What does your work have to say to those who might envision it as relevant to the history of queer or trans experience? We wonder if you could talk more about what fantasies or fictions in history do for us in these works, or more broadly.*

MM: To write this film, Carlos and I wrote letters to each other in character as Martina and Nour over a period of months, producing pages of correspondence that were eventually pared down to a script. As we wrote to each other, we were corresponding through a historical/future longing: a desire for the possibilities of

archival research, and the possibilities of history outside archives, a desire for the unexpected and yet ordinary (Cvetkovich 2003). However, we were not trying to find queer ancestors, or "ghosts" in our archives (Arondekar 2009; Freeman 2010); rather, we claim a place for Martina and Nour in the national histories of Lebanon, Syria, and Colombia and in the imperial and colonial histories of the Ottoman and Spanish Empires. We use "national history" with attention to both the spectacular and mundane aspects of national production in the nation-state era (an era that produces the nation as previous to, and desiring of, a state), and with a deep knowledge of the power of "national history." Martina, in fact, is written as a hero of the independence struggle.

This is not a film that speaks (only) of a transnational queer experience, particularly as "transnational queer experience" is a highly racialized and classed category and seems to largely operate in the temporality of the now and its futures. Rather, *Deseos* / رغبات assumes that nonnormative, queer, and female experience is always deeply rooted in place—and invites viewers to experience and imagine the multiple ways that "queer" is always connected to its specific locality, both in place and time. Islam, as a highly translocal/transregional religion and practice, has been and is a framework out of which queer practice can emerge. To put it in another way, any hegemonic sex/gender system contains within it the conditions of possibility for play within that system. For example, there is a line in *Deseos* / رغبات in which Nour is telling Martina about her happiness and her sense of excitement that her lover is marrying her brother, while Nour herself is marrying her lover's brother. Her excitement emerges from the constraints and possibilities inherent in the time and place she lived in. Nour says to Martina that she and her lover will breast-feed each other's children and thus make a family—articulating a well-

known precept of Islamic law—that breast feeding from the same women creates a marriage prohibition, the definition of kinship. There are many moments in our script that speak specifically to non-Western audiences (including my failed attempt to imagine and perform a pre-nation-state, Levantine dialect in the voice-over), and part of the cacophony of temporality of our film is the cacophony of audience reception. For example, in our script and film we also wanted to draw attention to the historical relationship, a history much longer than the nation-state, between Beirut and Damascus. This was important to us because at the time of making and conceptualizing the film (and still, to this day) there are over 2 million Syrian refugees and displaced peoples in Lebanon, and they are subject to a xenophobic, highly racialized and sexualized security state. In fact, a discourse of homophobia is emerging transnationally as a critical securitizing, racializing, and dehumanizing tactic aimed at Syrian refugees. Over one-fourth of the current population of Lebanon are refugees from different parts of the region (Palestinian, Syrian, Iraqi, Sudanese). In our film we wanted to give an account of the pre-nation, and pre-state-system history of the area (and perhaps also pre-homo- and heterosexual), but also to remind the contemporary viewer that, historically, Damascus was the cultural, economic, intellectual, and cosmopolitan sun around which Beirut orbited. We also provided a different location from which to rethink what we now understand as transnational histories and genealogies of sexualities and gender systems.

CM: On finding Martina's legal case, filed in one of the "Criminal Cases" folders in the Colombian National Archives in Bogotá, it was apparent to me that I could learn about her today only because of her misfortunes. Martina was tried for

being a "hermaphrodite" in 1803, and her encounter with the colonial legal system turned her into an instructive case for the future. Martina and others who were defined by the legal, medical, and religious establishments are exceptional cases that give us some insight about queer lives in the past, but these legal documents reduce their experiences to anomalies and entirely erase their subjectivities. Bothered by this fact, I felt that using this document as a point of departure to construct a more nuanced, fictional narrative about Martina would be an interesting device to resist the reductive power of the archive—and of history at large. Giving Martina agency and the chance to resist the bruising language of the law felt like an act of intergenerational queer solidarity. At the same time, I was aware that this "solidarity" could also be interpreted as another act of violence on her. I remained paralyzed by this contradiction for a while until Martina appeared in my dreams one night and told me, "Do it."

Maya and I were surprised to learn that cases of female same-sex relations did not exist in the Ottoman archives (at least those we had a chance to research). The absence of these cases, however, taught us that the Ottoman legal system considered these cases as something to be dealt with within families. Creating a fictional story about a lesbian woman in Beirut at the time seemed again an act of solidarity. Nour's story tries to address the complexities of her time as well as our decision to imagine her as a historical subject absent documentation of her existence.

Although we live in a (Western) world where stories of same-sex relations and gender nonconformity are widely discussed, I still believe queer lives continue to be defined by legal frameworks of social inclusion. The LGBTIQ agenda is entirely constructed within a legalistic purview in which citizenship equals legal

equality. Undoubtedly, there are some benefits to this approach, but, not unlike colonial times, this perpetuates a narrowing effect of the experience of difference. These cyclical repetitions were on my mind as we wrote *Deseos* / رغبات. While Martina's and Nour's stories are anchored in a seemingly anachronistic experience, in my opinion they are mirrors of patriarchal systems that have partly evolved but not entirely progressed.

LD and ZT: *Your work seems to offer us forms of transfiguration, ways of remaking the past and reorienting the future. The film, for example, is invested in what we might call a "happy ending" that is perhaps at odds with the reality of history (i.e., it emphasizes the power of friendship and affective relations over time instead of the tragic tropes of queer suffering, martyrdom, or death). What do we do when history doesn't give us what we want or produce the images and documents that we ourselves desire? How does desire structure your work and impel research and creative production?*

MM: Attuned to ways our own historical longings structured *Deseos* / رغبات, we worked against the notion of "unthinkability" as it relates to histories that would, in the present moment, be called "queer." Our character, Martina, is twice arrested. She is arrested by colonial authorities on charges of having an unnatural body. She—her life—is arrested again by the archive, caught within a discourse of the natural, of criminality, and of the imperial state.

    The closing of a case file does not have to be the end of a person's historical or contemporary significance. In my academic work I also use court archives and am struck by the same question, namely, that in those moments our closest encounters are not with the people found in a case file but with the regime of power that structures legal and archival systems (Steedman 2002; Trouillot 1995). In fact, the people encountered in legal case files are somewhat interchangeable, and that is the point of both the legal genre of writing and the regime of power. In *Deseos* / رغبات we play with the idea that it could be possible to "know" someone who is found in the archives, that is, to play with a fantasy (our fantasy) that Martina in fact had a life outside the structure of our encounter—the archive. A researcher's pull toward the archive is not coincidental. This pull, this desire, is itself melancholic (Eng and Kazanjian 2002). The archive is a temporal order: what we find in the archive, what we want to find in the archive, even what frustrates us about the archive, shifts as what it means to be a reader, a researcher, a person in the world, changes.

CM: Martina was set free after the trial, as they weren't able to prove her body was "unnatural," and this is where her story officially ends. In our fiction, however, her traumatic experiences are the fuel that gives her an emancipatory force and turns her into an agent of the proindependence resistance, gives her a loving partner, and lets her get lost in her "freedom," forever. Nour's husband dies, and she is able to live her life next to her lover, raising their respective children together in the family structure they desired. We felt very strongly about giving both of their stories "happy endings," precisely to resist the prevalent tropes of tragedy that are typical in historical accounts of same-sex lives and within the present day's legalistic frameworks, in which tragedy and trauma are ways to raise funds and enact equality campaigns. Our characters want to resist society and history's desire to pity them and find ways to develop full lives beyond their official histories.

LD and ZT: Deseos / رغبات *is a scholarly-artistic collaboration that emerged from a conference that you both attended. Can you talk a little about the experience (or productive possibilities in general) of collaboration across disciplinary or professional boundaries? To what extent do you envision your work as a kind of transformation or transmutation?*

MM: Carlos and I met through the structure of our collaboration: we were both invited to be part of an interdisciplinary workshop that brought together artists, lawyers, and academics on the concept of the "unnatural" (curated by Council[1])—convened in Beirut, Lebanon, in 2015 at a conference titled "The Manufacturing of Rights" (Ashkal Alwan 2015). We were drawn to each other as friends and as practitioners troubled by similar questions and methods but in different vocations and institutions. We later started hanging out in New York, and actually conceived of the film during one of those hangouts in Washington Square Park when we were discussing friendship, technology, and the important work of the Sylvia Rivera Law Project (in particular, the organization's prison penpal initiative, a direct inspiration for our letter-writing script). I have worked in film and theater for years in Lebanon and the United States, both before and concurrently with my academic career. We made the film over the course of a year, and it wasn't necessarily the smartest thing to do while I was a postdoc and supposed to be writing my book (by and large the academy does not reward these types of projects).

CM: Maya and I met and started our collaboration before the conference you mention. In fact, our dialogue with the core participants of the inquiry "The Against Nature Journal," convened by the Council in Beirut, led to the decision to produce an interdisciplinary conference to discuss the impact of Law 534, a (dormant) law in the Lebanese penal code that criminalizes same-sex relations as being "against nature." This project brought together a dozen professionals from different fields to contextualize the role that colonial legal legacies play within contemporary societies. *Deseos* / رغبات is the result of this dialogue, and its script reflects these informed positions.

Interdisciplinary collaborations have been an important part of my work for over a decade. I am a firm believer in the power of bringing multiple and different perspectives together when producing artistic projects, in particular when these deal with political topics that are addressed by different professions. This kind of exchange is not only nurturing for the work, it is also a fuller way of engaging a topic and of addressing a public.

MM: I found the experience of working with Carlos vital and vitalizing—it was important for me to remember (and keep remembering) that academia does not own knowledge production, and that so much of the vitality of theory, critique, and method occurs outside academic space. Academics know this because we are often inspired by art and visual and performance culture, but it is quite different to collaborate and produce work within and toward that space. I found that thinking and writing about archives in two different genres—academic writing and script writing—to be incredibly generative.

Leah DeVun is an associate professor of history at Rutgers University. She is the author of *Prophecy, Alchemy, and the End of Time* (2009), winner of the 2013 John Nicholas Brown Prize, as well as articles in *GLQ, WSQ, Osiris, ASAP/Journal, postmedieval,* and *Radical History Review,* among others.

Zeb Tortorici is an associate professor in the Department of Spanish and Portuguese Languages and Literatures at New York University. He is the author of *Sins against Nature: Sex and Archives in Colonial New Spain* (2018). He recently edited *Sexuality and the Unnatural in Colonial Latin America* (2016) and coedited *Centering Animals in Latin American History* (2013).

Note

1.   Council, founded in Paris in 2013, is an art organization and curatorial program that seeks to foster better understandings of societal issues by assembling people and knowledge from the arts, sciences, and civil society. It regularly curates exhibitions and public programs and commissions new work by artists, researchers, and activists. Their website is www.council.art.

References

Arondekar, Anjali. 2009. *For the Record: On Sexuality and the Colonial Archive in India*. Durham, NC: Duke University Press.

Ashkal Alwan. 2015. "The Manufacturing of Rights: Beirut." Conference, May 14–16, Beirut. ashkalalwan.org/events/the-manufacturing-of-rights-beirut/.

Cvetkovich, Ann. 2003. *An Archive of Feelings: Trauma, Sexuality, and Lesbian Public Cultures*. Durham, NC: Duke University Press.

Eng, David L., and David Kazanjian, eds. 2002. *Loss: The Politics of Mourning*. Berkeley: University of California Press.

Freeman, Elizabeth. 2010. *Time Binds: Queer Temporalities, Queer Histories*. Durham, NC: Duke University Press.

Fuentes, Marisa J. 2016. *Dispossessed Lives: Enslaved Women, Violence, and the Archive*. Philadelphia: University of Pennsylvania Press.

Gordon, Avery F. 2008. *Ghostly Matters: Haunting and the Sociological Imagination*. Minneapolis: University of Minnesota Press.

Motta, Carlos, dir. 2015. *Deseos* / غبات ر. Written by Maya Mikdashi and Carlos Motta. carlosmotta .com/project/2015-deseos-%D8%B1%D8%BA%D8%A8%D8%A7%D8%AA/.

Steedman, Carolyn. 2002. *Dust: The Archive and Cultural History*. New Brunswick, NJ: Rutgers University Press.

Trouillot, Michel-Rolph. 1995. *Silencing the Past: Power and the Production of History*. Boston: Beacon.

"Trans*historicities"

A Roundtable Discussion

M. W. BYCHOWSKI, HOWARD CHIANG, JACK HALBERSTAM, JACOB LAU,
KATHLEEN P. LONG, MARCIA OCHOA, and C. RILEY SNORTON

Curated by LEAH DEVUN and ZEB TORTORICI

Abstract "Trans*historicities: A Roundtable Discussion" offers reflections on how thinking about time and chronology has impacted scholarship in trans studies in recent years. Contributing scholars come from numerous disciplines that touch on history, and have expertise in far-ranging geographic and temporal fields. As a broad conversation about some of the potential possibilities and difficulties in seeking out—and finding—trans in historical contexts, this discussion focuses on the complex interrelations between trans, time, and history.
Keywords trans*, historicities

TSQ: *As early as Leslie Feinberg's 1992* Transgender Liberation, *scholars and activists have looked to the past for antecedents that might legitimate and inform present trans* identities (albeit, at times, in romanticizing, Orientalist, and colonialist ways). More recently, scholars have pointed to the genealogical significance of cross-dressers, hermaphrodites, bearded women, and others who have confounded binary gender, exploring continuities and discontinuities with respect to current notions of queer and trans* subjectivity. Given the rise of trans studies in recent years, and given that we're starting to see a move toward writing and visualizing trans history, how has history shaped your view of transgender, and vice versa?*

Jack Halberstam: Actually, going back to Feinberg is really important but not to the clunky arguments in *Transgender Liberation* where they imply that gender management emerges out of early capitalism, but rather, this is a good time to look back at *Stone Butch Blues*. In *Stone Butch Blues* Feinberg insists that the liberation of butches and femmes, transpeople and intersex people, depends not on an identity politics oriented toward recognition but on a politics of solidarity. In the age of neoliberal inclusivity and at a time when the protection of LGBT peoples can often be predicated on the management of "foreign" populations, we need the broader view of transgender history. And after all, transgender variability has often marked the shared space of homophobia (directed at queens and butches) and transphobia.

Historical accounts of gender variability are crucial at a moment when change happens at a blistering pace. A student informed me recently that the term *cisgender* was so "old," it was, they suggested, "very two years ago" and no longer in use. Whether or not the student gave an accurate assessment of the viability of the term, the comment sheds light on the very short life of current ideologies. For two years to represent a massive period of change (and nowadays it can) means that longer histories become almost irretrievable. I believe that without a longer historical view of the arc of transgender activism, we are stuck with squabbles about the significance of Caitlyn Jenner and internecine conflict. We need transgender history now more than ever.

Howard Chiang: Some of the bracketed words in your question might serve as a useful point of entry into unravelling the reciprocal shaping of transgender and history. *Romanticizing, Orientalist,* and *colonialist* all point to the variegated differentials of power and how their operation diverges or intersects in our scholarly agenda to write and research trans history. These terms call attention to the urgency of questioning the standpoints from which serious scholarly conversations about queer experience emanate and whose interest such dialogues serve. The centrality of these representational, redistributive, and epistemological effects to documenting subjects who bear a long-standing injurious or concealed past cannot be overstated. Any synthesis of their historicity must engage with the peripheries of otherwise.

Of course, the kind of social and political legitimation we now seek through our work in trans history is always already informed and enabled by the past. But how that past is made comprehensible and relevant to the present demands a rigorous reflection on the logic and political content of the very methodological hermeneutics that promise the delivery of such a promise. From editing *Transgender China* (2012) to authoring *After Eunuchs* (2018), I have become increasingly aware of the genealogical burdens of treating China—not unlike the way other scholars have approached the West—as a "field site" (a geographical aporia), as well as the ongoing tension, mutual imbrication, and productive opposition such a procedural turn generates between "transgender" and "history." If the past can be mobilized to serve the experience of the present, what are the stakes of counting on divides of culture—or race, ethnicity, nationality, and even language—for the purpose of bringing normative legibility and comfort to claims of alternate being? It is high time to recalibrate our views of transness and history—and their intermodalities—from decentering the axis of geophysical belonging.

C. Riley Snorton: This question points to at least two impulses in trans historiography. On one hand, it underscores an impulse to disarticulate the origins of transness from the clinic. On the other, albeit relatedly, it opens up a line of questions about the capaciousness of *trans* to refer to "cross-dressers, hermaphrodites, bearded women, and others who have confounded binary gender." In my own work, this has meant pursuing a historiographical practice that identifies how events, actors, and places illustrate the conditions of possibility for gender transformation. As it relates to the discipline (or disciplining) of trans studies, this kind of methodological consideration also evidences a vast and disparate genealogy for the field's formation—in black feminist studies and women-of-color feminisms, queer theory and queer-of-color critique, crip theory, and cultural studies, among others.

M. W. Bychowski: Liberation means to me a reforging and reforming of critical relationships across the boundaries we have built between and around ourselves. Much of my work has taken a genealogical approach to trans history and literature, connecting the present and the medieval past, largely because my first encounters with transgender life and history were as things to which I wasn't sure I had any access. Am I trans enough? Am I medieval enough? Building such access points and tools for the journey has since become my goal. This takes the form of theories, narratives, and histories—what I call "genres of embodiment"—that touch on certain instruments (e.g., knives, clothes, diagnoses) that cut across many of us in different ways, or certain figures (e.g., hermaphrodites and eunuchs) that are used to signify us in different ways, or stories (change, hybridity, revelation) that are used to give us voice in different ways. These genealogies and genres of embodiment affirm "yes, one can be trans in *this* way" or "yes, one can be medieval in *that* way." As critical praxis, trans people have long found ways to live with community and tools that were not built for us. Likewise, medieval people regularly reached across time and cultural differences to find people, ideas, or histories to engage. Taking that first step across divisions of time and humanity takes a degree of courage—courage to be wrong, to be challenged, to be changed—but this is how we survive, and this is how we find liberation.

Among these genres and genealogies of trans genders, one figure and praxis that I find useful in this discussion of trans ventures into the past is the trans pilgrim, the *peregrinus*, meaning the perpetual "foreigner." The "trans" here works with the pilgrim to signify this vaulting of gendered time and place, as though we are perpetually between or across. Genealogies are inroads that often cut across and depend on old paths, sites, and back roads. We connect them but learn from them. The transgender back roads have things to teach us about the ways trans life moved around and between the major charted thoroughfares. Some of these places and trails are hard to get to and require genealogies to bring us there, but once we arrive, the whole landscape will begin to seem different. On the way back, we begin to modify the genealogies that first carried us there or else create new ones that were not apparent until we accessed the perspective of these old trails and back roads. Indeed, it is no small wonder that in becoming a pilgrim through trans history we become increasingly aware of our foreignness to the present moment of transgender. What begins as "imposter syndrome" may be replaced with a commitment to hospitality for all those who, like us, do not belong here because neither the here nor now is ours to own. In mapping these genealogies, I try to remain aware that we are crossing the places, times, and lives of others. This may mean sharing the road where multiple paths intersect, overlap, or fork. As we build tools and maps and roads, we must do so in conversation with others past and present, ready and willing to be revised as we revise. The pilgrim must learn to participate without belonging—more on this later.

Marcia Ochoa: For me, like Riley, it's been important to disarticulate trans from the current forms of medical governmentality available to first-world subjects—the clinic, transition, treatment. This wasn't the way I really experienced how most trans people in US Latinx and Latin American social contexts emerged. First, because people simply didn't have access, and, second, because they didn't express a need for this kind of recognition to validate their existences. I think working with historical methods is indispensable to understanding and contextualizing contemporary forms of existence, and I don't see this as a kind of presentism, but rather as an acknowledgment that the forms of power we encounter today are not immutable. I think the problem with presentism is actually one with determinism—when we assume our categories hold up across contexts (time, space, cultures, materials), we engage in deterministic historiography. I find David Getsy's concept of trans "capacity" very helpful in thinking about our use of the category trans as an analytic: "Transgender capacity is the trait of those many things that support or demand accounts of gender's dynamism, plurality, and expansiveness" (2014: 47). To begin with gender as an empirical question allows us to suspend the kinds of assumptions we make about embodiment and gender based in our own categories and to be open to how and through which forces people have been rendered legible in different categories.

TSQ: *What is your engagement with questions of time and chronology, and how has your view shifted over the years (especially since the publication of the 2007 "Theorizing Queer Temporalities: A Roundtable Discussion" in* GLQ *[Dinshaw et al.*

2007])? What do you see as the tension between, on the one hand, historicism, and, on the other hand, queer temporality and asynchronicity?

Halberstam: I have been interested in queer temporality since the 1990s when I wrote about the life and death of Brandon Teena in my book *In a Queer Time and Place*. While the book began as an attempt to grapple with the murder of a young transman, it quickly became a meditation on temporality, spatiality, and subcultural lives. Because the rural is so often represented as a space "before" the modern, in writing about Brandon Teena I had to think through this spatialization of temporal regimes. I am not sure I see specific tensions between historicism, queer temporality, and asynchronicity, but I do think that queer notions of time put pressure on the organization of historical knowledge. Riley Snorton's new book, for example, *Black on Both Sides*, uses the uneven and incomplete archives of black fugitivity to retell the history of black gender variability. If, as Hortense Spillers (1987) has argued, the black body was "ungendered" by capture and exchange, then, Snorton proposes, this ungendering gives access both to narratives and methods of fugitivity and marks gender instability as part of the history of blackness itself. Refusing to separate out histories of race from histories of gender variance, Snorton provides a very different arc for transgender history.

Snorton: I appreciate Halberstam's cogent reading of how multiple temporalities animate my recent work, *Black on Both Sides*. I'll add that my considerations of temporality are deeply shaped by black study,[1] such as when the unnamed protagonist in Ralph Ellison's *Invisible Man* (coincidentally winning the National Book Award at the height of Christine Jorgensen's media story) describes time as a boomerang that leaves its impression through violent reencounter. Or in Kara Keeling's noted essay "Looking for M—: Queer Temporality, Black Political Possibility, and Poetry from the Future" (2009), which appears in *GLQ*, and takes Frantz Fanon's articulation of interval temporality as an occasion to think about how it feels to be in time and to gesture toward a historiographical practice that holds in tension the relationship between the past and future of black queer and trans narratives. These are only a couple of examples that have been particularly resonant in my thinking, but one of the critical lessons of black study is a critical posture toward linear time. History—as a procedure of marking change over time—is also confounded by careful studies of blackness.

Kathleen P. Long: Riley Snorton's work provides a crucial critical perspective on historiographical practices and how they might be transformed and confounded by considerations of black queer and trans experiences. *Black on Both Sides* has helped me rethink how I approach the texts I encounter, and their problematic relationship both to linear notions of history and to the historical context in which they appear. I have much work left to do in this regard, as I come at this question backward, having begun my work on gender from the perspective of history. Working as an early modernist, I was always drawn to the texts that remained outside the canon, at too great a distance from it to be integrated into it or normalized. Trans* studies has given me the ability to analyze the gendered components of this marginalization of certain texts from a critical perspective, and to understand how the texts themselves propose alternative ways of understanding gender. Early modern French materials present theories of gender that call into question bigendered ways of organizing the world. This is particularly striking because of the way in which everything is gendered in French: masculine or feminine, rather than having the range of possibilities, including neuter or common or doubly gendered nouns, found in Latin. So, a questioning of bigenderism in early modern medical and philosophical materials signals an understanding of how French society is constructed on this model, as well as of the limitations of this model. Certain forms of what we might call transgender were accepted in French culture; a number of medical theorists believed that women could become men. But this transition played out in a very rigid cultural context, one that demanded a very precise, almost ritualistic, discourse. This makes the case of Marin le Marcis, misread by Michel Foucault (2003: 68–70) and Stephen Greenblatt (1988: 73–86), particularly interesting: a man who was baptized and raised as a woman, who lived and worked as a woman for a number of years, and who uses this precise, authorized discourse to establish his right to live as a man. This story also brings together the representation of an intersex individual, called a hermaphrodite at that time, with his own self-representation as a man who was once a woman, raising questions about the relationship between gender mobility and the complex materiality of the body. Trans* theory, particularly with its emphasis on the importance of varied and mobile experiences rather than fixed identity and abstract frameworks for that identity, has opened the way to seeking the narratives early modern trans* people have told about themselves.

History has a purpose in this regard, for example, in the archival search for materials that have not yet been considered. Mathieu Laflamme, at the University of Ottawa, has found the court documents for the Marin le Marcis case, which gives us access to the "unmediated" testimony of Marin himself. How many other documents exist that could give us insight into the lives of trans* people? Montaigne scholars would think of the case of Mary (described in his *Journal de voyage*, 1983: 77; the name itself could be masculine or feminine), who was tried and hanged for impersonating a man sometime around 1580. This case is strikingly significant because Mary (whose name is an alternate spelling of the French word for husband) refused to return to living as a woman (Ferguson 2013).

But trans*historicities also draw us to consider these documents with a critical eye toward the complex relationships between gender normativity and early modern trans* discourses. Susan Stryker and Aren Aizura note that "self-identified trans people found new ways to enter into conversation with others about the objective and subjective conditions of gendered embodiment, rather than remaining mere objects in the discourses of others about them, or continuing to speak in constrained autobiographical modes that, for the most part, narrated diagnostic categories from first-person perspectives" (2013: 1–2). In Jacques Duval's account of Marin's testimony, Marin has mastered the diagnostic discourse that will make his transition acceptable to the authorities because his life depends on this discourse; thus, his own experience of gendered embodiment remains somewhat opaque to us (1612: 384–89). We can imagine trans* subjectivities by navigating between these documents and contemporary accounts of trans* experiences, but we cannot know with any certainty what these past experiences have been.

Jacob Lau: My work argues for reading trans-of-color narratives as the "b-roll" experience of gendered, classed, and racialized time, always glimpsed through state-enacted forms of time that regulate and discipline the experience of embodiment through processes such as immigration and administrative documentation. I am calling this methodology "trans-temporality." One of my primary engagements in theorizing trans-temporality as a trans* historicist method is to understand trans narratives, bodies, and lives as informed and coconstituted by postcolonial historicism, queer-of-color critique, and racialized asynchronicity. In the ways in which queer temporality (and I am thinking in particular of Jack Halberstam's *In a Queer Time and Place*) has been understood as backward and adolescent, and trans subjectivity constituted through contingent communal acknowledgment (often in direct contradiction to the times of the state), I see critiques of historicism as formulated in that creative tension. For instance, in my current project I analyze California's Respect after Death Act (2012), which was passed after pressure from the family of Christopher Lee, a gender-nonconforming mixed-race Asian American trans man who cofounded the San Francisco Transgender Film Festival. Lee's film *Christopher's Chronicles: Christopher Does Dallas* (1997) is one of the earliest documentaries by a transmasculine subject of their transition. The fascinating thing about the film is the ways in which Lee both gives a transnormative narrative of transition in familiar scenes of trans becoming (shaving and recounting wanting to wear a tie as a child, discussing discomfort with menstruating in the toilet of the men's restroom, the family room with his mother, shopping with his girlfriend), yet contests this narration at the same time. The contestation is done through both music cues relying on a 1980s and 1990s pop soundtrack and inserting a scrolling text across the bottom of the screen (snarkily informing the viewer of cruising in the men's room, breaking up with his girlfriend, contesting reliance on visual narratives by informing the viewer of his mixed-race, disabled, pansexual, faggy body). The tension between Lee's spoken narrative and the textual-visual narrative functions as a means to give two histories at the same time.

In a similar way, after his death Lee was misgendered on his death certificate, leading his family to contest state practices of gendering after death. I see trans*historicity as operating in the gaps between the misrecognition of Christopher Lee's gender on his death certificate and the ways Lee's queer families contested that misrecognition as well as challenged how the state recognizes who is next of kin. As Halberstam put so wonderfully in the *GLQ* roundtable, "[Queer time] is a theory of queerness as a way of being in the world and a critique of the careful social scripts that usher even the most queer among us through major markers of individual development and into normativity" (Dinshaw et al. 2007: 182). As such I think queer temporality can and does operate within the normative scripts of historicism yet lends itself to nonnormative historicities by pushing against the social scripts enacted on queer and nonnormative subjects already feeling out of sorts with the paths they are told to follow.

What I think what other scholars engaged in questions of colonialism, imperialism, and temporal critique such as Bliss Cua Lim (2009) and Dipesh Chakrabarty (2000) point to (as well as Carolyn Dinshaw in the roundtable cited in the question), are the ways the enchanted, monstrous, and nonsecular push theorizations of historicity to render visible historicism's imbrication within racialized, postcolonial, and settler colonialism, which allows for a multiplicity of affective fronted histories to surface. As Dinshaw describes, "Thinking nonlinearity over and against linearity is hard enough, but figuring out the criteria by which different nonlinear temporalities might meaningfully be brought together —figuring out how to make heterogeneity analytically powerful—is exponentially harder" (Dinshaw et al. 2007: 186). Reading historical documents retrospectively claimed as "trans" for their racialized, sexualized, gendered, and nationalized temporal underpinnings is what I am doing in my current book manuscript, and to some extent what Cameron and I were trying to do in our introduction to Michael Dillon/Lobzang Jivaka's 1962 memoir *Out of the Ordinary: A Life of Gender and Spiritual Transitions* (2016).

I also think it might be worth asking a variation of Chris Nealon's question about how our theorizations of alternate temporalities are legible not only as attempts to think through the possibilities of movement and community but also as attempts to think around or against the time of the commodity (Dinshaw et al. 2007: 188). Especially since trans* histories and cultural production tend to go through cyclical patterns of "rediscovery" and commodification every couple of years in American media. We saw this with Christine Jorgensen, Thomas Beatie, Chaz Bono, and, more recently, Caitlyn Jenner. I think we should also be wary of the ways in which these figures can surface as commodifiable, owing to the sorts of trans narratives they produce, as they often cite a white middle-class hetero-normativity as part and parcel of their marketable transness. My work is of course interested in some of these figures, particularly Michael Dillon, whose memoir was understood as a kind of lost piece of trans masculine history. I was reticent about how to approach and characterize the Dillon/Jivaka memoir, or even if it should be published, since the author clearly was reluctant to write it. Cameron and I had to wait until an upwelling in interest in trans cultural production and autobiography before we could even find a publisher. So a lot of our work in the academy is based on what we do as marketable to university presses. But also Dillon's life was lived in retreat; literally at the end of it he was a Buddhist monastic waiting on higher ordination in Ladakh. His memoir arrived on the desk of his literary agent after news of his death in 1962. Characterizing his memoir as transgender is tricky because the medical techniques practiced on his body can only retrospectively be understood as those for trans masculine people or as constituting "transsexuality." His memoir is really more of a transnational and spiritual one, and one that I argue in my larger project demonstrates the colonial and imperial conditions making up white transmasculinity (especially female-to-male transsexuality).

I find that many points of discussion in "Theorizing Queer Temporalities" remain important in theorizing trans*historicity and historicism. Particularly, Roderick Ferguson's warning that "recruiting previously excluded subjects into a nationalist regimen can be a way of using time to unmake forms of nonnationalist relationality" (Dinshaw et al. 2007: 185). I think Eric Stanley put it best during *TSQ*'s roundtable on decolonizing the transgender imaginary, when he suggested that those of us working in the academy should be asking what an insurgent trans studies project might look like (which brings down the political order) lest we partake in historicizing previously excluded subjects into a nationalist regimen and use time to unmake forms of nonnationalist relationality (Boellstorff et al. 2014: 425). One of the animating impulses of my theorization of trans-temporality is to understand that other ways to be have always existed beyond the record of the state: for instance, Sylvia Rivera discusses the important moment of meeting Marsha P. Johnson as the birth of a strong sistership that marked the beginning of her entrance into community. I wonder how sistership as a mode of survival, providing a kind of insurgent trans politics and historical project, might also be understood as specific trans-of-color affect.

Chiang: My work is deeply inspired by the ongoing debates in historicism and queer temporality. For one, it pulls us out of a protean investment in queer and trans history as a modality and politics of recuperation. Because subjects of power, knowledge, and experience emerge out of not just historical junctures of interpellation but also the highly differentiated praxes of historiographical displacement, the restorative enterprise of social historical impulses must always be confounded with the kind of critical historical thinking that questions how differences are constructed and categories arise in the first place. This is what Joan Scott (1991) has called the "evidence of experience."

I have drawn on this genealogy of feminist and queer theoretical reappraisals of time and historicity to provide an alternative chronology of Chinese history. Beginning with eunuchs in late Qing Peking and concluding with transsexuals in Cold War Sinophone Taiwan, *After Eunuchs* advances a new reading of twentieth-century Chinese history that supersedes dominant narratives based on the socialist/postsocialist paradigm (Chiang 2018). The tendency among Chinese historians to focus on developments solely within Maoist China overlooks the historical context in which the tensions between the "centers" and "peripheries" of the People's Republic grow over time. By traveling to Taiwan (where the purported "first" case of Chinese transsexuality was reported) with the Nationalist government in the late 1940s and 1950s, the Sinophone perspective encapsulated in the ending of *After Eunuchs* offers a fresh interpretation of twentieth-century "China" beyond the conventions of China-centered historiography: whereas in the early twentieth century, the transmission of foreign sexual knowledge and identity politics was mediated primarily via Japan (as thoroughly captured through the lens of colonial modernity), these processes of cultural translation were subsequently rerouted through—and rerooted in—Sinophone communities in the Cold War period. Taking Japan and China as new agents of imperialism seriously, this reframing also speaks to one of your questions about the "coloniality of the present" by asking us to pay more—not less—attention to forms of colonialism and empire beyond the Western-centric configurations of colonial modernity. In the age of the rise of China, what is preventing us from provincializing China?

Bychowski: As scholars of history we are much like builders (including builders of stories) trying in many ways to preserve and highlight existing structures while also annotating, amending, and activating these foundations so as to help the past deploy critical presences in our futures. There is no easy answer if faced with a choice between historicism and queer (or trans) alternatives because even as far as accuracy and meaning are concerned there are rarely easy and complete answers given by any one method. In my experience, tools and methods of study and storytelling must time and again be adapted (if not outright reinvented) to accurately depict elements of history. This challenge is compounded when the historians who have previously and currently established the patterns of a certain school of history (such as historicism) do so with aims and audiences other than those more closely identified with the object of study. This is one of the accomplishments of *Black on Both Sides*, as noted by others: holding in tension the desire (or social compulsion) to tell and hear linear narratives with the nonlinear resources given to and retained by those whose stories are being told. Even sympathetic projects, such as queer readings of figures acknowledged as "trans" in some respect, often do more to address the ways in which the figures are queer than tell their narrative in a way that highlights the transness. To continue on this example (there are many others), I have had to remind fellow queer theorists for whom I have a warm respect that transgender does more in society, history, and art than merely disturb cisgender people and norms. Likewise, trans experiences can challenge us with slippages in subjectivity, time, relations, and identity so that a presumed objective telling does much to remove critical elements (cherry-picking data) in order to create linear historicist narratives. Important points have already been made about ungendering and other forms of erasure that may also amount to untransing, unqueering, or even uncripping to make our past and presences easier to incorporate or outright ignore.

Yet as a builder and preserver I am optimistic. What seems to benefit the goals of historicism as well as queer (and trans) alternatives is a range of tools for analysis and communication. In conceiving of "trans genres of embodiment," I recognize how some histories function by giving us a beginning, middle, and end. Other stories require events to be engaged in other orders, sometimes starting with our present moment and looking back at how we got here. Then there are stories told (necessarily) from a state of uncertainty, including (if not especially) histories of the past. Our present moment is only one of many potentially imagined (or, rather, imaginable) futures for those living in moments of the past. Being able to think with asynchronicity, even speculatively, about the uncertainty of the future of the past allows us to better appreciate the significance of decisions, actions, and consequences of the past in the subsequent history. In other words, historicism is one tool and genre for telling trans histories. In my own life, I see the daily utility of telling with near-objective detail the contexts and sequence of events so that what happened after cannot have happened before. Yet my own life and history does not only function that way. How do I respond to a friend who picks up a photo of us from our youth and asks, "Who is that?" That person she points to is me and yet not me. Do I call that person by my current name or by her/his/our name? That person used a different name and lived in different contexts. Yet the revelations of my present change how we view the past, even to the extent that the past seems strange and unrecognizable to some of us. Even our own friends may not be able to recognize us. Transgender plays with time, history, and temporality in a multitude of ways that demand intentional and multiple ways of telling trans histories and narratives. I begin to wonder if "trans temporality" might in some ways function with but distinctly from queer temporality.

Ochoa: I first encountered historiography when I took a colonial Latin American historiography class in grad school. I knew that I didn't want the twentieth-century focused account of the failure of modernity (democratic institutions, markets, citizenship, technology, commodities) in Latin America to frame how I understood the people I was proposing to work with in Venezuela. Focusing on the colonial period was essential for my understanding of contemporary forms of governmentality in the region. Trans studies was not yet constituted as a field. William B. Taylor, the historian who introduced me to historiography, put a then-recent translation of the 1626 memoir attributed to Catalina de Erauso/Alonso Díaz de Guzmán in my hands and suggested I write my seminar paper on the figure. The last thing I wanted to do was claim a Basque conquistador as a transgender ancestor! That set up my engagement with Erauso as a way to think about trans outside the contemporary political, economic, and technological structures that shape our understanding of the category. Since I was also working in media studies, I saw that Erauso also helped me get out of media presentism—what does trans mediation look like when we don't have YouTube or hormones to work with? This work developed in a few years, and I published it as a consideration of the memoir and its implications for the survival of gender-variant people in the Americas (Ochoa 2007).

TSQ: *What are your scholarly, activist, personal, and political (or other) concerns about, or investments in, trans history? Does the question of queer (cross-temporal or trans∗historical) kinship play a role in your scholarship and sense of community formation and sustenance? If so, how?*

Snorton: When pressed, I explain that the political investments of *Black on Both Sides* are twofold: to highlight trans studies' varied genealogies (and to particularly illustrate how black feminism has mapped out the implications of racialized gender for trans experience) and to revive or invent strategies for black and trans life in the present/future. The second is a persistent preoccupation, framed as a question of how does one chart a life (or, as it relates to the consternating question of agency, what Jennifer Morgan [2004: chap. 6] writes in terms of resistance or accommodation) that has been dominantly expressed as unlivable and unimaginable. The process of writing trans history required an active participation in political work, including working with Black Trans Lives Matter movements, the Black Trans Advocacy Coalition, and addressing the life chances of black and trans people who grapple with issues of homelessness, criminalization, and other modes of state and institutional violence.

I would add that as, on some level, *Black on Both Sides* is invested in presenting a usable past for more livable black and trans lives, then placing myself in political communities with black and trans elders, youths, and peers was a kind of fieldwork that simultaneously served as a training ground for thinking methodology according to an ethical imperative of being with.

Halberstam: Queer kinship plays a huge role in my new book, *Trans*: A Quick and Quirky Account of Gender Variability*. There, I argue that because kids are coming out as transgender at earlier and earlier ages, they access the meaning of transgender bodies through online sources and through their parents, many of whom rush to educate themselves and their child about what this may mean. As a consequence, as Tey Meadow's (2018) new work on the parents of trans* children shows, trans kids occupy extremely different relations to queer community and kinship than generations before them. Meadow argues that the support that many trans children now enjoy from their families and communities allows them to "disidentify with transgender history" and forge a direct identification instead with, potentially, more heteronormative social forms. This tendency to skip identifications with trans* elders creates a massive gap in the transmission of knowledge outside family networks, from one generation of queer or trans* people to the next. I believe that we need to rethink kinship now along the lines that Marilyn Strathern offers in her sense of a "merographic method." Strathern herself in the introduction to *Partial Connections* explains the function of this method in terms of always "thinking about what is implicit or explicit or about what is hidden or made visible" (2004: xxix). It is a method that is built on parts, recognizing parts rather than wholes and thinking through partiality in terms of connections and relations. This kind of method would allow us to look for queer kinship connections beyond the family and biology and think about the partial and arbitrary nature of all description and theory and to the complex interactions between people and technology, human bodies and other nonhuman animal forms, scales and intensities.

Long: I just want to say that Riley Snorton's formulation of a "usable past for more livable black and trans lives" and Howard Chiang's call for "critical historical thinking that questions how differences are constructed and categories arise in the first place" underscore the ethical concerns of trans*historicity that seem to move all of us. As someone whose scholarly and activist focus is on the violence that normativity inflicts on bodies and minds, I often feel much more a part of the disability studies community, and of disability rights activism, than I do in any particular field of gender studies. Yet my work on the early medicalization of disability connects strongly with intersex, which was medicalized from the medieval period on; and well into the twentieth century, intersex is connected with other "nonnormative" bodies. There are some brilliant scholars who connect queer and crip experiences (Robert McRuer leaps to mind); M. W. Bychowski has been doing important work in this regard, connecting postmodern, modern, and medieval texts. But I think queer and trans* theory has more to gain from intersections with disability studies, particularly considering more than just contemporary materials and narratives. I worry that the distancing from disability studies that sometimes takes place in gender studies signals an anxiety about stigma that pushes queer theory into a normative direction, something that is antithetical to its motivations.

One simple example of how this connection can be made across history is Rosemarie Garland Thomson's concept of the normate, the body unmarked by difference. The normate as Thomson describes it resembles Aristotle's ideal type (from his treatise on *The Generation of Animals*; the section on the generation of monsters, or what we would call nonnormative bodies): an aristocratic, Greek, male body without any marked differences from an idealized father. Aristotle makes it clear that nonmasculine bodies are already nonnormative, then moves on to bodies that are missing parts or have too many, or that are different in other ways. Here, the intersex body (the "hermaphrodite") is mentioned as one of these monstrous forms. Thus, gender and disability are conceptually associated from the first philosophical discussions of embodied difference. This holds true in medical treatises from the early modern period, and well past the Enlightenment into the twentieth century. Arguably, this association of gender difference in all its forms and disability still resonates today in the pathologization of forms of trans★ embodiment and experience by means of terms like "gender identity disorder." Foucauldian approaches to disability and gender studies are useful in the analysis of institutions and social networks that frame and shape nonnormative bodies. I would suggest that greater focus on Georges Canguilhem's critique of medical philosophy and its formulations of the normal and normativity, the pathological, and disease as they play out in scientific research on and medical treatment of bodies is also necessary to understand fundamental and long-standing conceptual frameworks of gender and disability. Trans★historicity considered in this light can help us understand the sedimentation and naturalization of concepts of the type, the ideal, and the normal, but also the immediacy of these concepts. Here again, trans★historicity can reveal how these concepts and the frameworks built on them come to seem fixed over time, as well as explore their inherent instability.

Elizabeth Bearden has offered a compelling analysis of the ways in which "definitions of natural and unnatural bodies and behaviors have disabled people for millennia" (2017: 33). These definitions implicate differently gendered bodies (from a narrow masculine ideal) as well as other "nonnormative" bodies. But these long-standing concepts also had their critics, from Augustine to Montaigne, who saw monstrosity as a human concept that revealed only the limitations of human understanding rather than any underlying truth about nature and human nature.

The risk we run in untethering transgender theory from disability and intersex theories is a continuation of the long-standing regime of normalization that Bearden identifies. Trans★ and intersex studies, along with disability studies, have the power to destabilize normalization, rendering the elusive "normal" the only true "abnormal."

In her introduction to a forthcoming volume on *Ovidian Transversions*, Valerie Traub describes the "hermeneutic counterpoint" of a focus on "the fundamental instability of concepts, categories, and practices," inspired by Deleuze, and "the historical and theoretical consequences of the culture's emergent attraction to fixity, classification, and regulation," delineated by Foucault. As Traub makes clear, these two theoretical approaches are not mutually exclusive. The insistence on classification and the desire for fixity that it reflects suggest the instability that subtends our ontological and epistemological systems. Montaigne made this clear in his critique of legal and medical systems of thought in his essay "Of Experience" ("De l'experience"), which evokes the limitations of knowledge as a system of "classification and regulation" in his image of children playing with mercury: "Who has seen children trying to divide a mass of quicksilver [mercury] into a certain number of parts? The more they press it and knead it and try to constrain it to their will, the more they provoke the independence of this spirited [generative] metal; it escapes their skill and keeps dividing and scattering in little particles beyond all reckoning" (Montaigne 1965: 816; mercury was often considered to be the metal that mediated between gold, considered masculine, and silver, considered feminine, in alchemical thought). For Montaigne, embodied experience is both generative and fugitive, to gesture toward C. Riley Snorton's masterful conception of the fugitivity of black trans* experience, which should be central to our understanding of trans*historicity.

Gender is one of our oldest systems of classification of embodied experience, yet this experience itself always escapes such classification and lives beyond the realm of regulation and containment. Our more generous and generative selves confound the systems that purport to define us, creating ever more possibilities for life, adapting to new circumstances and environments; this is how we survive.

Bychowski: Generosity for me begins in the trans necropolis and works outward. How may I be generous to the dead? How might this generosity teach us to be more "generous and generative" for those living or who may yet live. In this, I want to again affirm what Snorton calls "the ethical imperative of being with." My response takes off from the minor rewording (present in the wider statement) that we consider the responsibility and necessities of the ethical imperative of *living* with. How does the work of my life make, not make, or unmake the liveability of another's life? How can history help us better live together? Too many trans, intersex, nonbinary, and genderqueer people (especially trans people of color and trans people with disabilities) are denied livable lives. Too many bodies are stolen. Too many voices in our present moment and our past are silenced, even after death. Our work begins by listening. I've publicly described myself as someone who spends her day listening to marked, badly marked, and unmarked graves. I find this work of finding trans futures in the past to be sad and hopeful. Sad because in listening to a certain trans affinity in the medieval narrative of "Narcissus" by John Gower (2006: lines 2275–398) or to the suicide note of Leelah Alcorn, I know how the stories and histories proceed; how they (in)form narrative expectations. I am sad because I do not fully know if or how they might have proceeded differently. I am hopeful because by listening to these stories, I hear moments in which the future we know (our present future) may not have been the only future. I imagine these other potential futures to the past. Sometimes the histories tell us directly, other times we must hear them from the environment. And often, such as in the case of Narcissus and Alcorn, the dead also imagined other futures and hoped that we might find what they could not reach. Gower's "Narcissus" uses the word *otherwhiles*. These otherwhiles include the time in which I live but also the time in which Alcorn lives and the times of countless other trans and nontrans people who find selves in such woods of isolation. By so imagining, these otherwhiles become connected. We begin by existing with and yearn for a living with each other. The call of Narcissus and Alcorn for help and life may be heard by such otherwhiles. We learn how to better listen. We learn how to help relics and lost tales to speak in terms that might be heard and incite more livable lives. We learn the histories that are and those histories that might be. I have a button I wear that says, "Transgender Can Save the Middle Ages," and I believe that. But I also believe that the Middle Ages can save transgender, as a collective of ideas, communities, histories, and futures. Trans lives can be found and reclaimed, heard and imagined in the necropolis of the past. The past is not so set in stone (even tombstones) that trans youths cannot engage with its telling. Otherwhiles is a way in which we might begin to grow out of the necropolis with better inroads to the past and future in forms like what Halberstam calls "queer kinship." How might we give past and future generations better than we've received?

Ochoa: I think it's dangerous to project one's sense of kinship onto this work. While historical antecedents are politically important in many struggles (and are very much what students come into my classes desiring), I think the most important political commitment we should have with history is to complexity and messiness. If we are going to use a form of queer kinship to animate the work, let it be that spinster aunt, or the pervert cousin who got put away, the dashed lines, empty spaces, and question marks on the genealogy chart. That said, yes, it's important for people to know that "we" have a past, that "we" have survived, but for me that question should always lead us to how forms of power have worked in people's lives and what kinds of responses people have come up with, both redemptive and hopeless. Trans history for me helps build an account of how things get to be the way they are.

TSQ: *What might be gained or lost by thinking about time, history, and trans* (as an identity or, especially, as a model or method for theorizing various types of crossings) together? Do you see a role for speculation or imagination in researching, writing, and theorizing trans* history?*

Snorton: The question of consequence as it relates to thinking about time, transness, and history begs a consideration of Sylvia Wynter's work. Particularly when she writes about the sociogenic principle as a science for a new rhetoricity of identity. Wynter's call for a project of new humanism—against its biocentric and ethnocentric overrepresentations—is also a way to think about the porosity of fact and fiction, scientific certitude and its underlying speculative assumptions and projections. The intersubjectivity of history and imagination is also present in Audre Lorde's notion of "dreams/myths/histories" in the introduction to *Zami* (1982), which, if we are to apply Jafari Allen's (2012) cogent analysis of the "stroke" in his introduction to *GLQ*'s "Black/Queer/Diaspora" special issue to Lorde's formulation, underscores the intimate relations among and between history, myth, and dream. Approaching this question slightly differently, one might reflect on the affects and desires that accompany any encounter with the archive or the process of "writing up." Let us consider that an archive serves as "proof" not only of the questions we bring to it but also of a set of political procedures and institutional forces that make it available to us. The evidence of the archive's political and institutional contexts has given rise to several generative formulations for bridging the supposed distinction between history and imagination, of which I would be remiss not to note Saidiya Hartman's notion of "critical fabulation." As Hartman relates in "Venus in Two Acts," sometimes imagining the otherwise of documentary evidence is the ethical requirement for engaging particular assemblies of materials, which have been organized to diminish and disparage certain kinds of lives.

Lau: I find that some level of speculation and imaginative acts are always part of researching, writing, and theorizing trans* history mainly because, frankly, many of the figures I study have died. And in many ways speculation and open conjecture is a good guide through archives that, as Riley Snorton noted earlier, have institutional restraints. I have always felt that affect is a means of navigating time, history, and trans*ness, especially when the figures you are looking for are in essence written out of time. In my work, and in ways similar to how many folks in this roundtable are discussing, I understand cisnormative time as a particular form of state-time that, while far from static or linear in process, does align itself with the progress notion of Western telos and ontology. For instance, I think about the ways state documents such as birth certificates, social security cards, travel visas, and death certificates provide a linear narrative of a gendered, racialized, and classed life and also are key parts of the national historical record, meant to outlive the trans subject. While often we think of these documents in terms of spatiality for trans people (providing access to spaces, providing the means for transnational movement), I primarily approach them through the ways they narrate about trans lives in cisnormative time. Particularly, why have Marsha P. Johnson's death certificate and social security card been such contested documents? How has trans-of-color affect been generated in ways unrecognized by the state before death, and how does it demonstrate means of livability in the midst of necropolitical conditions?

In ways similar to what other folks have mentioned here, I also find that approaching cis time as a racializing as well as gendering process intimately bound to citizenship and recognizable subjectivity, vis-à-vis Dipesh Chakrabarty's *Provincializing Europe: Postcolonial Thought and Historical Difference* (2000), Kara Keeling's "Looking for M—: Queer Temporality, Black Political Possibility, and Poetry from the Future" (2009), and Walter Benjamin's "Theses on the Philosophy of History" (1968), indexes the sort of historicist practices that lend themselves to situating trans-of-color precarity in ways that help illuminate the necropolitical present. In turning backward to understand our present moments and whatever futures they may portend, what affective modes can the dead use to announce their presence? How does trans*historicity account for these?

Chiang: Perhaps one of the most illuminating consequences of the recent turn toward writing and visualizing trans history has been the questioning of key assumptions hidden in the shadow of an earlier generation of queer history. Thinking about time, history, and trans together challenges the way that same-sex desire/relation has come to monopolize the historical analysis of nonnormative gender and sexual experience. This intellectual interrogation of what Susan Stryker (2008) calls "homonormativity" opens up new ways of thinking about the past and makes room for critical distances from the present. Like the way any other field of history is executed, researching, writing, and theorizing trans history *demands* robust speculation and imagination. This is especially pressing for a field that has long been oppressed by the hegemonic protocol of modern historiography. This also might just mirror the creative ways with which subjugated historical actors have had to speculate or imagine ways of survival across time and place.

Bychowski: Trans life seems to give master classes in metaphor. Indeed, all those who must live or exist in a world not built for them learn in diverse ways how to identify with protagonists and histories that do not represent us, how to translate experiences, how to take tools and stories to use for other purposes in the benefit of other bodies, and how to tell multiple stories for different audiences. Metaphor is a function of carrying across and living between meanings. Thus beyond the social status as a marker of identity, trans and transgender has long functioned as a verb, a method of doing. The experience of dysphoria—one possible and precarious element of trans life among many—often involves a degree of revisiting the past in response to later realizations, crystallizations, or liberations and may also involve a degree of strong desire for certain elements joined with a strong repulsion to others. A nondysphoric transgender history (as we might characterize historicism's desire for nonsubjective near-objective storytelling) may then be concerned with revisionism or cherry-picking. Yet to disregard dysphoria (among other trans ways of reading the past) as a disordered and psychotic approach to history is to undermine the validity, reality, and utility of one currently prominent trans form of cognizing history. That we must learn to tell stories in nondysphoric and other cisnormative ways is a professional and personal necessity that many of us learn very young. But if we are to use our full and varied faculties to dismantle the transphobic, queerphobic, misogynistic, and ableist presumptions in how history is told, then it is not enough that we merely write about transgender through the eyes and tools of cisgender. To put a sharper point on it, if we do not want to merely be the objects of historical study but the tellers—and given that our place in the academy is often precarious if acknowledged at all—then we must not be shy in saying that we have perspectives to share.

This brings us back to transgender and metaphor as critical to thinking through trans history. Beyond dysphoria and trans methodologies in general as real and subjective approaches to history, transgender histories (on the personal and large scale) benefit greatly from acknowledged and tactical use of the imagination. History does not come to us fully fleshed out in useful and wholly accurate narrative forms. Historians often have to use a degree of imagination (checked by evidence) to fill in the gaps and silences. History as it reaches out to us through texts, relics, traditions, and absences will often work symbiotically with a historian's speculations to tell their story. All the more so it seems for transgender history. In society, transgender issues a call for stories. News outlets reporting on a trans celebrity will want the secrets. Scholars will want the facts, contexts, and implications of a historical person. Friends and family will want to know what has and will happen to their beloved. Trans people too can wrestle with mysteries, lived contradictions, and multiple views on their own past, present, and future. Amid all of these details, the connective tissue is often fluid, amorphous, and semitranslucent. Imagination and story is how we find ways of functioning, ways of making connections, and getting from yesterday to tomorrow. We reach out with our imaginations to see the materials we will use in our stories to build livable lives—materials, stories, and lives we share with those who come before and will come after. Narrative is one way transgender functions and forms, but it is also that which society and history demand of transgender. Transgender was at times and in ways unthinkable and unspeakable in the past, but that does not mean it was nonexistent. If silence were the same as nonexistence, many of us would not be here. Other times, transgender is thought and spoken between words, in appropriated words, in metaphors and suggestions. Our job is then not only to help the past speak but to learn to read the ways the past gives us signs and gestures. Working symbiotically between past and present, textual and imagined histories, the trans historian and trans history can co-operate in the telling.

Ochoa: I have proposed in another essay informed by colonial historiography the idea of time travel as a historical method (Ochoa 2016). I think we do this by disentangling our given sense of temporality from the questions we're asking, and broadening into an extended present that includes moments in time often considered to be distant and separate. I'm also very influenced by Leslie Marmon Silko's *Almanac of the Dead* (1991), which proposes a sense of cyclical time. In the same way as we need to undo our given sense of gender categories to resist determinism in our historical work, we need to undo our given sense of time. This undoing is a fundamental contribution of trans studies to scholarship in general.

TSQ: *Jack Halberstam, in a lecture a few years ago, suggested that readers now often approach the past through the "coloniality of the present," in which we project ourselves and our desires backward in time or onto a particular historical text. How have you in your own work managed questions of self-interest or desire as you have engaged with historical subjects? What are your thoughts on the search for "origins" or for trans pasts (understanding trans as a category of identity, anti-identity, and/or methodology), which have clearly become an animating force in both academia and popular culture?*

Halberstam: I have found María Elena Martínez's (2014) work on Juana Aguilar instructive in this regard. Martínez examined the case of a gender-ambiguous person in Guatemala who was accused of unnatural acts with women in 1803. Arguing against a presentist reading of the case, Martínez directed our attention to the colonizing gesture of absorbing differences from a historical distance. Colonial power, she reminds us, claims the right to name and to know. We should resist reproducing that form of power in our archival reclamations. In my own work, early on in *Female Masculinity*, I made the case for what I called "perverse presentism," or the application of what we do not know in the present to what we cannot know in the past. So rather than taking knowledge from our current context and using it as a template for the past, we must recognize how much we do not know about gender variability now and use that as a tool for withholding the imposition of knowledge onto vastly different cases from the past.

Snorton: I hear Jack's critique as an ethical one—that is, not so much about the need for historians to disabuse themselves of the temporal contexts from which they engage in narrating the past but about a rightful concern over what work we are requiring historical figures to do for the present/future. This concern unfolds in a few ways—the mobilization of the archive as a tool to argue for an(other) inevitable present, the impulse to reveal the past in terms of an unassailable certainty based on what we can see/find, an insufficient consideration of what Édouard Glissant described as the "right to opacity" for historical actors.

Long: Where this "coloniality of the present" is most evident to me is in our assumption that only now are we theorizing gender in complex ways. In medical and philosophical discourse of sixteenth- and seventeenth-century Europe, particularly France, there were intense debates over the nature of gender, and whether it was a simple binary of male and female, or whether it was more capacious and more mobile. The constructed and potentially illusory nature of gender was presented in a range of works, including novels and poetry. All of these discussions arose in the context of competing philosophical discourses; Aristotelian and Neoplatonic modes dominated both the universities and the courts, respectively, but skepticism (particularly Pyrrhonian) arose as an alternative model in the second half of the sixteenth century and was used to call into question philosophical authority, cultural and social institutions and systems, and systems of knowledge themselves. This critical approach to accepted philosophical conceptions of the world was promulgated by Montaigne and those who followed his work; it was present in larger philosophical debates well into the seventeenth century. This mode of questioning authority informed a number of works that questioned gender norms and bigenderism itself, thus popularizing skeptical approaches to gender. I strongly agree with the ethical concerns expressed above by Halberstam and Snorton, particularly the caution against the "imposition of knowledge" or the "impulse to reveal the past in terms of an unassailable certainty." But the past also draws us to engage with it, and that engagement has its own forces of attraction and aversion; is it possible to avoid bringing these forces into play?

Bychowski: The question of the past's relation to the present offers two dangers immediately to my mind. On the one hand, I think of those trans, intersex, and nonbinary people who have been told, like women, people of color, and people with disabilities (to name a few), in various ways and times that whole eras of history are not theirs. The very mention of medieval transgender studies raises the question, "Were there any trans people in the Middle Ages?" I can face these questions and respond also to the more interesting question, "*How* were people trans in the Middle Ages?" But I see the looks in my students' faces when they are told that transgender is only a recent modern invention, "just a phase" historically. I also see their defiance to this presumption. This brings me to another danger, that any one of us should claim the past is "ours." This raises the ethical problem of re-creating the same exclusiveness that kept us out of historical studies to start with, and the further problem of being inaccurate. We may share experiences, relics, traditions, ideas, and stories with the past, but we do not occupy their skin, feel their pain, witness history as they witness. There is ever contingency in our points of contact. Between these two expressions of the same exclusive possessive impulse, there needs be room to say that the past is not so fundamentally "other" that we can do nothing for it and it for us, yet also respect that the past is different enough to teach us and we are different enough to contribute something to the past beyond merely repeating what the past says in the same way.

At this contingency, solidarity arises. Those in the past have power over us (we need them), and in encountering them they make demands of us. In developing theories on trans genres of embodiment, I have returned to the idea of participation without belonging from Jacques Derrida's "Law of Genre" (1980). One participates in womanhood (and this is important), but womanhood does not belong to any one person. This is all the more important when we participate in the lives of communities with whom we do not share the same contexts and contingencies. History may be understood as an extension of this present truth. As in any relationship, our strength is in our (temporal and contextual) differences, and we can do things the other cannot or cannot alone or cannot any longer. By maintaining a sense of participation without belonging across eras and arenas of history we can articulate a sense of "us" that nonetheless preserves the immense power of the "thou" that continues to attract the "I." Our roads meet and even overlap, but to call one an "origin" or another an "heir" is to isolate and dominate the flow of power in ways that limit where we, you, or I may go.

Also, in regard to historical fields prior to the coinage of words such as *transgender*, the question of language also arises. At first blush, the demand to learn and use the language available or utilized by people of the past is as important as it is persistent. We hear people say, "We must speak with premodern language." This challenges us to learn how transgender functions in the past through constructs such as eunuchism, hermaphroditism, chivalry, or a monk's vows. The dilemma, then, is that we function as historical polyglots, but our insights are still not recognized. Our borrowed words and accents and our code-switching trigger some to set up barriers that extend the request to "speak with premodern language" to the ungenerous and ungenerative demand to "speak only with premodern language." Such walls seem easier to build between the past and trans studies for those who do not depend on such crossings and for those for whom such walls excuse ignorance on the grounds that there is nothing there to learn on the other side. For some, the demand that we speak premodern means that we should completely abandon the accent of trans studies. The claim that one can be transgender in a medieval way is rebuffed by those for whom transgender is definitely modern. In the process of working between medieval and transgender studies, I have found allies with wisdom and support, and warnings in fields such as postcolonial studies and translation studies. They know the dangers and feel the significance of the polyglot, the need to code-switch, but also the power that comes with thinking through trans-lation: the bringing across, the living between, the hybridity, and fluidity. Trans historical studies as well as transhistorical studies echo and intersect with transnational and trans linguistic experiences. In the position of the historical polyglot we see the shimmering edges between identities like eunuch and transsexual, when we must speak with trans accents when we may say eunuchs are trans in this way or with premodern accents when we may say that transsexuals are eunuchs in that way—even as we are caught silent or grasping for new or modified language when there are no words yet to speak of the transitions in between.

Ochoa: I agree, I think the determinism that I discussed above is very similar to the "coloniality of the present" in Jack's lecture. I appreciate M. W. Bychowski's use of code-switching as a metaphor for this kind of (inter)disciplinarity. To do this work, we need to be agile, fluent, fluid, and thoughtful. We can translate to facilitate multiple kinds of exchange, not to create equivalences. But the work of translation is tricky—while we may have dexterity with multiple codes, we have to be attentive to the meaning we produce in the translation, as even putting, to use M. W.'s example, transsexuals and eunuchs in the same frame can be received as a hurtful or violent act. Sel Hwahng (2009) does this in his work about people he calls Korean sex slaves to the Japanese army in World War II, often called "comfort women." In the article, he makes an early posthuman move that I think is jarring to many readers, essentially describing these people as a kind of sanitary device. I so appreciate this article, and I think, analytically, he is very right in terms of how the Japanese army saw them. He asks us to think of these people within the frame of trans studies not to support an identitarian claim but to understand how power, institutions, technologies, and empire shape bodies and genders. However, there is inherent violence in referring to people who use the term *comfort women* (and a number of other terms) to refer to themselves, and who employ the discourse of humanism and human rights to advocate for themselves. Sel is able to do the cultural translation necessary to reduce the harm of this act, but many readers will stop at the claim and understand the move to be a dehumanizing one. I don't think this means we should shy away from doing this hard work, but it's not easy.

TSQ: *Susan Stryker and Aren Aizura's formulation of "trans-historicity" in their 2013 coedited* Transgender Studies Reader 2 *served as a partial impetus for us to explore the topic of "trans*historicities" here in this issue of* TSQ. *How might the concept of historicity speak to you in ways that "history" itself might not? What does* historicity *do for you, in your thinking, that the term* history *itself might not?*

Long: I particularly appreciate Stryker and Aizura's emphasis on the "strangeness of the past." I think this vision of historicity is a call to respect that strangeness, rather than colonizing it (to pick up on Halberstam's formulation cited above). We are likely to see more in the past, representations and formulations that we could not imagine to be there from within our own framework, richer experiences of trans* and intersex than we assumed would be there. Our practice of history seems to tend to see a movement in a particular direction or toward a particular conceptual goal; historicity allows us to hold in our minds (and yes, our imaginations) disparate moments of others' experiences that we cannot fully experience ourselves, and which we can try to understand, but over which we cannot have mastery.

Snorton: One way to distinguish history from historicity is to think about the difference between an account of the past and an accounting for an account of the past. As Kathleen Long states, historicity cannot be a performance of mastery, as it will always be a rhetorical and methodological practice that reads the political dimensions of history. That is to say, historicity implies that time is not the only (or even primary) coordinate of the past.

Bychowski: The roundtable that we share here is an excellent example of trans*-historicity, one that by design should continue to grow and consider those whose place at the table has not yet been recognized or actualized. Like a roundtable, history sometimes gives (or tries to give) a sense of a common shared story and experience of time, which, while allowing for different perspectives, amounts to a cisgender-centric and cis-subjective account presented implicitly as objective reality. On the other hand, Stryker and Aizura frame historicity alongside "temporality" to interrupt the givenness that might otherwise lead to compulsory-cisgender histories. How might different histories present different senses of temporality? Historicity seems to designate a wide range of stories and experiences of time that work together, next to, or against one another to more accurately reflect historical pasts, more so than one master narrative or even representative (i.e., token) narratives that are present, asked to merely stand (or sit) and be counted. In short, trans*historicity works to leave space for the narratives not yet at the table or to leave time for other senses of time to not only be counted but to transform what counts as history. I begin to imagine a table of trans*historicity that is not simply round but recursive, growing and bending back on itself but ever veering beyond the circles that came before.

Ochoa: History is to historicity as time is to temporality. The notion of historicity allows me to pay attention to how people *experience* history, how they walk around with it, and what the structure of those stories might be. In thinking through this idea long ago, I was very influenced by the anthropologist Victor Turner's essay "Religious Paradigms and Political Action" (1976), in which he uses his concept of social drama to analyze what I ended up thinking about as the walking-around history of everyday people. In the essay, he suggests that these paradigms—these story structures we carry around with us—animate and inform our behaviors. Trans*historicity, then, is not only the desire to augment those paradigms; it is also about embedding senses of temporality that emerge from trans existences in historiography more broadly, and developing ways of seeing/sensing/detecting historical materials relevant to these stories. In the end it's to reshape paradigms of historicity and transform history as a field of study.

M. W. Bychowski is an Anisfield-Wolf SAGES Fellow and full-time lecturer at Case Western Reserve University. She is the author of ""Unconfessing Transgender" from *Accessus: A Journal of Premodern Literature and New Media* (2016) and "The Isle of Hermaphrodites" from *post-medieval: a journal of medieval cultural studies* (2018). She has several forthcoming articles, including ones on transgender saints, premodern sex change operations, medieval manuscripts, and trans suicide in the Middle Ages. Currently, she is developing a book length study of transgender in medieval literature and history.

Howard Chiang is an assistant professor of history at the University of California, Davis. He is the author of *After Eunuchs: Science, Medicine, and the Transformation of Sex in Modern China* (2018) and editor of *Sexuality in China: Histories of Power and Pleasure* (2018).

Jack Halberstam is professor of gender studies and English at Columbia University. He is the author of *Skin Shows: Gothic Horror and the Technology of Monsters* (1995), *Female Masculinity* (1998), *In a Queer Time and Place* (2005), *The Queer Art of Failure* (2011), *Gaga Feminism: Sex, Gender, and the End of Normal* (2012), and, most recently, a short book titled *Trans*: A Quick and Quirky Account of Gender Variance* (2018). Halberstam is currently working on several projects, including a book titled *Wild Thing: Queer Theory after Nature*, on queer anarchy, performance, protest culture, and the intersections between animality, the human, and the environment.

Jacob Lau is a Carolina Postdoctoral Fellow through the Program for Faculty Diversity in Women's and Gender Studies at the University of North Carolina at Chapel Hill. Along with Cameron Partridge, he is coeditor of Michael Dillon/Lobzang Jivaka's 1962 trans memoir *Out of the Ordinary: A Life of Spiritual and Gender Transitions* (2016), for which he also coauthored an introduction.

Kathleen P. Long is professor of French at Cornell University. She is preparing a translation into English of *The Island of Hermaphrodites* (*L'isle des hermaphrodites*) and a book-length study of the relationship between early modern discourses of monstrosity and modern discourses of disability.

Marcia Ochoa is associate professor of feminist studies at the University of California, Santa Cruz, and founding advisory board cochair of El/La Para Translatinas, a transgender Latina social justice organization in San Francisco's Mission District. An anthropologist specializing in the ethnography of media, Ochoa is the author of *Queen for a Day: Transformistas, Beauty Queens, and the Performance of Femininity in Venezuela* (2014) and coeditor of *GLQ*. She is at work on a new project, *Ungrateful Citizenship*, which documents the work of El/La Para Translatinas and the terms on which transgender women from Latin America who live in the United States and Europe participate in, belong to, and are recognized by society.

C. Riley Snorton is professor of English language and literature at the University of Chicago. He is the author of *Black on Both Sides: A Racial History of Trans Identity* (2017) and *Nobody Is Supposed to Know: Black Sexuality on the Down Low* (2014).

Note

1.   In chorus with others, I use *black study* to refer to the antidisciplinary production of black thought that appears in, across, and beyond the disciplines of black studies, Africana studies, African American studies, and African diaspora studies.

References

Allen, Jafari S. 2012. Introduction to "Black/Queer/Diaspora at the Current Conjuncture." Special issue, *GLQ* 18, nos. 2–3: 211–48.

Bearden, Elizabeth B. 2017. "Before Normal, There Was Natural: John Bulwer, Disability, and Natural Signing in Early Modern England and Beyond." *PMLA* 131, no. 1: 33–50.

Benjamin, Walter. 1968. "Theses on the Philosophy of History." In *Illuminations*, edited by Hannah Arendt, translated by Harry Zohn, 253–64. New York: Schocken.

Boellstorff, Tom, et al. 2014. "Decolonizing Transgender: A Roundtable Discussion." *TSQ* 1, no. 3: 419–39.

Chakrabarty, Dipesh. 2000. *Provincializing Europe: Postcolonial Thought and Historical Difference*. Princeton, NJ: Princeton University Press.

Chiang, Howard. 2012. *Transgender China*. New York: Palgrave Macmillan.

———. 2018. *After Eunuchs: Science, Medicine, and the Transformation of Sex in Modern China*. New York: Columbia University Press.

Clare, Eli. 2015. *Exile and Pride: Disability, Queerness, and Liberation*. Durham, NC: Duke University Press.

Cua Lim, Bliss. 2009. *Translating Time: Cinema, the Fantastic, and Temporal Critique*. Durham, NC: Duke University Press.

Derrida, Jacques. 1980. "The Law of Genre." Translated by Avital Ronell. *Critical Inquiry* 7, no. 1: 55–81.

Dillon, Michael/Lobzang Jivaka. 2016. *Out of the Ordinary: A Life of Gender and Spiritual Transitions*, edited by Jacob Lau and Cameron Partridge. New York: Fordham University Press.

Dinshaw, Carolyn, et al. 2007. "Theorizing Queer Temporalities: A Roundtable Discussion." *GLQ* 13, nos. 2–3: 177–95.

Duval, Jacques. 1612. *Des hermaphrodits et accouchemens des femmes: Et traitement qui est requis pour les relever en santé* (*On Hermaphrodites, Childbirth, and the Treatment That Is Required to Restore Women to Health Afterwards*). Rouen: David Geuffroy.

Ferguson, Gary. 2013. "Early Modern Transitions: From Montaigne to Choisy." In "Transgender France," edited by Todd Reeser. Special issue, *L'esprit créateur* 53, no. 1: 145–57.

Foucault, Michel. 2003. *Abnormal: Lectures at the Collège de France, 1974–1975*. Edited by Valerio Marchetti and Antonella Salomoni. Translated by Graham Burchell. New York: Picador.

Getsy, David J. 2014. "Capacity." *TSQ* 1, nos. 1–2: 47–49.

Gower, John. 2006. *Confessio Amantis*. 3 vols. Edited by Russell A. Peck. Translated by Andrew Galloway. Kalamazoo, MI: Medieval Institute.

Greenblatt, Stephen. 1988. *Shakespearean Negotiations: The Circulation of Social Energy in Renaissance England*. Berkeley: University of California Press.

Hartman, Saidiya. 2008. "Venus in Two Acts." *Small Axe* 12, no. 2: 1–14.

Hwahng, Sel. 2009. "Vaccination, Quarantine, and Hygiene: Korean Sex Slaves and No. 606 Injections during the Pacific War of World War II." *Substance Use and Misuse* 44, no. 12: 1768–1802.

Keeling, Kara. 2009. "Looking for M—: Queer Temporality, Black Political Possibility, and Poetry from the Future." *GLQ* 15, no. 4: 565–82.

Lorde, Audre. 1982. *Zami: A New Spelling of My Name*. Watertown, MA: Persephone.

Martínez, María Elena. 2014. "Archives, Bodies, and Imagination: The Case of Juana Aguilar and Queer Approaches to History, Sexuality, and Politics." *Radical History Review*, no. 120: 159–82.

Meadow, Tey. 2018. *Trans Kids: Being Gendered in the Twenty-First Century*. Oakland: University of California Press.

Morgan, Jennifer. 2004. *Laboring Women: Reproduction and Gender in New World Slavery*. Philadelphia: University of Pennsylvania Press.

Montaigne, Michel de. 1965. *The Complete Essays of Montaigne*. Translated by Donald Frame. Stanford, CA: Stanford University Press.

———. 1983. *Journal de voyage*. Edited by Fausta Garavini. Paris: Gallimard.

Ochoa, Marcia. 2007. "Becoming a Man in Yndias: The Mediations of Catalina de Erauso, the Lieutenant Nun." In *Technofuturos: Critical Interventions in Latina/o Studies*, edited by Nancy Raquel Mirabal and Agustín Laó-Montes, 53–76. Lanham, MD: Lexington.

———. 2016. "Los Huecos Negros: Sodomy, Cannibalism, and the Failure of Modernity in Tierra Firme." *Genders* 1, no. 2. www.colorado.edu/genders/2016/05/19/los-huecos-negros -cannibalism-sodomy-and-failure-modernity-tierra-firme.

Scott, Joan. 1991. "The Evidence of Experience." *Critical Inquiry* 17, no. 4: 773–97.

Silko, Leslie Marmon. 1991. *Almanac of the Dead: A Novel.* New York: Simon and Schuster.

Spillers, Hortense. 1987. "Mama's Baby, Papa's Maybe: An American Grammar Book." *Diacritics* 17, no. 2: 64–81.

Strathern, Marilyn. 2004. *Partial Connections.* Walnut Creek, CA: Alta Mira.

Stryker, Susan. 2008. "Transgender History, Homonormativity, and Disciplinarity." *Radical History Review*, no. 100: 145–57.

Stryker, Susan, and Aren Z. Aizura, eds. 2013. *The Transgender Studies Reader 2.* New York: Routledge.

Traub, Valerie. Forthcoming. Introduction to *Ovidian Transversions: "Iphis and Ianthe," 1300–1650*, edited by Valerie Traub, Patricia Badir, and Peggy McCracken. Edinburgh: Edinburgh University Press.

Turner, Victor W. 1976. "Religious Paradigms and Political Action: The Murder in the Cathedral of Thomas Becket." In *The Biographical Process: Studies in the History and Psychology of Religion*, edited by Frank Reynolds and Donald Capps, 153–86. The Hague: Mouton.

Feeling Backward with *Albert Nobbs*

ANSON KOCH-REIN

Abstract Drawing on Heather Love and Dan Irving, this piece argues that Rodrigo García's film *Albert Nobbs* has a place in transgender studies because it offers a cinematic opportunity to engage in feeling backward, to view sadness, dysphoria, and loneliness as part of an important, (re)current register of transgender affect.
Keywords transgender affect, capitalism, Heather Love, *Albert Nobbs*, *The Well of Loneliness*

> The experience of queer historical subjects is not at a safe distance from contemporary experience; rather, their social marginality and abjection mirror our own. The relation to the queer past is suffused not only by feelings of regret, despair, and loss but also by the shame of identification.
> —Heather Love, *Feeling Backward*

The marginality and abjection of the queer subjects in *Albert Nobbs* mirrors our own despite layers of historical distance. Rodrigo García's 2011 film, based on a 1927 novella by George Moore, which had previously been adapted into a play by Simone Benmussa ([1979] 2012), stars Glenn Close, who, having played the role of Albert in the 1982 off-Broadway production, coproduced and coauthored the film's script. The almost thirty-year delay between Close's first encounter with the role and the movie adaptation is not the only way in which *Albert Nobbs* is belated, queerly fallen out of time, and yet not at a safe distance. With a story that's contemporaneous with Radclyffe Hall's 1928 novel, *Albert Nobbs* feels—relates to the queer past—like a 2011 *Well of Loneliness*.

Albert Nobbs (Glenn Close) works as a butler at the Morrison Hotel in late nineteenth-century Dublin, saving up money for his dream to buy a tobacconist shop. When his employer, Mrs. Baker, orders him to share his bed with house painter Hubert Page (Janet McTeer) for a night, Albert, in fighting off a flea, reveals his chest binder and swears Hubert to secrecy. The next day, Hubert shares that he, too, has been living as a man since escaping from an abusive husband and now lives with his wife Cathleen. Albert hesitantly tells Hubert about his traumatic backstory of having been gang raped before starting to live as a man. Inspired by the domestic bliss at the Pages' household and imagining a wife behind the counter of his future tobacconist's shop, Albert soon begins awkwardly courting Helen Dawes, a maid at the hotel. Helen is newly in love with Joe Mackins, who, passing himself off as a boilerman, had arrived at the hotel the same night as Hubert. Joe encourages Helen's "walking out" with Albert to see if she can get some money off her unwanted suitor for emigrating to America together. Helen, uncomfortable with the arrangement, goes on a few dates to receive presents from Albert. Nobody's dreams come true: typhoid quarantines the hotel and puts Albert out of commission for a while. On recovering, he finds that Hubert has lost Cathleen to the disease. Helen gets pregnant from Joe. Albert offers to marry her but is rejected. Joe is desperate and wants to run off to America alone. When Albert tries to break up a fight between Joe and Helen, Joe pushes him against a wall, cracking his skull. In the commotion, Albert crawls off into his bedroom and dies. Alone. In the epilogue, Hubert comes to the hotel, which Mrs. Baker is now renovating with the money she took from Albert's room. He finds a destitute Helen, who has been blackmailed into working for free because she is afraid the baby will be taken from her as a single mother. He promises to take care of Helen and the child, little baby "Albert Joseph."

This plot summary only insufficiently conveys how viscerally the film engages all the elements of "backwardness" that Heather Love recommends to our attention in *Feeling Backward*: "Shyness, ambivalence, failure, melancholia, loneliness, regression, victimhood, heartbreak, antimodernism, immaturity, self-hatred, despair, shame. I describe backwardness both as a queer historical structure of feeling and as a model for queer historiography" (2007: 146). This historical structure of feeling, contested when it comes to readings of *The Well* as a classic source for lesbian, transgender, and queer scholarship, received almost no scholarly mention when presented in *Albert Nobbs* in 2011. For movie reviewers, the intensity of backward feelings proved too much, not distant enough. While praising Close's and McTeer's performances, most reviews reject the titular character harshly. Mick LaSalle characterizes Albert as so "out of touch and desperate" as to create "an undeniable ick factor" for the audience, a "repellent person, one who is alert to others in a way that would freak people out" (2012). Angie Errigo calls the film "not only sad, sad, sad but dreary and unpleasant, peopled with largely unsympathetic characters," including "a central character so miserable and pathetic it is hard to care" (2012). In her discussion of *The Well*, Love notes the "underlying discomfort with the extreme sadness" (2007: 101) present in critical readings of the novel. In the reviewers' responses to *Albert Nobbs*, this discomfort is at the heart of the overall reception of the film.

In one of the few academic takes on the film, Charlotte McIvor (2013) follows the tradition of classification established by readings of *The Well*, arguing that, in its portrayal of "Hubert and her wife," *Albert Nobbs* "decisively centralizes the lesbian and queer undertones of Moore's novella" (94). Indeed, Hubert and Cathleen are presented as a loving couple figuring moments of queer happiness. Even after Cathleen's death, Hubert's masculine swagger and flirty confidence set a hopeful tone in the movie's final scene. McIvor reads this comparatively successful sexual model as lesbian and changes Hubert's pronoun accordingly. But unlike movies that offer lesbian/sexual redemption through a desiring lover in ways that can feel like trans erasure (I'm looking at you, *Boys Don't Cry* [dir. Kimberly Peirce, 1999]), *Albert Nobbs* does not resolve Albert's challenges into an alternative past and future, even if Albert is inspired by Hubert's having a wife. What "having a wife" would mean for Albert—who wonders to himself if Hubert told his wife "that he is a woman" before or after they got married—remains open. Hubert and Albert are not portrayed simply as mirror images. They are not just the failing, inhibited, and romantically successful versions of the same story. They both live as men, but how, why, and what this means for them cannot easily be put into identity labels. Of course, all the familiar scripts of historical or theoretical identification can be run on the film: Is Albert trans? Is he a lesbian? Is he "cross-dressing" for economic reasons or as a result of sexual trauma? The film offers fodder for all these narratives. There is even a truly cringe-inducing scene of Hubert and Albert walking awkwardly to the beach dressed in Cathleen's dresses. On the beach, Albert breaks into an uncharacteristic run, exploring the freedom of movement unencumbered by the trappings of binders and masculine reserve, until he trips and falls. They both return to their lives after this moment of what it looks like when a 2011 film imagines a character considering detransitioning in the late nineteenth century. If based on all these tropes, McIvor wants to call Hubert's version of female masculinity "lesbian," it at least marks the way in which sexuality seems central to Hubert's life. However, Albert's experience is quite clearly not centered on sexual desire and instead is a lonely experience of gender, inviting viewers into the queer historical structure of feeling that Love calls backwardness. As in the following exchange with Hubert, while Albert seems often out of touch with how to fit into the social world, his identification is firm: "What's your name?"—"Albert."—"Your real name?"—"Albert." It is difficult to look backward through the lenses of twenty-first-century identities at *Albert Nobbs*. Love encourages us to instead feel backward: "Backward feelings serve as an index to the ruined state of the social world; they indicate continuities" (2007: 27). Feeling backward, queer historiography is then not about identifying Albert, but about identifying with Albert through the continuities of a—still—ruined social world.

Unlike the upper-class story of *The Well*, *Albert Nobbs* weaves its story of dysphoria and social alienation into a working-class fabric. If, as Dan Irving (2008) suggests, "scholars within trans studies rarely contextualize trans identities, subjectivities, and activism within historical and contemporary capitalist relations" (39), then *Albert Nobbs* offers a story with much need for such a contextualization. To see Albert's masculinity in relation to class, we must pay attention to how the film compares Albert and Joe. The scene in which Hubert catches Albert struggling with the flea in his binder/corset is intercut with scenes of Joe Mackins's frantic attempts to fix the boiler. In fixing it, Joe passes as a boilerman and secures a position as the hotel's handyman. In realizing that Hubert will keep his "secret," Albert sustains his passing, which has allowed him to work there, as well. Intercutting their visible sense of relief, the film suggests that passing is not just for people like Albert. Albert and Joe, in other words, have a lot in common: they are both courting Helen (even if, in the case of Joe this means kissing her before even asking her name, and in Albert's this means barely kissing her even after she has complained that this would have to precede a marriage proposal), they both pass under conditions of capitalist exploitation, and neither one can make good on his dreams or his promises to Helen. Joe cannot get capital to pay for his dream to go to America, or even step into the role of provider for the baby, and Albert cannot convert his savings into social or sexual capital. Irving writes that "appeals to mainstream society to accept transsexuals as legitimate subjects often emphasized their valuable contributions to society through their labor" (2008: 40), and the movie appears to establish Albert's deservingness through his work, following a logic of productivity as value under capitalism and as a signal of masculinity. The movie opens with Albert working meticulously, and he is repeatedly shown to remember guests' particular preferences and allergies. He also keeps working through the first stages of typhoid. However, saving money, the accumulation of capital to start his business, is ultimately not presented as a commendable trait. Rather, Albert is shown as a miser, repeatedly counting money on his bed and caring more about tracking his budget in a little black book than about his date with Helen. He does not have sexual capital, nor does he demand sexual favors in exchange for the presents to Helen, which creates discomfort in Helen, who is used to heterosexuality as a market exchange. He has no capital, he just has money, hidden under the floorboards of his room only to be stolen after his death by his employer. As much as Albert strives to be what Irving calls "the good, deserving citizen who cultivates an entrepreneurial spirit" (2008: 52), this spirit remains stuck in the role of server rather than entrepreneur. His respectability as an almost invisible worker ("Such a kind little man"—"Who?"—"Nobbs") is turned into disgraced notoriety when his death causes a scandal reported in newspapers. His labor amounts to nothing either in life, because his capital cannot be converted, or in death, when he cannot use heteronormative structures of inheritance, accumulation, and intergenerational wealth to pass it on.

Albert Nobbs has a place in trans studies, not to rehash, defend, or question the historical opacity of "living as a man" but because it offers a filmic opportunity to engage in feeling backward: to view sadness, dysphoria, and loneliness not with open hostility but as an important (re)current register of transgender affect. Feeling backward, Love refuses "to write off the most vulnerable, the least presentable, and all the dead" (2007: 30). Writing off dead Albert for the promise of a future with Hubert leaves us in denial of the ways in which Albert's marginality and abjection continue to resonate sometimes, somewhere, for some. You are feeling backward with *Albert Nobbs* when the survival skill of being "alert to others" makes you repellent, when passing gives you safety but invisibility feels like crushing loneliness, when shyness and inexperience are creepy, when your money is worth nothing. What's at stake is the question of "how to make a future backward enough that even the most reluctant among us might want to live there" (Love 2007: 163). Let's make the future backward enough for those who may feel the shame of identification with *Albert Nobbs*.

Anson Koch-Rein is a visiting assistant professor of gender, women's, and sexuality studies at Grinnell College.

References

Benmussa, Simone. (1979) 2012. *The Singular Life of Albert Nobbs*. Richmond, UK: Alma.

Errigo, Angie. 2012. "Albert Nobbs Review." *Empire*, April 10. www.empireonline.com/movies/albert-nobbs/review/.

Hall, Radclyffe. (1928) 2015. *The Well of Loneliness*. London: Penguin Classic.

Irving, Dan. 2008. "Normalized Transgressions: Legitimizing the Transsexual Body as Productive." *Radical History Review*, no. 100: 38–59.

LaSalle, Mick. 2012. "'Albert Nobbs' Review: Story a Little Too Creepy." *SFGate*, January 27. www.sfgate.com/movies/article/Albert-Nobbs-review-Story-a-little-too-creepy-2728101.php.

Love, Heather. 2007. *Feeling Backward: Loss and the Politics of Queer History*. Cambridge, MA: Harvard University Press.

McIvor, Charlotte. 2013. "'Albert Nobbs,' Ladies and Gentlemen, and Quare Irish Female Erotohistories." *Irish University Review* 43, no. 1: 86–101. doi.org/10.3366/iur.2013.0057.

Moore, George. (1927) 2011. *Albert Nobbs: A Novella*. Harmondsworth, UK: Penguin.

Sex Time Machine for Touching the Transcestors

JULIAN B. CARTER

"Sex Time Machine" is an archival experiment originally created as a gallery take-away for visitors to curator E. G. Crichton's exhibit Out/Look and the Birth of the Queer *(September 2017–January 2018) at the GLBT History Museum in San Francisco. It depicts embodied intimacy as the center of the local queer/trans cultures it documents—a sliver of the early 1990s, layered into a few months of 2017. It attempts to enact, in text and illustration, something of the social experience of bringing the past into the present. It also explores how bodies both are and are not archives and how archives do and do not have room for our bodies in them.*

Prologue

EG's email 12/15/16

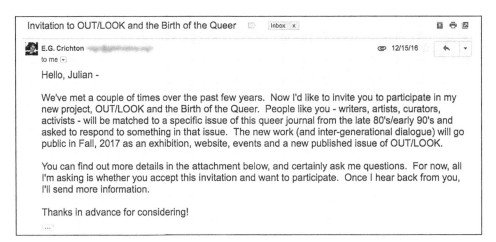

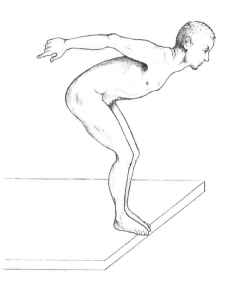

We invite you to dive into the archive, think about our queer history, and use the issue we send you as a score for creating something new and provocative in the medium of your choice.

Time travel is not simply fun. Relics of early 1990s SF crackle with intense affect, unresolved and irresolvable. In 1991 it seems like everyone is stimulated, everything is urgent, we're too young to die and we never thought we'd make it this far, we are angry and hurt by the straight world and we don't always know how to stop fighting when we try to get close to other queers. We turn to one another anyway. We're dazzling, we crackle, we rustle and gleam with the energy of battle. Crazy sexy cool, we fuck because that's how we know we're still alive. I keep making bad jokes about having an issue with the past. Diving in, I confront how lonesome I was at the interface between erotic terri- tories defined and defended by gen- der. Leather helped protect me from the friction burns. Holding on tight with my thighs, my teeth, I braced against the fear that even queer wasn't big enough to hold me. Rememory is hard. It brings back the full force of my grati- tude for the company I found there in the gender DMZ. The love. The lessons in survival.

Chapter 1: Out of the Archives, into the Sheets

I couldn't deal with Queer Nation meetings—too much righteousness in too small a space. But the protest culture rocked. We were glorious in our defiance, our outrage and our outrageousness, our determination; I'm still proud of the way we made a new kind of beauty in all our exhaustion and grief.

That fall, a full scholarship with stipend made it possible for me to start a PhD program in history at Irvine. At a welcome reception with strawberries and white wine, a kindly senior faculty member tried to engage me in conversation by asking what I'd been doing since I graduated from college. I said "making sex toys for gay leathermen." The party went silent as though I'd screamed

RAVING HOMOSEXUAL

but I swear I wasn't trying to be confrontational. I just couldn't see the virtue in disappearing myself. My unruly genderqueer embodiment, my class alienation— these were enough to navigate in that white-genteel space without taking on the responsibility for resolving the discomfort my presence raised for others. The project of erasing queerness from the world didn't need my help. Over 20,000 people died of AIDS-related infections in the United States in 1991, bringing the total AIDS deaths in the US to 156K (amfAR 2018; FACT 2018).

These days, my corner of the queer cultural web vibrates at regular intervals with commentary on the desire to have everybody feel safe. I can't help but remember how we once articulated the difference between "safe" and "safer" in relation to sex. We knew safety wasn't possible. That's why we developed social techniques to take care of ourselves and each other. Simple things you could whisper to a stranger, like *cum on me, not in me*.

Cum on me, not in me: a Dionysian statement, at once an invitation and a battle cry. I love the way it reframes the link between sexual community and infection. The normative assumption in those days was that we wouldn't be dying if we'd kept our pleasures silent and invisible and isolated, the way straight people felt comfortable with us. Against the reproach that queer freedom caused the AIDS crisis, it flaunts our erotic creativity as a solution to the epidemic. *Cum on me, not in me* brings the risk to the party, splashes it across the surface of the skin.

The rhetoric continues to thrill me—so much that sometimes I forget that JJO parties weren't my thing. Phallic faggotry wasn't socially or emotionally available to me in Orange County, and if there were LA scenes that might have been welcoming, I didn't know how to find them. Instead, I flowered in the Mission, five hundred miles north in the purple Edwardian where my hybridity made sense.

More accurately, I was allowed in the door on the first Saturday of every month. The rest of the time 455 14th Street was a faggot faerie sex palace. I longed to go work the glory holes at Tuesday Sucks. It was so close; but my leather daddy had persuaded the owner to allow pansexual kink parties there and was reluctant to risk his privileged access by sneaking me into men's events. When he brought me along for the hippie-casual conversations where business got discussed, I had strict instructions to keep my mouth shut and melt into the background like a good boy. They never asked about the stickers on my jacket, FAGDYKE and FUCK YOUR GENDER. I didn't mind. I had enough experience of disenfranchisement to feel at home in that particular erotic and historical margin, soaking up the past, listening to my elders talk about their dead and swap stories about sexual feats that took place when I was in day care.

Maybe that's why I've been dreaming about throwing a cross-generational JJO party at the archives.

THE GLBT HISTORICAL SOCIETY ARCHIVES & MUSEUM
PRESENTS
CUM ON ME NOT IN ME
a queer cross-generational

JACK & JILL OFF

touch the
queer past!

pass on
the pleasure!

LEARN WHY ARCHIVES REALLY STOCK GLOVES!

Such a party couldn't be a direct reenactment or reconstruction of the cultural moment; sexual communities morph as people age, or die, or move out of town, or just move on. But a carefully crafted event could re-create the sexual affect of the time and stimulate a kind of contemporary reflection that would let us explore the difference between now and then. *Out/Look* #11 ran articles documenting the emergence of Queer Nation, analyzing how gay men's porn informs lesbian erotics, describing the social dynamics of group masturbation. In fact, the whole issue crackles with all the boldness and discomfort of the early 1990s. What better way to reactivate both than to ask midlife queers to open themselves to the sexual energies of a new generation? The mix of vulnerability and bravado it arouses feels exactly right. So does the sense of humor teetering on the edge of bitter impossibility. Then, it was about the hopelessness of resisting mortality. Now we have to add the practical challenges of making the party work for everyone. What would persuade aging queers to make the energetic investment in going out? And how could I help people bridge gaps in generational experience and individual comfort with public sexual expression?

In my dream, the difficulties magically resolve themselves so the productive awkwardness has room to unfold. People joke about wearing gloves in the archives. Someone sits on the Xerox machine. We let our different mores rub up against one another, shyness and variations in sexual culture present among us in their fullness and without apology. Gradually the words slow down and we begin to transfer our lived queer sexual culture to one another directly, body to body; the young touch the accumulated past in the living flesh of the aging.

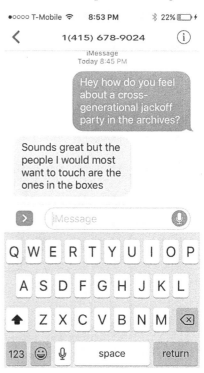

My dream, like Queer Nation itself, is about the collective power that's released when people get easy with both causing and experiencing salutary discomfort. Exploring the boundaries of what we're allowed to do is about more than the adrenaline rush of a loud *fuck you*. It is a countercultural ethic and a learned skill basic to building durable and diverse communities, and it's been developed in different ways with every resistant generation. Curious about how such dynamics play out in the present, I started texting my young friends.

Chapter 2: Transgenderational Touch and the Paper Body

My friend Zach has a thing about Lou Sullivan, the man who talked the medicopsychiatric establishment into expanding access to institutionally assisted transition to people who wanted to live gay lives. Lou died in early 1991, while the editors were collecting materials for *Out/Look* #11; a volunteer at the Gay and Lesbian Historical Society was processing his papers while Zach's body was taking form in his mother's uterus.

Zach has been fascinated by Lou for several years. He has read every word of Lou's diaries and all the secondary literature he can find; he has a rich sense of how his

peers imagine him, even struck a Saint Lou medal to comment on his current place in young transmen's cultural memory. But for all his studying Zach has never met anybody who knew Lou or who ran in his circles.

I decided to try to hook him up.

I started with my old friend Robert because while he wasn't personal friends with Lou, they overlapped in the community of San Francisco sex nerds—historians, sexologists, therapists, and the like. Against the common American tendency to valorize the individual personality it felt important to generate and transmit a sense of Lou's larger socio-sexual context. That, and Robert was unapologetically effeminate in a way that would have drawn Lou like honey. I liked the idea of Zach getting fucked by someone Lou would have wanted.

But Robert's neuralgia was pretty bad, so we went out for Thai food instead.

The only extant video of Lou shows him earnestly outlining the case for gay transsexuality to a medicopsychiatric audience. Watching him perform in an implausible blue suit, you would never intuit that he was an aspiring kinkster who named himself after Lou Reed. There's a chasm between Lou's rock&roll self-image and his much more restrained public presence. So Zach and I were especially delighted by Robert's memory of Lou kicked back, laconic, and funny, giving a talk with his feet up and his hands clasped behind his head.

The next morning I began to draw the Lou that Robert described. It felt right to materialize that cocky body on paper. Thus flattened and simplified, his sexual confidence can slip tidily into a box with other archived memories.

Drawing gave me a way to develop a physically engaged interactive relationship with Lou, who is otherwise unavailable to touch. Two dimensions are better than none. I trace his contours with my eyes, run my hands over his planes, curve his fingers under mine, and watch his smile develop in response. Only then do I recognize, by contrast, how much pain his face usually registers. Charmed to discover Lou's lighter side, and intrigued by drawing's power to document the reality of fantasy, I began making paper dolls of the different people he might have become. Then Zach showed me a photograph of a topless presurgery Lou. I wanted to draw him, and Zach said *He would have hated that.*

Then again Lou might have appreciated the joke. The paper breastplate sits on his paper torso awkwardly, like the misfitted garment it always was—and the sheer relief of removing tits so effortlessly! No justification or anesthesia required.

In contrast to the indexical claims that photographic images make, drawing lets me document the potency of the imagination. When I pick up a pencil I claim fantasy's world-generating force. When I add my drawings to the archive I expand its capacity to serve as an index to the motivating dreams of the dead. Still, there are limits to such expansion. Archives have truth standards to uphold and rules about who can add what to the collection. No filing system can hold the sadness of waking up to discover that, yet again, your body hasn't magically reconfigured itself; no acid-free box contains the full sensuous and affective range of gender rebellion at the beginning of the 1990s. We need more than one kind of repository for our longings.

So I drove Zach to rural Mendocino to spend two nights with Jordy and Marty at Twisted Timbers, their kinky art gallery, erotic playground, and columbarium. In 1991, when Lou was dying, Jordy gave up on the gender clinics. No blue suit for him; his leather paired better with black-market hormones. Now he

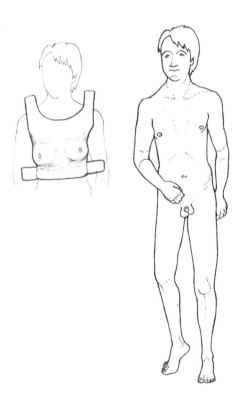

and Marty are grey and courteous custodians of queer intensities spanning seventeen decades.

They invite us to fondle the tip of that history. The leather jacket hanging from the ceiling; dead lovers under glass; books and paintings everywhere—they answer all our questions, and unearth more. Their sensual appreciation animates the relics with which they surround themselves and whose tales spring easily to their tongues, eager to pass into new mouths, looking for a chance to replicate in fresh contexts. Their home is less an archive than a provocation. There are moments when it seems that something might happen. But Jordy injured his knee and they've been cooped up inside too much lately, and they opt to take us to the local drive-through tree. They invite us to return in summer, when the dungeon has shaken off its winter dormancy and the meadow throbs with men.

Chapter 3: Between Before and After (for Jordan)

You said "It's odd how queer generations work; one of my housemates is ten years younger than me but he transitioned seven years ago so I'm the baby." I nod. This kind of temporal pleating is common and amusing in my social world, where creative life paths result in unpredictable generational sequences. You were born when I was twelve but we met as peers; your step-kids are close to my daughter's age. Now as you prepare for top surgery the texture of our connection changes and I find myself reconstituted as the daddy in this relationship.

Score: The consultation before the consultation before surgery. A sculpture for 5 hours in three trans lives.

1. *Gathering*: Intentional shared silence, reading in the sun. (2 hours)
2. *Closeness*: Rest your head on my chest while I lean on my boyfriend's broad shoulder in a breathing braid. (20 minutes)
3. *Call*: Tell us what you fear and what you want to know about top surgery. (10 minutes)
4. *Response*: We share the parts of our stories relevant to your questions. (20 minutes; may continue over dinner)
5. Nourishment: Dinner. (40 minutes)
6. *Release:* Our naked skin opening together in the sauna. (45 minutes)
7. *Anticipation*: Write out a list of questions to ask the surgeon. (30 minutes)
8. *Conclusion*: You have 60 seconds to tell us what concerns remain for you. You then turn your back and listen for 3 minutes as we discuss your concerns with each other. (4 minutes)

—April 17, 2017, Oakland, California

I tend to you with weekly phone calls, a half-day performance made just for you, bodywork and dinners, company and note-taking during consults, rides to and from the hospital. I offer you the nurturance my son can't accept, his adolescent drive for separation rendering him hostile and mute. And you respond with the gratitude of an adult, recognizing the preciousness of recognition.

There were several reasons I didn't get top surgery in 1991, when it first became clear to me that that needed to happen. Obviously the money was an issue. So was the fact that I didn't recognize myself in the guys I saw transitioning around me, or the chests that resulted from the available mastectomy techniques. Mostly, I didn't want to run from my embodiment. I wanted to know its painfulness and its erotic capacity alike, accepting my own bodily intensity and complexity the same way I'd accept those qualities in other queers. The dykes I knew called this "being in your body."

The erotic ethos of the early '90s leather community encouraged me to bring my breasts into focus in all their materiality, their substance as blood and lymph and nerves like my fingers and face. I always knew I'd cut them off; I just thought I owed it to myself to make friends with them first. I prepared myself for surgery by encountering the reality I wanted to change.

Did my young self confuse top surgery with dissociation? If so, there might have been a grain of truth in my error. Like shock, surgical procedure protects us from experiencing pain in the moment of trauma, and in so doing creates a kind of pocket in time.

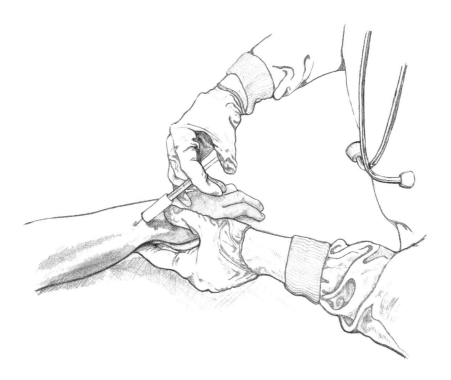

Your anesthesiologist is a lesbian my age or a little older. Her gloved hands are tender and firm as she enters your flesh. The drugs she administers induce amnesia, then excitation before your breathing slows. She inhabits those spacious seconds with you, standing still by your head, observing the steadiness of your pulse. It would be boring if your life weren't at stake.

I spend the same five hours drawing in a café, acutely alert to the clock, contemplating the experience of before becoming after.

A TIME LINE

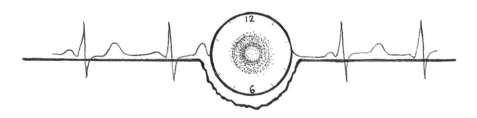

It's funny—I come to all your appointments but no matter how I try I can't seem to get there on time. Something about this surgery seems to mess with my sense of when I am.

I become your happy anchor, drawing on my past to hold you to now while you stretch yourself forward in trust and hope. Witnessing, I relive the ways my present was not my past's intended future. We mix retroactivity and anticipation. Our shared between is like a game of slip-and-slide on a wet timeline—we can't predict or control our trajectory. Occasionally the slide is pocked with trauma potholes when everything slows to a nightmare crawl. I'm not jealous of your easy healing, just a little bitter, and doing my best to stay with the startling love in your eyes.

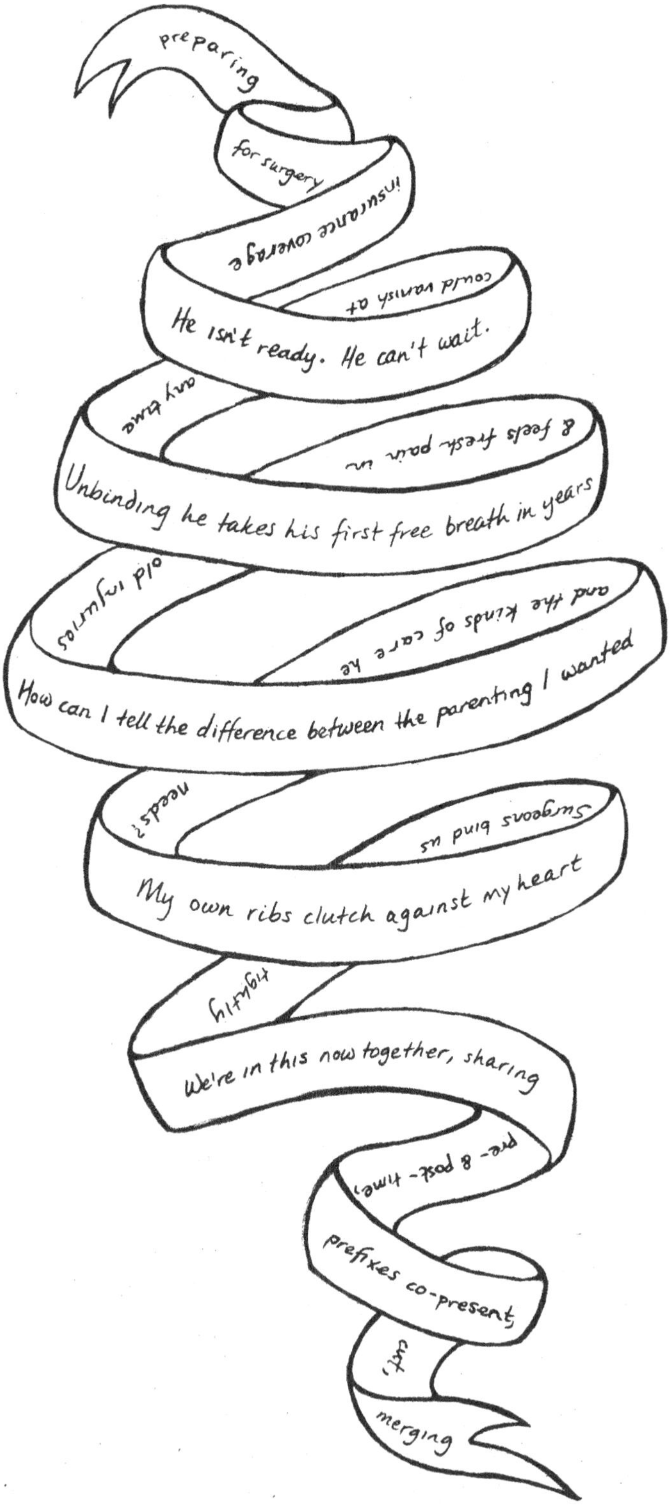
preparing
for surgery
insurance coverage
could vanish at
He isn't ready. He can't wait.
any time
& feels fresh pain in
Unbinding he takes his first free breath in years
old injuries
and the kinds of care he
How can I tell the difference between the parenting I wanted
needs?
Surgeons bind us
My own ribs clutch against my heart
tightly
We're in this now together, sharing
pre- & post- times,
prefixes co-present,
cut,
merging

Postscript

When I accepted the curator's invitation to respond to *Out/Look* #11, it wasn't entirely about the magazine and its contents. The thing that moved me was the larger event of opening this queer archive of the late 1980s and early 1990s.

Re-creation seemed more promising than documentation. I embarked on the *Transgenderational Touch Project*, a social sculpture/durational intimate performance piece exploring the relationship between interpersonal connection and individual change. I chose two younger trans-identified artists who were on the brink of major personal shifts (as I was in 1991) and committed myself to responding tenderly to their processes while they moved into new phases of their lives. My partners and I spent three months sharing their projects. As their dreams of impending futures merged with our varying knowledges of the past, their individual trajectories began to connect to larger historical and theoretical arcs. And while the frame of our exchange kept enlarging, its energy and contents grew more and more intimate. Another way to say this is that we entered one another's timelines.

Such work feels acutely necessary to me at this time. Right now we in the United States are looking at an enormous change in the embodied experience and practical meaning of transsexuality: the first cohort of trans children is transitioning before puberty at the same moment that economic support for access to health care is undermined and the sociocultural space for free exploration constricts. We have no way to anticipate what these accidentally synchronous changes will mean for how we collectively understand trans becoming and movement potential, but we do know we will need to pay extra attention to connecting across trans generations.

The *Transgenderational Touch Project* is therefore a gesture toward several different pasts, and a promise to nurture several different futures.

Julian B. Carter teaches embodiment theory and social practice at the California College of the Arts. Both his scholarship and his creative practice examine pleasure, power, and the bodily ways of being through which people experience self and community belonging. He is the author of *The Heart of Whiteness: Normal Sexuality and Race in America, 1890–1940* (2007) and shorter works in *GLQ, TSQ,* and the *Journal of the History of Sexuality,* as well as various anthologies, blogs, and zines. Carter dances, draws, and makes social sculptures as principle instigator of the performance group PolySensorium.

List of Drawings

p. 691: Jordan reading *Out/Look* #11 at their preconsultation retreat. Oakland, Spring 2017.

p. 692: Julian diving into the archives.

p. 693: Julian coming home from 455 14th St. at dawn. San Francisco, Summer 1991.

p. 695: JJO flyer is based on the ones we used to advertise parties at 455 14th St. Terminology of the JJO was coined in the 1980s by the Institute for the Advanced Study of Human Sexuality.

p. 697: Robert Lawrence posing in front of his big rig. Suisun Bay, California, Summer 1978.

p. 698: Lou Sullivan smiling. The chair is the one he sat in for his videotaped interviews with Ira Pauley, 1988–90. Excerpts available courtesy of the GLBT Historical Society at www.youtube.com/watch?v=SxgZNNX-v2g.

p. 699: Lou Sullivan paper doll and breastplate. Derived from photographs in the Louis Graydon Sullivan collection, GLBT Historical Society, San Francisco.

p. 700: Zach and Marty at the drive-through tree. Mendocino, Spring 2017.

p. 701: Score for Jordan's preconsult retreat, coauthored and co-led by Evan Lutz. Oakland, Spring 2017.

p. 702: Anesthesiologist installing IV port for Jordan's top surgery. UCSF, Spring 2017.

p. 703: Nipple timeline.

p. 704: Text ribbon drawn during Jordan's surgery. San Francisco, Spring 2017.

References

amfAR (American Foundation for AIDS Research). 2018. "Thirty Years of an HIV/AIDS: Snapshot of an Epidemic." www.amfar.org/thirty-years-of-hiv/aids-snapshots-of-an-epidemic/ (accessed June 19, 2018).

FACT (Fighting AIDS Continuously Together). 2018. "A Brief Timeline of AIDS." www.factlv.org/timeline.htm (accessed June 19, 2018).

A Journey beyond Normativity
The Syncretic Possibilities of Trans Studies

DAVID PRIMO

Trans Studies: The Challenge to Hetero/Homo Normativities
Edited by Yolanda Martìnez-San Miguel and Sarah Tobias
New Brunswick, NJ: Rutgers University Press, 2016. 255 pp.

Given the exponential growth in scholarship about gender and sexuality, there is still a paucity of works dealing extensively with the complexities of trans studies. The book *Trans Studies: The Challenge to Hetero/Homo Normativities*, edited by Yolanda Martínez-San Miguel and Sarah Tobias and published in 2016, fits perfectly in this gap. This anthology stems from the trans studies lecture series organized by the editors and Aren Aizura in 2012–13 at Rutgers' Institute for Research on Women. Taken together, the essays engage in a rich interdisciplinary debate that deals with several political, theoretical, and methodological issues that are crucial for this field of study.

The thirteen chapters here are organized in five sections. The first section, "Gender Boundaries within Educational Spaces," discusses how to create inclusive higher education environments for transgender people. This section interlocks academia and social policy with the intent of offering concrete proposals to transform university organization. The "Trans Imaginaries" section includes three essays that adopt the trans studies lens to interrogate the imaginaries created by canonical and innovative cultural production in theater, narrative, and cinema. These chapters offer thought-provoking insight to understand the role of literary theory and cultural studies in addressing the intersections between identity work, the burden of the colonial experience, and the racialization of desire. The "Crossing Borders/Crossing Genders" section offers a discussion on the ways in which normative assumptions about the body inform the creation of social policies

TSQ: Transgender Studies Quarterly ∗ Volume 5, Number 4 ∗ November 2018   **707**
DOI 10.1215/23289252-7090171   © 2018 Duke University Press

in the post-9/11 fight against terrorism. The three chapters in this section show that regulations and security technologies incorporate gender norms and racial stereotypes that hinder and inhibit the mobility of gender-variant people across national thresholds. "Trans Activism and Policy Work" addresses the intricacies of the relationship between trans activism, broader LGBTQ+ movements, and health issues (HIV). Finally, the "Transforming Disciplines and Pedagogy" section adopts the trans studies framework to rearticulate medical research and educational practices.

The brief description of the contents of this anthology highlights the wide variety of topics herein presented. The heterogeneity of the contents of the book may unsettle the reader, but the introductory chapter and the concluding one are both helpful in identifying the common threads shared across the five sections. The chapters align with a concerted effort in gender studies toward a more refined understanding of normativity, and, more specifically, they take the reader into the heart of the productive instability of concepts such as heteronormativity and homonormativity.

Beginning with the introduction, this book scrutinizes the separations between theory and practice, and between politics and academia. Indeed, it contains works dealing with empirical research, social policy, and activism alike. Some chapters also try to bridge these areas, as, for example, offering critical accounts of biometric surveillance in airport security (chap. 6). These connections offer, in addition to a description of the socioeconomic context of trans activism, a refined depiction of the uneven access to political and economic resources by trans and LGB activism. Further chapters point out some of the most crucial tensions produced by the academic institutionalization of trans studies, which resulted in neither a substantial increase in the number of trans people as faculty members, staff, and students at universities (chap. 2) nor an actual transformation of medical praxis for what concerns gender variances (chap. 12).

The organization of the book also blurs the compartmentalization of trans, queer, and women's studies, which led to heated debates among the areas' respective proponents. While recognizing the historical and political significance of the distinctions between these fields, the editors suggest that their mutual friction and magnetism—the challenge to gendered and sexual oppressive assumptions, and the attention to the complex interrelations among embodiment, bodies, and identities—might offer an opportunity for "a multivocal continuation of the problematization of gender" (4). The book does not define what should count as trans studies in a neat way. The theoretical entanglements, which are not limited to the three above-mentioned fields—including, for example, postcolonial studies—broaden the hermeneutic potential of trans studies. What I found to be most remarkable is that trans studies cease to be merely defined by the focus on gender-variant people. It becomes a fully fledged and privileged analytical frame for a "complex disarticulation between the definition of biological sex, culturally constructed gender and normative or nonnormative sexual desires" (7). As an illustration, Lucas Crawford's literary analysis of *The Unnamable* by Samuel Beckett (chap. 3) clearly shows the potential of trans studies, in conjunction with queer theories, to grasp the simultaneity of stickiness and instability in identity projects.

This theoretical engagement maintains and extends previous accounts of the multilayered divisions that are at play in a multitude of contexts, such as college policies (chap. 1) and airport security norms (chaps. 6 and 7). To put it another way, this book unpacks the LGBTQ+ acronym, with a specific focus on the trans category, pointing out that there is no easy dichotomy between emancipation and reproduction of the norm. For example, Aren Z. Aizura points out the underlying nationalist epistemic violence in trans-focused documentaries aimed at raising awareness about trans migrant asylum seekers. We can identify previous attempts in this direction, for instance, in the study by Eleonora Garosi (2012) about hegemonic transnormativity in politics of transitioning in the Italian context, which resulted in a tripartite model of gender transition trajectories—gender conformers, gender innovators, and gender benders. Nevertheless, *Trans Studies* overcomes the categorical approach—first and foremost the transsexual-transgender dichotomy—focusing on the processual dimension of the articulation of gendered subjectivation. Rather than enumerating a typology of gendered nonconformities, the essays expressively stress the relevance of the stratification processes at play. They unfold the entanglement of—by way of example but not limited thereto—persistent colonial inheritances (chap. 4), medical praxis (chap. 12), late capitalistic transnational economic strategies (chap. 5), and security policies (chap. 6) in which the production of the trans category takes place. Likewise, they markedly destabilize the very process of identification and self-naming by showing the pervasive interweaving of disciplinary strategies and lines of flight: "At the same time, the imposition and policing of this complex array of gender, racial, and sexual categories coerce both belonging to and transgression of their boundaries" (70). Last but not least, this volume lays the ground to transform these thick theoretical, empirical, and political dissertations into actual changes in social policies and practices, in particular for what concerns education (chap. 13) and the academy (chaps. 1 and 2).

A major issue with this book is the almost exclusive focus on North American countries and English-language texts —excepting the essays written by Keja Valens (chap. 4) and Jian Chen (chap. 5). For this reason, it is not easy to extend the discussions included in this book in other geographical contexts. Nevertheless, it would be unfair to consider this an actual limitation, and I believe that the eclectic theoretical exchanges offered in this anthology might be a powerful stimulation for further debates about trans studies in other countries.

In Italy, trans studies is extremely underrepresented and nearly absent in academic programs. Despite this, I am persuaded that a dialogue between trans studies and the so-called Italian theory (Gentili and Stimilli 2015)—a wide array of philosophical and political thoughts that emerged from the *operaismo* (an Italian working-class antiauthoritarian grassroots political movement that emerged in the 1970s from a rearticulation of Marxism)—would be highly productive, as demonstrated by previous attempts in this direction (Arietti et al. 2010). Italian theory shares with trans studies not only an enmeshment of theoretical engagement and political praxes but also the nonontological understanding of social categories. Notably, Italian theory conceptualizes social class more as an investment of social desire than a mere effect of social structure (Gentili 2002). This epistemological frame, in conjunction with the disarticulation of sex, gender, and sexuality, might draw attention to the process of subjectivation and self-constitution as a site to contest and unsettle gendered and sexual norms (Negri 2015), in dialogue with the "Trans Imaginaries" section in this book. Furthermore, a dialogue between these strands of study might, on the one hand, help locate trans studies within the context of neoliberal late capitalist governmentality and, on the other, balance the disembodied cisgender gaze that is still prevalent in Italian theory.

Overall, I deem this book to be an essential and complex contribution to the field of gender studies. Given the heterogeneity of its contents and the intricacies of the theoretical trajectories herein collected, this work might not be suitable as an introduction to trans studies for those new to this field. However, as a young researcher in gender studies and an LGBTQ+ activist, I found the reflections contained in this anthology very useful, notably because they offer a comprehensive overview of the intersections between trans subjectivities and communities, and cultural production and social policy. For this reason, the essays are extremely helpful and thought-provoking for researchers, social workers, practitioners, and activists willing to engage in a critical exploration of the analytical, practical, and syncretic opportunities of trans studies.

David Primo is a PhD student at the doctoral course Social Sciences: Interactions, Communications and Cultural Constructions in the Department of Philosophy, Sociology, Education, and Applied Psychology at the Università degli Studi di Padova (Italy). He studies queer perspective on critical studies on men and masculinities and LGBTQ+ youth cultures.

References

Arietti, Laurella, et al. 2010. *Elementi di critica trans (Elements of a Trans Critique)*. Rome: Manifestolibri.

Garosi, Eleonora. 2012. "The Politics of Gender Transitioning in Italy." *Modern Italy* 7, no. 14: 465–78. doi.org/10.1080/13532944.2012.706998.

Gentili, Dario. 2002. *Italian theory: Dall'operaismo alla biopolitica (Italian Theory: From the Operaismo to the Biopolitics)*. Bologna: Il Mulino.

Gentili, Dario, and Elettra Stimilli, eds. 2015. *Differenze Italiane. Politica e filosofia: Mappe e sconfinamenti (Italian Differences. Politics and Philosophy: Maps and Trespassings)*. Rome: DeriveApprodi.

Negri, Toni. 2015. "A proposito di Italian theory" ("About Italian Theory"). In Gentili and Stimilli 2015: 21–29.

The Shape of Desire

RAMZI FAWAZ

Abstract Bodies: Sixties Sculpture in the Expanded Field of Gender
David Getsy
New Haven, CT: Yale University Press, 2015. 372 pp.

David Getsy's magisterial book *Abstract Bodies: Sixties Sculpture in the Expanded Field of Gender* begins with a seemingly straightforward argument: in the 1960s, American sculptors turned to a range of nontraditional materials, and abstract or nonrepresentational sculptural forms, to reimagine the human body outside binary constructions of gender. These artists took up materials such as scrap metal, aluminum sheeting, crushed car parts, worn leather, zippers, buckles, and fluorescent bulbs in large-scale sculptural works that often appeared as assemblages of seemingly incompatible or chaotic parts, thereby invoking the human body without ever directly representing it. In so doing, they imagined the body taking on numerous shapes that could never be accurately pinned down as distinctly male or female, or else imagining so-called male and female body parts as interchangeable or fitting in unexpected ways that upended any easy ascription of gender to a material form. For instance, in chapter 3, Getsy explores how, in her early assemblage work, feminist sculptor Nancy Grossman produced massive three-dimensional canvases on which she carefully glued rubber tubes weaving in and out of zippers, the openings of leather shoe parts and biker jackets. These visually suggestive pieces invoked genital parts and orifices but confounded any straightforward attribution of particular genders to the components, or clearly defined points of entry, thereby allowing for a playful unhinging of parts from gendered bodies. As Getsy explains:

> The practice Grossman used to engage with abstraction—that of assemblage—increasingly brought her back to bodily imagery in the form of detached parts. . . .

TSQ: Transgender Studies Quarterly ★ Volume 5, Number 4 ★ November 2018
DOI 10.1215/23289252-7090626 © 2018 Duke University Press

> Her works do not look backward to a past wholeness from which her parts came. They wryly recombine them into new futures. The items she used, from the horse harnesses to the boots to the clichéd leather jackets, all pointed to the bodies they once clothed and held but also celebrated the new constellations they had become. (177)

Such innovations in abstract sculpture, Getsy stresses, were not merely self-serving or aesthetically sealed formal experiments but extended attempts to materialize emerging conceptions of nonbinary genders that were flooding the American imagination in the 1960s. This attempt to expand the range of ways that gender could be conceived and represented preoccupied the conceptual thought of artists as diverse as David Smith, John Chamberlain, Nancy Grossman, and Dan Flavin (the four central figures explored in Getsy's study), despite the fact that none of these artists explicitly claim to be, or directly identify with, the historical label *transsexual* or the more contemporary term *transgender*. Rather, Getsy states,

> The artists I discuss offered abstract bodies and, with them, open accounts of personhood's variability and possibility. . . . [T]hese works evoke the concept of the body without mimesis, producing a gap between that calling forth of the human and the presentation of artworks that resolutely refuse to provide an anchoring image of a body. In that gap, there grew new versions of genders, new bodily morphologies, and a new attention to the shifting and successive potentials of these categories. (41)

While seemingly simple on its face, Getsy's argument explodes two widely held assumptions in both art history and the study of gender, with monumental intellectual consequences. On the one hand, Getsy pushes back against the long-running assumption that the emergence of abstraction in contemporary sculpture and art was an attempt to escape the limits of bodily representation into a realm of nonrepresentational meaning. Rather, Getsy shows that the increasingly abstract sculptural forms repeatedly referenced the body in terms of size, scale, and allusion to abstracted human body parts; simultaneously, in interviews, journal entries, and personal notes, the artists themselves talked about their sculptures as fictional "people" or sexual objects, or else dedicated their work to actual persons, thereby linking an abstract work of art to a human being in the everyday world, even if only through reference to a proper name. Getsy's aim is to show the extraordinarily generative capacity of abstraction to call forth new ways of conceiving and inhabiting the gendered body, rather than its assumed tendency to alienate the viewer or refuse "reality" through reference to nonrepresentational forms. Writing about the innovative sculptural work of the contemporary transgender artist Cassils in his conclusion, Getsy sums up his position this way: "As the artists discussed in this book suggest, abstraction has capacity. It is productive and proliferative. Rather than an avoidance of representation, it must be considered an embrace of potentiality and a positing of the unforeclosed. Abstraction makes room. Because of this capaciousness, abstraction has emerged as urgent for a growing number of transgender and queer artists in recent years. It offers a position from which to imagine, recognize, or realize new possibilities" (277).

On the other hand, Getsy's claim boldly asserts that notions of gender transitivity and nonbinary genders can be perceived far outside immediate representations of human morphology or personal, lived experiences of embodiment. The radical implication of this latter argument is no less than this: gender transitivity is not only a lived or material experience attached to the bodies of those who claim transgender identity or embodiment (though it is certainly and urgently that); it *also* describes a set of logics, or ways of thinking and perceiving the world, outside binary conceptions of gender that can potentially be shared by everyone and identified in a vast range of cultural forms, aesthetic materials, and art practices that have implications for material bodies and subjectivities. Transgender as a mode of thinking is everywhere, then, but always apparent in particular and distinct ways, depending on how it is materialized or brought into being. As Getsy points out in his preface, "A transgender history attends not just to the evidence of gender non-conforming lives but also—as this study does—shows how accounts of transgender capacity are produced (sometimes inadvertently) through attempts to reconsider how bodies and personas can be imagined or evoked. It also asks its questions broadly with the understanding that all genders must be characterized differently once mutability and temporality are recognized among their defining traits" (xvi). Getsy understands sculpture to be an especially potent site for such materializations because it is arguably the single art form most preoccupied with registering the human body in its full three-dimensionality, whether in forms that replicate the body like Greek statuary or forms that index or reference an abstract notion of the body, or else the actual body of the viewer, without representing it directly.

Getsy's canny conceptual move is a deliberate one intended to accomplish two tasks with one sweep: to make plainly visible to art historians how deeply questions of gender and sexuality, and gender mutability in particular, inhabit the conceptual thought and material production of abstract artists in the late twentieth century; and to encourage the fields of transgender studies, queer studies, and feminist theory to see how the history of art and its ongoing concerns over representing the human body provide some of the most innovative and sustained mediations on gender and sexual variability in existence. Moreover, Getsy seeks to make transgender studies more attentive to the problem of materiality beyond the human body, that is, to account for the ways that actual aesthetic materials like clay, leather, metal, or canvas—the literal tools of an artist's practice—can also conjure new ways of understanding or conceiving the fleshy materiality of the body itself. As a result, Getsy's book is fundamentally interdisciplinary and nonidentitarian. It does not merely apply one set of tools from art history to study transgender logics, or simply transpose transgender theory onto artworks; rather, Getsy deftly shows how distinct works of art and the material histories that surround them pose questions that can only be fully explored and answered by taking up both fields in tandem, or else allegorize key ideas, concepts, and values of transgender thought in formal innovation.

This is captured most vividly in Getsy's signal conceptual term, *transgender capacity*. Getsy uses this concept to describe "the ability or the potential for making visible, bringing into experience, or knowing genders as mutable, successive, and multiple." He continues, "It can be located or discerned in texts, objects, [and] cultural forms . . . that support an interpretation or recognition of proliferative modes of gender nonconformity" (34). By conceiving gender transitivity not only as an identity or lived experience but also as a formal capacity of artistic pro-duction, Getsy opens up the possibility of seeing queer genders and sexualities as legible in everything from aesthetic mediums to the specificities of a given art practice. Transgender capacity, then, is a theoretical tool that allows us to register when nonbinary understandings of gender become visible, legible, or translat-able through particular formal practices. When we pursue instances in which transgender capacity is at play, we are fundamentally tracing *logics of nonbinary gender*, rather than locating particular gendered identities; far from losing sight of the bodies and lives such logics shape, inform, and produce, this method pro-vides a thicker attention to the sites where new ideas about inhabiting gender differently appear and potentially help bring into being the conditions that support the flourishing of transgender life.

Consequently, *Abstract Bodies* is organized around four such logics, which Getsy links to four key artists in the development of sculptural abstraction in the 1960s and after: first is *the logic of gender variability*, which Getsy sees in David Smith's range of abstract metal sculptures composed of unruly appendages, shapes, colors, and erratic lines that offer numerous variations on what the human body might look like beyond gendered ascriptions: "Smith's works willfully eschew mimesis of the body as means of creating new, previously unimagined, configurations, which nevertheless allude to or invoke the human figure. . . . The abstract body prompts different and divergent nominations depending on who is doing the assigning and for what reasons" (44, 93). Second is *the logic of fitting or coupling*, which Getsy finds in John Chamberlain's famous crushed car works,

massive multicolored, jagged-edged balls of composite metals that visually alle-
gorized the unruly fitting or conjoining of gender-nonspecific bodies: "The parts
are not securely identifiable as male or female, or even penetrative or receptive. . . .
[Chamberlain] refers to the sexual fit as 'squeezing and hugging,' often leaving his
description of erotic activity outside of ways that gender might be neatly assigned
to parts or activities . . . the fit was generative, not prescriptive" (122). Third is *the
logic of disembodied parts*, which Getsy sees on display across Nancy Grossman's
career in both her large-scale, found-material assemblage works and her noto-
riously misunderstood series of disembodied leather heads, composed of thickly
layered leather masks tightly zippered or buckled over elaborately carved wooden
sculptures: "Her work—both abstract and representational—prompts projective
identifications of gender and sexuality only to complicate and confound them.
Remarkably, she does this without representing the body at all. Her head sculptures abstract and suggest the body, and viewers rush to fill in what they think
that body should be" (150). And finally is *the logic of interchangeability*, which
Getsy identifies in Dan Flavin's iconic fluorescent light sculptures, multicolored
arrangements of large-scale light tubes that could be infinitely interchanged for
one another, yet were given nominal particularity through their dedication to
specific people and their coloring in distinct hues: "These names that [Flavin]
kept attaching to his systematically interchangeable works produce—in excess
of Flavin's intentions—a logic of transformational personhood and mutable
gender, that, like his lights, places value on sameness and interchangeability
made particular through naming" (211). In each chapter, Getsy carefully unpacks
how a distinct artist became invested in particular logics of gender transitivity or
variability at the conjuncture of a wide range of sites, including their individual
biographies, public accounts of transsexual or transgender life circulating at the
time of their creative production, their engagement with distinct materials, and
the art world's reception of their work. Getsy shows how distinct expressions
of transgender capacity have rich histories that can be traced through a careful
reconstruction of their varied creative, intellectual, and political contexts and
across multiple archives far beyond the limits of a single artistic work.

The great intellectual gift of *Abstract Bodies* is not only its conceptual
innovation, captured in Getsy's theorization of "transgender capacity," his
commitment to seeing abstraction as a space of openness and possibility, and
his precise tracing of abstract logics of gender transitivity, but also in the book's
methodological dynamism and creativity. Simply put, *Abstract Bodies* is an
extraordinarily imaginative book. It makes unexpected yet absolutely compelling
links between artworks and transgender logics or ways of thinking that are easily
overlooked or misperceived from traditional disciplinary approaches: the idea
that Dan Flavin's fluorescent light tubes, seemingly wholly nonrepresentational

light forms sentimentally dedicated to different people in the artist's life, might actually put forth a fully formed theory of interchangeable gendered nomination is, quite simply, astonishing, yet utterly convincing. It can only be so, however, because Getsy shows the reader how Flavin's art practice (which Flavin wrote extensively about in his journals and spoke of in interviews throughout this career) reflects his investment in experimenting with generic, mass-produced light tubes that could produce surprisingly distinct visual effects while also simultaneously all being functionally the same. Through a meticulous analysis of Flavin's developmental thinking about his own work, as well as his curious practice of dedicating each piece to a different person, Getsy shows how the artist became increasingly inclined toward exploring this interplay between generality and particularity, which is a fundamental feature of gendered self-nomination: namely, that gender is a widely shared category of identification, but that naming oneself as a particular gender (through choice of pronouns or a new name) gives provisional, but meaningful, specificity to a given experience of gendered embodiment. Getsy underscores that,

> combined with Flavin's insistent system of sameness, the dedications signal Flavin's proliferation of difference and variability among his standard materials that can be recombined, paired, relocated, and exchanged—and that one never forgets are all, fundamentally, the same. . . . From the perspective of transgender theory and its accounts of successive states of identity and mutable and multiple genders, Flavin's practice of naming interchangeable units can be extrapolated into an inadvertent account of personhood that shares such priorities with transgender politics and culture. Both teach us that a name can, after all, make all the difference. (258)

The arguments Getsy makes in each chapter garner their high level of persuasiveness and conceptual daring in part because he vastly expands the coordinates through which we can make sense of, interpret, and do something with a work of art or a particular art practice: by taking into account the actual history of transgender life in the late twentieth-century United States, Getsy can show how a pervasive public discourse of gender transitivity in the 1960s influenced both the personal and creative investments of particular artists (and altered the ways they talked about their art in gendered terms). By studying what artists had to say about their work, especially how figures like Chamberlain and Grossman repeatedly refused gendered nominations of their artworks by a range of cultural critics, Getsy can underscore the complex discourses these artists developed regarding their engagement with nonbinary conceptions of gender. By studying the physical materials these artists use and the distinct ways they experimented with shape, form, and texture—such as Flavin's use of multicolored fluorescent light tubes and Smith's uneven aluminum cubes—Getsy illuminates how particular materials afforded unique possibilities for giving shape to gender-transitive ways of thinking. It is the exceptional range of variables that Getsy takes into account when assessing a single artwork that allows him to see something in it that speaks to broader cultural logics: history matters, discourse matters, materials matter, intellectual outlooks matter, embodied practices matter. All of these Getsy takes up, never isolating a given art object but considering how it produces meanings in relation to all of these factors as they take shape through, against, and in tandem with one another.

Abstract Bodies, then, is not for the intellectually lazy or for the singularly minded disciplinary thinker (though perhaps it is precisely suited to persuade such a thinker away from their rigid theoretical commitments); rather, it demands intellectual capaciousness and open-mindedness from its reader, which is perhaps unsurprisingly the affective stance Getsy claims (in common voice with transgender theory) that makes conceptions of nonbinary gender possible in the first place. Getsy's approach forces us to consider some of the larger ramifications of art and cultural production that actively makes particular identities more labile or mutable or else highlights what is already contingent in seemingly stable identity markers. We are left asking such key questions as does the kind of transformability of gendered nomination apparent in these artworks translate to categories like race and disability; is it possible to present these latter categories as mutable or contingent without falling into the trap of cultural appropriation; how can artwork that offers new ways of inhabiting particular identities and identifications provide the conceptual ground for equally innovative kinds of political activism, new ways of relating to others, and even new kinds of ethical practices; and what might be the positive consequences of incorporating the affective stance of irreverence, playfulness, and experimentation with the form and shape of particular identities that these artworks display?

One easy way to dismiss the magnitude of Getsy's intervention is to claim that the book fails on account of its refusal to centralize self-identified transgender artists. One might be tempted to inveigh: Why write a book that purports to develop a theory of transgender logics in modern sculpture but not develop case studies of trans artists? Setting aside the fact that Getsy does indeed provide a beautiful and in-depth discussion of contemporary trans artist Cassils at the book's conclusion, I believe such a criticism quite spectacularly misses the point: far from sidelining, making invisible, or denigrated trans artists, Getsy's approach elevates their investments, lives, and ways of seeing to the level of a philosophical imperative that has underwritten the production of Western art for numerous artists of many identity categories across time. Getsy is not blaspheming against transgender theory or politics (i.e., doing trans theorizing without actual trans people) but fulfilling its most radical goal, namely, to underscore the variability, mutability, and transitivity of all genders, perhaps even especially those that appear on the surface to be self-evidently normative or fixed. Perhaps, most importantly, by reading the logics of gender transitivity in works commonly assumed to have nothing to do with transgender thought and life, Getsy offers a reading practice attuned to multiciplity, thereby conceiving of transgender as an almost philosophical or ontological viewpoint from which to develop interpretation. Getsy willfully risks decentering a commitment to trans identity to illuminate something broader about the role that transgender plays as an operating logic in creative or aesthetic thought that finds countless expressions, modes, and forms. Abstraction, understood as a dynamic approach to form that stresses "the unforeclosed," is echoed in Getsy's own approach to gender. When gender is even provisionally abstracted from particular bodies, we can potentially conceive of it more dynamically, which in turn has salubrious effects for the flourishing of actual embodied people, who may very well be the spectators, creators, or critics of the very abstract works of art before us, but also might not. As Getsy compellingly states, "One of the central questions of this book has been how to visualize transformation and its potential. In other words, when we question the limitations of dimorphism or of binaries and when we recognize that personhood is not static, how do we look?" (279) Put another way, *Abstract Bodies* tells a story about how abstract sculptors in the 1960s gave shape to the desire to live, be, and feel outside the logic of binary gender; that story gives us permission to use our scholarship, our art practices, and our politics to give shape to new and unexpected desires, even those we haven't yet imagined.

Ramzi Fawaz is associate professor of English at the University of Wisconsin–Madison. He is the author of *The New Mutants: Superheroes and the Radical Imagination of American Comics* (2016) and coeditor (with Darieck Scott) of a recent special issue of *American Literature* titled "Queer about Comics" (2018).

Printed and bound by CPI Group (UK) Ltd, Croydon, CR0 4YY

13/04/2025

14656485-0005